Energy Economy in China

Policy Imperative, Market Dynamics, and Regional Developments

Energy Economy in China

Policy Imperative, Market Dynamics, and Regional Developments

Kang WU
East-West Center, USA

World Scientific
NEW JERSEY • LONDON • SINGAPORE • BEIJING • SHANGHAI • HONG KONG • TAIPEI • CHENNAI

Published by

World Scientific Publishing Co. Pte. Ltd.
5 Toh Tuck Link, Singapore 596224
USA office: 27 Warren Street, Suite 401-402, Hackensack, NJ 07601
UK office: 57 Shelton Street, Covent Garden, London WC2H 9HE

British Library Cataloguing-in-Publication Data
A catalogue record for this book is available from the British Library.

ENERGY ECONOMY IN CHINA
Policy Imperative, Market Dynamics, and Regional Developments

ISBN 978-981-4335-67-6

In-house Editor: Zheng Danjun

Typeset by Stallion Press
Email: enquiries@stallionpress.com

Printed in Singapore.

To my two lovely daughters Joyce and Emily

Contents

Preface

China has a huge energy market. The world's most populous country consumes more coal, power, and energy as a whole than any other country in the world. Accompanying this large market is a growing economy, which has expanded substantially for over three decades since the late 1970s. While the Chinese economy is facing many challenges, it is expected to grow continuously over the next 10 years and beyond. As a result, China's energy needs will increase at a faster pace, creating bigger challenges to the environment and making energy security a greater concern to China and the world at large.

With 20 years of research experience, Dr. Kang Wu has deep knowledge on energy issues in China and the Asia-Pacific region. He is familiar with every aspect of the energy sector and economic development in China. In this book, Dr. Wu offers a unique analysis of challenges facing the Chinese energy industry with a special focus on oil, gas, and regional developments inside the country. The book provides detailed studies of China's oil and gas demand, supply, and trade at the national and regional levels, with additional coverage of other key energy fuels such as coal, hydroelectricity, nuclear power, and other renewable energy. In my view, no other study can match the breadth of coverage and depth of analysis offered by this book. The study will serve as a major guide to our readers in understanding the complexity of China's energy sector at present and in the future.

Fereidun Fesharaki, Ph.D.
Chairman, FGE
Senior Fellow, East-West Center
July 2012

Acknowledgments

The author wishes to thank the many colleagues and collaborators who have helped to make the publication of this book possible. Great recognition is due to Dr. Fereidun Fesharaki, Chairman of FACTS Global Energy (FGE) and Senior Fellow of the East-West Center, whose long-term support and mentoring has been essential. The East-West Center is the author's home base, while FGE is where a comprehensive database has been made available to the author to ensure that the book be rich and accurate in data and analysis. The author is grateful that to World Scientific Publishing Company for moving ahead with the publication of the book and providing editorial support along the way.

From the East-West Center, FGE, and regional energy institutions in Asia, the author has a long list of researchers, professionals, and research assistants to acknowledge, who provided assistance, gave their critiques, engaged in discussions with the author, and shared their views on various issues concerning the energy sector development, energy security, environmental issues, and future growth in China. The list, by no means exhaustive, but important to acknowledge, includes (alphabetically) Alexis Aik, Rouben Azizian, Sara Banaszak, Michael Barry, Jeff Brown, Raymond Burghardt, Guy Caruso, Xavier Chen, Elizabeth Van Wie Davis, Tilak Doshi, Lee H. Endress, Shi Fu, Shixian Gao, Fereidun Fesharaki, Shasha Fesharaki, Tomoko Hosoe,

Yoon Hyung Kim, Xiaoli Liu, David Isaak, Xiaoming Ke, Bo Kong, Ken Koyama, Sarah Ladislaw, Mark Lewis, Diana Lu, Chris McNally, Charles Morrison, Jane Nakano, Caleb O'Kray, David Pumphrey, Denny Roy, Keith Schneider, Dan Shi, Rob Smith, Ian Storey, Gayle Sueda, Elspeth Thomson, Jennifer Turner, Lijuan Wang, Sidney Westley, Xiaojie Xu, Chi Zhang, Liutong Zhang, ZhongXiang Zhang, and many others. That said, all errors remain the responsibility of the author.

Kang Wu
July 2012

About the Author

Dr. Kang Wu is a Senior Fellow at the East-West Center and a Senior Advisor at FGE. He conducts research on energy policies, security, demand, supply, trade, and market developments, as well as energy-economic links, oil and gas issues, and the impact of fossil energy use on the environment with a focus on the Asia-Pacific region. Dr. Wu is an energy expert on China and supervises the China Energy Project at the Center. He is also familiar with energy sector issues in other Asia-Pacific economies. Dr. Wu's work includes energy modeling and Asia-Pacific energy demand forecasting. In 2003, Dr. Wu testified before the U.S.-China Economic and Security Review Commission at Capitol Hill in Washington, D.C. on the impact of China's energy demand on the rest of the world. He received his Ph.D. in Economics in 1991 from the University of Hawaii at Manoa and B.A. in International Economics in 1985 from Peking University.

Dr. Wu speaks frequently at international conferences, forums, workshops, and training programs. His research has been widely cited by the press and industrial media, including *Time*, *The Wall Street Journal*, *New York Times*, *The Asian Wall Street Journal*, *International Herald Tribune*, *Far Eastern Economic Review*, *Journal of Commerce*, *The Strait Times*, CNN, *Financial Times*,

Reuters, Voice of America, BBC, CNBC, Radio Australia, Radio Free Asia, Dow Jones Energy Services, Bloomberg News, *Petroleum Argus*, *Oil & Gas Journal*, various Chinese media as well as Hawaii local TV stations, public radio, newspapers, and other media outlets. Dr. Wu is the author and co-author of numerous publications such as journal articles, research papers, project reports, books, and book chapters.

chapter 1

Energy and the Economy

China has a massive energy sector. In 2000, China's primary energy consumption was less than half of that of US, whereas its electricity generation was a little more than one-third of that of US (BP, 2011). After a decade of rapid growth, China first surpassed US as the world's largest carbon dioxide (CO_2) emitter in 2006 and then as the largest energy consumer in 2009 (BP, 2011; FGE, 2011a). This was due in part to the impact of the 2008–2009 global financial crisis, the worst since the 1930s, which led to shrinking energy use in US for two years in a row. In 2010, China's gross generation of electricity came close to that of US, and it surpassed the latter in 2011 for the first time. Over the next 10 to 20 years, the Chinese economy is likely to expand continuously, which will further drive the growth of energy use in this huge country (Ma *et al.*, 2008).

This chapter provides a context for the entire book, i.e., the overall energy production, consumption, and gap, the state of the economy, and future growth. We will discuss the current situation and future prospects of primary energy production (PEP) and primary energy[1] consumption (PEC) — where PEC is the focus as against PEP — and provide an overall picture of the energy economy in China. The roles

[1] Primary energy, as defined in this book, includes oil, gas, coal, hydroelectricity, nuclear power, solar, wind, and other commercially viable renewable energy resources, as well as noncommercial biomass. For this chapter only, gas includes both conventional gas and unconventional CBM and shale gas.

of oil and gas in China's total primary energy demand and supply will be assessed, along with coal, hydroelectricity, nuclear power, solar/wind/other renewable energy, as well as noncommercial biomass. The inclusion of noncommercial biomass is unique to this book, which seeks to provide a full picture of energy use in China. An overview of the economic development is also provided.

1.1. Primary Energy Production and Consumption: An Overview

In terms of total primary energy, where noncommercial biomass is included, China is currently the largest consumer in the world. In 2010, China consumed 52.8 million barrels of oil equivalent per day (mmboe/d) of primary energy, ahead of the United States' 47.5 mmboe (Fig. 1-1). The PEC for China is estimated to have reached 57.0 mmboe/d in 2011. On a per-capita basis, China's PEC is slightly above the world average and is around a quarter of the per-capita PEC of US. For instance, in 2010, the world's average per-capita PEC was around 14.0 boe per year; it was 55.9 boe per person in US and 29.2 boe per person in Japan, whereas in China, it was 14.5 boe, though it was much higher than India's 4.2 boe per person.

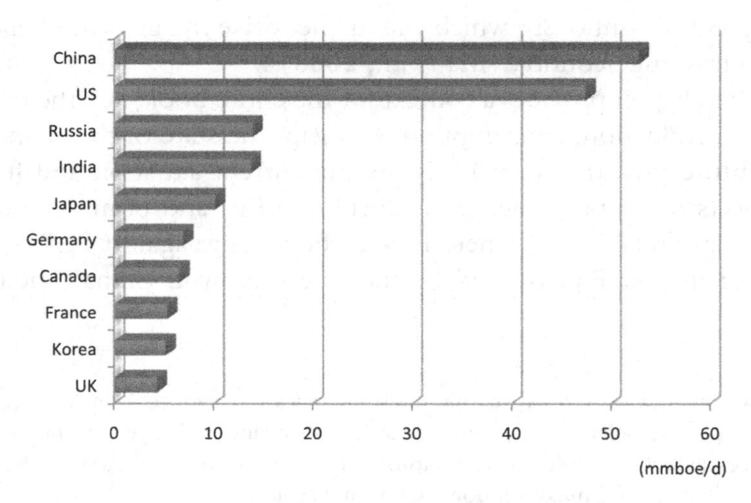

Fig. 1-1. The World's Ten Largest PEC Countries, 2010.

Coal plays a dominant role in both energy production and consumption. As the world's largest coal producer and consumer, the importance of coal for the country's economic development and energy use will not diminish overnight. In the meantime, China's coal exports have been declining since 2003, whereas coal imports have increased rapidly since 2001. In 2009, China became a net coal importer for the first time since the 1950s, and the imports increased in 2010 and 2011. The Chinese government has been trying to limit coal use and promote the use of other energy sources but has so far not been successful. This will pose a long-term challenge for the Chinese government.

Oil, which is the focus of this book, is the second largest source of PEC and production in China and is very important to the economy. Driven by transportation, petrochemical, and residential sectors, China's use of petroleum products has been rapidly growing in the past two decades. Since the early 1990s, the country's growing dependence on imported oil is a concern for the Chinese government. As the net imports are growing, it is challenging for the Chinese government to deal with the issue of energy security for the forthcoming 10–15 years and beyond.

Gas, which is another focus of the book and includes both conventional and unconventional gas when total primary energy is discussed here, currently has a much lower share in the total PEP and PEC in China than oil and coal. The Chinese government vows to increase gas production (including the development of unconventional gas) and consumption drastically. Given that China's consumption and production have had double-digit growth per annum for a number of years, there is no doubt that the share of natural gas in China's overall primary energy consumption will continue to grow.

China has accelerated nuclear power development since the early 2000s after slow growth during much of the 1990s. Despite the call for reassessment during the aftermath of Japan's earthquake/tsunamis on March 11, 2011, that caused massive damage to the Japanese nuclear power plants, China's ambitious nuclear power program to increase the installed generating capacity by a factor of six between now and 2020 appears to remain steadfast. However, recent developments suggest that China has become more cautious in approaching the issue of future nuclear power plants developments.

Hydropower has traditionally been given much attention and a high priority by the government, which is planning to launch several large hydroelectric projects in Southwest China. Hydroelectricity will continue to be an important source of primary energy for China for the decades to come. Beyond hydropower, China has been aggressive in promoting the development of other renewable energies such as wind power, solar power, and biomass power (Ma *et al.*, 2010; Zhang, Zhou and Cao, 2011). In fact, China's total investment in renewable energy at present is already the largest in the world and has continued to remain so. The year 2011 was the first under China's 12th Five-Year Program (FYP). In order to meet the target for reducing carbon emission intensity by 40%–45% by 2020 from the 1990 levels and increase the share of renewable energy to 15% of total PEC also by 2020, China is set to make bigger efforts in this area. (The Climate Group, 2011; Lewis, 2011; Climate Policy Initiative 2011).

1.1.1. *Primary energy production*

In 2010, China's PEP reached an estimated 46.6 mmboe/d, up from 18.4 mmboe/d in 1990 and 22.7 mmboe/d in 2005 (Fig. 1-2). In

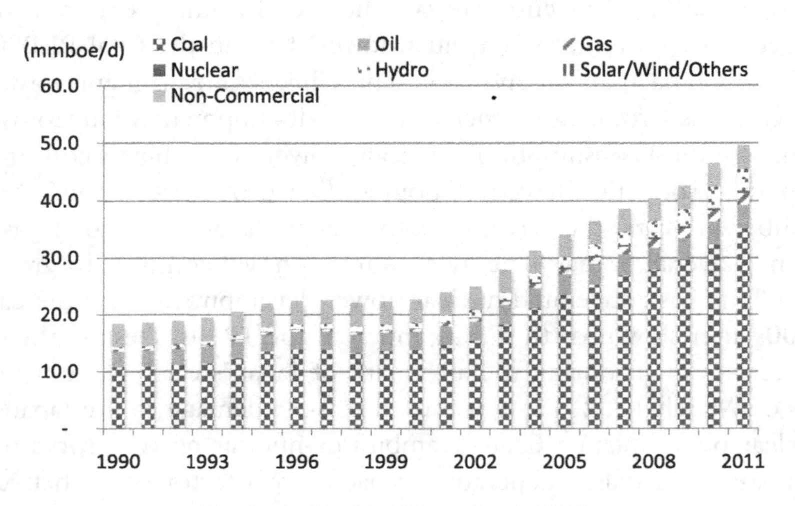

Fig. 1-2. PEP in China, 1990–2011.

Note: 2011 data are priliminary.

2011, China's PEP is estimated to have increased to 49.7 mmboe/d. China is now the largest primary energy–producing country in the world.

Since the late 1970s, there has been an increase in coal's share in total PEP. The share averaged 54% in the 1980s, 60% in the 1990s, and reached a high of 66% in the 2000s. In 2010, the share of coal in total PEP reached 69.5%, among the highest in China. Despite an unprecedented increase in production, in 2010, oil accounted for only 8.7% of China's PEP, down from the peak level of 17.0% in 1980. Even in 2000, oil still retained over 14% in the total PEP.

Apart from oil, hydroelectricity accounted for 7.0% of the PEP in 2010, gas (including both conventional and unconventional gas) 4.2%, and nuclear power 0.8%, solar, wind, and other renewable energies 1.1%. Over the forthcoming decade or two, coal will continue to be the largest source of PEP, but its share will decline. The share of oil will decline likewise Shares that will rise are hydroelectricity, nuclear power, and gas. The total PEP is projected to increase to 68.0 mmboe/d by 2020 and 85.7 mmboe/d by 2030 under our base-case scenario.

1.1.2. *Primary energy consumption*

In 2010, China's total PEC reached an all-time high of 52.8 mmboe/d, which was about 6.9 mmboe/d higher than PEP. In 2011, China's PEC is estimated to have increased to 57.0 mmboe/d, 6.3 mmboe/d higher than the PEP. The size of PEC in 2010 was up from 17.4 mmboe/d in 2000, 22.6 and 35.5 mmboe/d in 2000 (Fig. 1-3). Between 2000 and 2010, China's PEC was nearly doubled, with an annual average growth rate (AAGR) of 8.8%. Like PEP, coal dominates the PEC scene in China as well. In 2010, coal accounted for 63.4% of the total PEC, up from 60% in 1990 and 57% in 2000.

As the second largest source of primary energy, oil accounted for 17.1% of the total PEC in 2010, up from 12% in 1990, but down from nearly 19% in 2000. The changes in the share of oil are largely affected by the ups and downs of coal use in China and rising demand for natural gas.

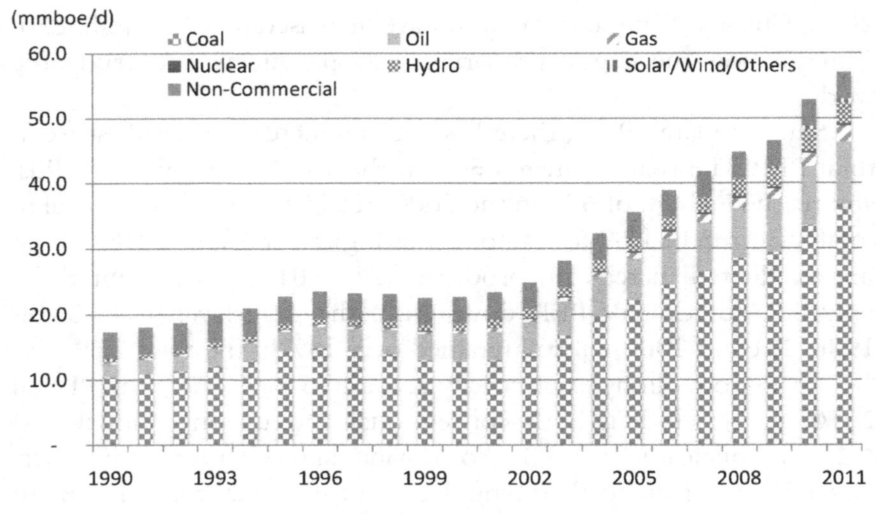

Fig. 1-3. PEC in China, 1990–2011.

Note: 2011 data are preliminary.

In 2010, gas (including both conventional and unconventional gas) accounted for 3.9% of China's PEC, which was up from 1.6% in 1990 and 2.0% in 2005. Despite the rapid AAGR of 16.7% between 2000 and 2010, including an impressive growth of some 23% for 2010, China's share of gas in total PEC is one of the lowest among the major Asia-Pacific countries.

In 2010, the shares of hydroelectricity and nuclear power in total PEC were 6.2% and 0.7%, respectively. Solar, wind, and other commercial renewable energy resources had only a small share of 0.8% in 2010. Meanwhile, noncommercial biomass accounted for 7.7% of the total PEC in 2010, which was down from 23% in 1990 and 18% in 2000. China's PEC is expected to increase to 82 mmboe/d in 2020 and 106 mmboe/d by 2030 (Fig. 1-4) under our base-case scenario.

The share of coal in primary energy consumption is forecast to decline In comparison, the share of oil is forecasted to increase slightly to stay flat until 2020 but go down gradually. For hydroelectricity and nuclear power, the shares are forecasted to increase substantially by 2020 and 2030. The share of gas will also increase significantly.

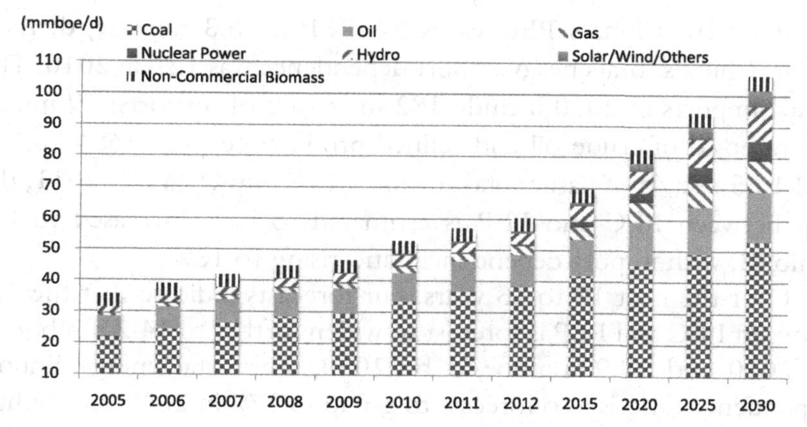

Fig. 1-4. Outlook of PEC in China Base-Case Scenario, 2005–2030.

Note: Data for 2011 are preliminary; data for 2012–2030 data are forecasts.

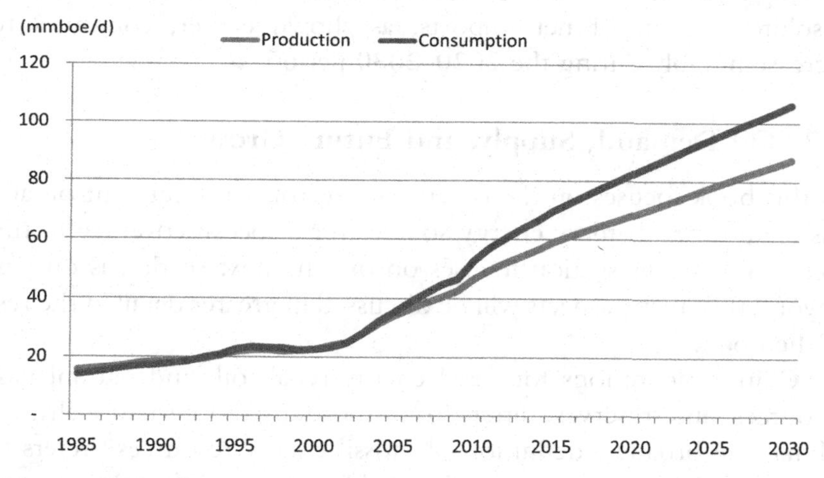

Fig. 1-5. PEP vs. PEC for China: Past and Future, 1990–2030.

Note: Data for 2011 data are preliminary and data for 2012–2030 are forecasts.

1.1.3. *PEP versus PEC: Widening gap*

A simple comparison between PEC and PEP in China points to the widening gap between the two (Fig. 1-5). Until the mid-1990s, China had enjoyed surpluses to varying degrees, which peaked in 1985 at 1.5 mmboe/d. A deficit has emerged since the mid-1990s.

In 2010, China's PEC exceeded PEP by 6.3 mmboe/d. As a result, China's total energy import dependence was 12% in 2010. The actual imports in 2010 include 182 mmt of coal (exports: 19 mmt), 5.7 mmb/d of crude oil and refined products (exports: 686 kb/d), and 1.65 bscf/d of natural gas (exports: 387 mmscf/d). In 2011, the gap between PEC and PEP is estimated to have increased to 7.4 mmb/d, with import dependence ratio rising to 13%.

Over the next 10 to 15 years, our forecasts indicate that the gap between PEC and PEP is forecast to widen further to 14.2 mmboe/d by 2020 and 18.9 mmboe/d by 2030. The total energy import dependence ratio is also forecast to go up to 17% in 2020 but slightly under 18% by 2030, thanks to the continuous growth in renewable energy, nuclear power, and hydropower. It also reflects the projected slowing down of PEC growth between 2020 and 2030. However, the absolute amount of net imports, as shown earlier, continues to increase notably during the 2020–2030 period.

1.2. Oil Demand, Supply, and Future Growth

As this book focuses on the oil and gas sector, we single out oil and gas from other primary energy sources for a special coverage in this sector. While this section focuses on oil, the next section is on gas. Beyond this, many aspects will be discussed in greater detail in the rest of the book.

China's definitions for fossil energy (coal, oil, and natural gas) resources and reserves differ from those used internationally. In China, the broadest definition of "fossil energy resources" refers to fossil energy deposits under all possible geological conditions and belonging to all geological ages. The proven part of the resources is only a fraction of the total. The Chinese term for proven reserves is "proven geological reserves." Also, China's definition of proven geological reserves is not the same as the internationally used term "proven reserves." The typical definition of proven reserves of oil, gas, and coal outside China is the one used by BP, i.e., "generally taken to be those quantities that geological and engineering information indicates with reasonable certainty can be recovered in the future from known reservoirs under existing economic and operating conditions (BP, 2011)."

Similar definitions apply to natural gas and coal. The Chinese-defined geological reserves are broader — besides those quantities, similar to the internationally defined proven reserves, it also includes reserves that either cannot be recovered economically or do not meet existing operating conditions. Because of the broader definition, the proven geological reserves of oil, gas, and coal reported by the Chinese government are often higher than proven reserves published outside the country in accordance with the international definition. Finally, China's definition of proven recoverable oil, gas, and coal reserves is identical to the concept of proven reserves used internationally, like the one used by BP.

For both proven geological and proven recoverable reserves, China tends to use the concepts of "cumulative reserves" and "remaining reserves." On an equivalent basis, the term "remaining reserves" used in China is commonly referred to as just "reserves" internationally.

Since the 1970s, China has conducted at least three nationwide appraisals of oil and gas resources. The first appraisal was completed in 1987, followed by the second in 1997 and the third in 2006. In all three cases, the actual work started a few years earlier. According to the most recent appraisal, oil resources have reached 792 billion barrels or 108.6 billion metric tons (tonnes), up from 575 billion barrels in 1987 and 686 billion barrels in 1997. Of the 792 billion barrels of oil resources, 86% is located onshore. Offshore resources account for 14% of the total (Fig. 1-6).

As far as proven reserves are concern, in its 2011 annual report, BP listed only 14.8 billion barrels for China at the start of 2011. At 14.8 billion barrels, China's oil reserves were only 1.1% of the world total of 1.38 trillion barrels.

The expansion of China's modern oil industry dates from the late 1950s, when the Daqing oil field was discovered in Northeast China. After five decades of development, China has become the fifth-largest oil producer in the world in 2010 (after Russia, Saudi Arabia, US, and Iran). In 2010, China produced 4.06 mmb/d of crude oil, an increase

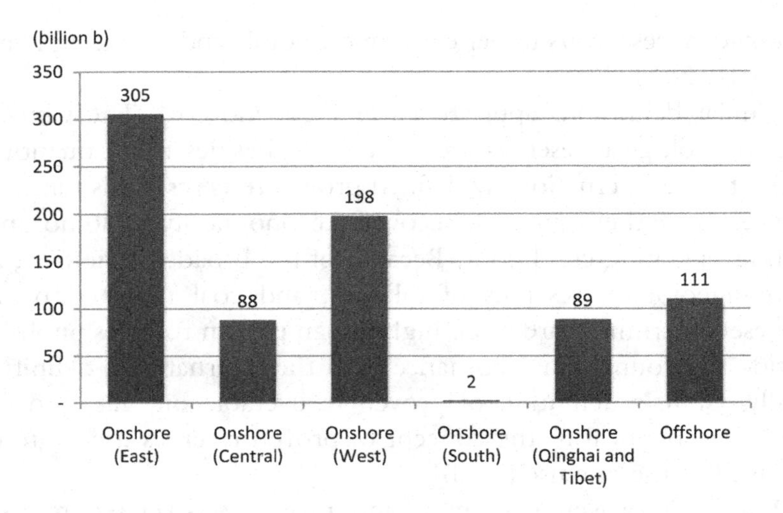

Fig. 1-6. Regional Distribution of China's Oil Resources in 2010.
Note: Based on China's latest government appraisal. Total is 792 billion barrels.

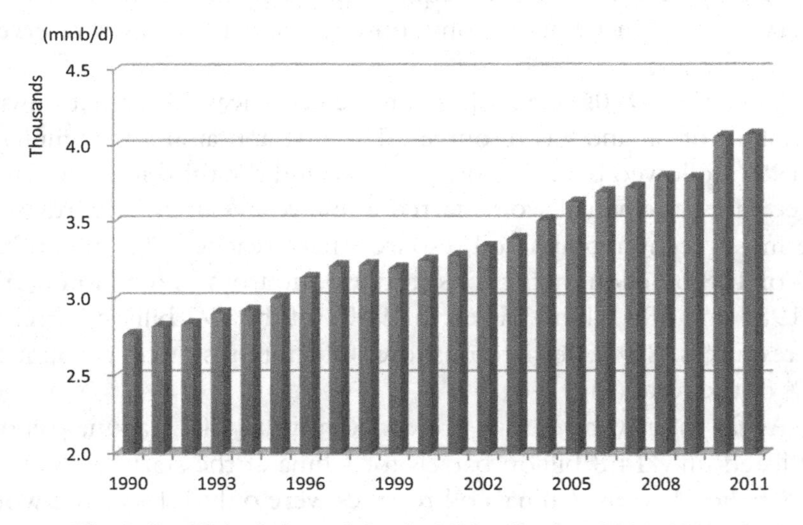

Fig. 1-7. China's Annual Crude Oil Production, 1990–2011.

of 7.1% from that in 2009 and up from 2.8 mmb/d in 1990 and 3.3 mmb/d in 2000 (Fig. 1-7). The year 2010 was record-breaking for China's crude oil production, due mainly to the new fields that were put into operation in offshore China during the year. It was thus the first year that China's crude oil production passed the mark of 4 mmb/d. Production growth averaged about 2.7% per annum for the period of 1980–1990, which slowed down to 1.6% per annum on average during the period of 1990–2000, but went up slightly to 2.2% per annum between 2000 and 2010. In 2011, however, the growth of China's crude oil production slowed down to merely 0.3%, thanks to the shutdown of the offshore Penglai 19-1 field due to the leakage with total output reaching 4.07 mmb/d.

Currently around 80% of China's crude oil is produced onshore and the rest offshore. In 2010, offshore production exceeded 800,000 barrels per day (kb/d), up from 29 kb/d in 1990 and 350 kb/d in 2000. The share of offshore production in the country's total crude output increased from 6% in 1995 to 15% in 2005 and an all-time high of 20% in 2010. About 60% of the country's incremental output during the period of 1990–2010 came from the offshore area, while from onshore areas, the contributions came from western Xinjiang Autonomous Region (including the Tarim Basin) and the Ordos Basin.

For most years since 1970, China was a net oil (crude and products) exporter until 1993 and a net crude oil exporter until 1996. The net oil exports (crude and products combined) peaked in 1985 at 708 kb/d. Since then, China's oil surplus has been shrinking. In 1993, China became a net oil importer for the first time since the early 1970s. Net oil imports increased from 200 kb/d in 1993 to 2.9 mmb/d in 2005, 4.4 mmb/d in 2009, 5.1 mmb/d in 2010, and an all-time high of 5.5 mmb/d in 2011.

Growth in oil demand has been strong in China since the early 1990s. Total petroleum product consumption, including direct burning of crude oil, amounted to 9.0 mmb/d in 2010, up from 2.2 mmb/d in 1990, 3.1 mmb/d in 1995 and 6.5 mmb/d in 2005 (Fig. 1-8). Petroleum product demand growth in China averaged at 7.6% per annum between 1990 and 2010. In 2011, China's petroleum product demand is estimated to have increased to 9.6 mmb/d.

Over the next decade and beyond, the growth areas for China's future oil production will come from the northwest (Ordos Basin), offshore, the west (Tarim and other basins), and other parts of the country. Part of the growth will compensate for the continuous

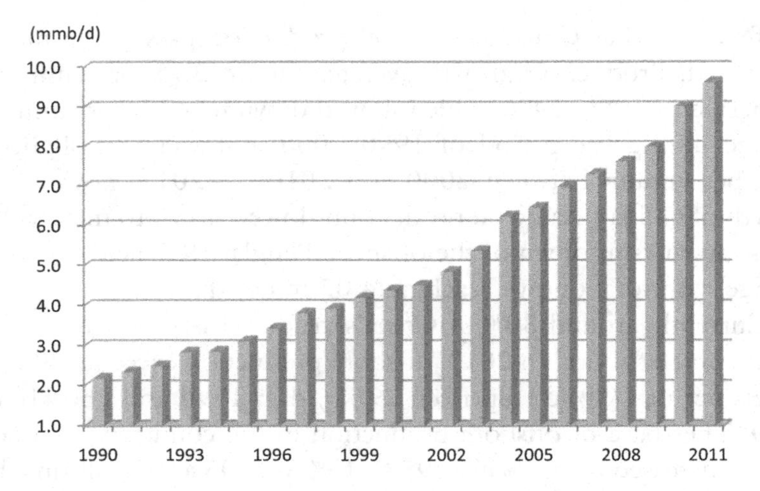

Fig. 1-8. China's Annual Petroleum Product Consumption, (1990–2011).
Note: 2011 data are preliminary.

decline in some of the aging fields in the east. However, the Chinese state oil companies are making efforts to stabilize production from Daqing, Shengli, Liaohe, Huabei, and other fields in the east.

Overall, however, it will become harder to sustain or increase the total production beyond 2020. Under our base-case scenario, China's crude production is forecasted to remain at under 4.3 mmb/d through 2030.

On the demand side, total petroleum product consumption is expected to increase to 14.0 mmb/d in 2020, but the growth is forecast to slow down after that, reaching 16.3 mmb/d by 2030 under our base-case scenario.

As a result of the above-mentioned scenario, the gap between the total petroleum product demand and the domestic crude output is widening rapidly. China's net oil imports, which are based on our forecasts of crude oil and product balances, are expected to rise to 10.0 mmb/d in 2020 and 12.3 mmb/d in 2030.

1.3. Gas Demand, Supply, and Future Growth

In this section, we cover primary energy resources other than oil, including gas, coal, hydroelectricity, nuclear, solar, wind, and other renewable energy. In the Chinese government's latest appraisal — as a result of the above-mentioned three appraisals and more recent work — it was reported that total natural gas resources amounted to 1,973 trillion cubic feet (tcf), or 55.9 trillion cubic meters (tcm), compared with the assessment of 1,187 tcf in 1987, 1,343 tcf in 1997, and 1,859 tcf in 2006. Of the 1,973 tcf of natural gas resources, 77% was located onshore. Offshore gas resources accounted for 23% of the total (Fig. 1-9).

In its 2011 report (BP, 2011), BP listed 99.2 tcf as China's proven reserves of natural gas in the beginning of 2011, accounting for 1.5% of the world total reserves of 6,609 tcf. This assessment is very close to the reported remaining proven recoverable natural gas reserves in China.

China's natural gas development started at the same time as its oil industry in the late 1950s. However, until the mid-1990s, the development of the natural gas sector had received far less attention than the oil sector. The gas sector development has since accelerated. In 2010, China produced 9.3 bscf/d of natural gas, up sharply from 1.5 bscf/d in 1990 and 2.6 bscf/d in 2000 (Fig. 1-10). In 2011, China's natural gas production increased further to 10 bscf/d.

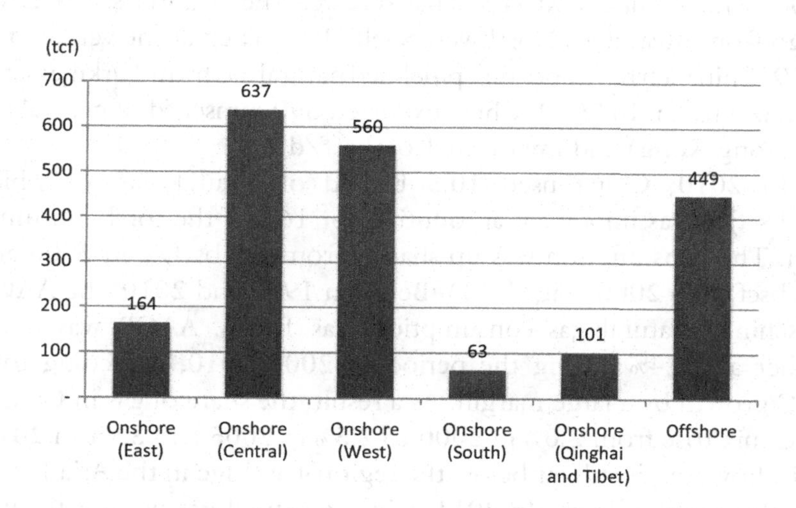

Fig. 1-9. Regional Distribution of China's Natural Gas Resources in 2010.

Note: Based on China's latest government appraisal. Total is 1,973 tcf.

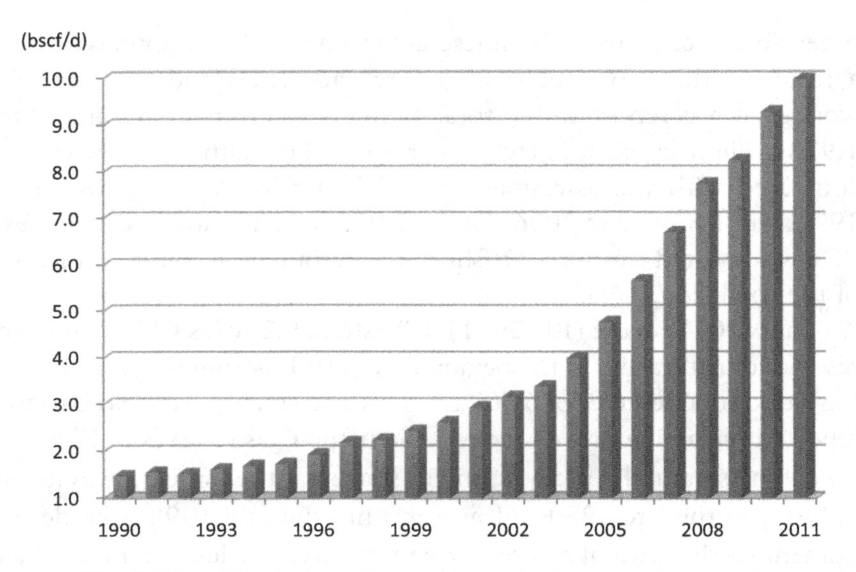

Fig. 1-10. China's Annual Natural Gas Production, 1990–2011.

Prior to 1996, China was not involved in the international natural gas trade. In 1996, China started supplying gas to Hong Kong from its offshore gas field Yacheng 13-1 via an underwater pipeline. In May 2006, China's first LNG terminal received the country's first LNG cargo from Australia's Northwest Shelf plant. Then at the very end of 2009, China started importing pipelined natural gas from Turkmenistan via Kazakhstan. In 2010, China exported 390 mmscf/d of natural gas (to Hong Kong) and imported 1.65 bscf/d.

In 2010, China used 10.5 bscf/d of natural gas, of which 1.7 bscf/d was imported, accounting for 16% of the total consumption. The consumption was up sharply from 1.5 bscf/d in 2000 and 2.3 bscf/d in 2000 (Fig. 1-11). Between 1990 and 2010, the AAGR of China's natural gas consumption was 10.4%. AAGR was much higher at 16.4% during the period of 2000–2010, exceeding total PEC growth by a large margin. As a result, the share of gas in China's PEC mix rose from 2.0% in 2000 to 2.5% in 2005 and 3.9% in 2010. This, however, is still far below the regional average in the Asia Pacific and the world at large. In 2011, China's natural gas use is estimated to have jumped to 12.6 bscf/d.

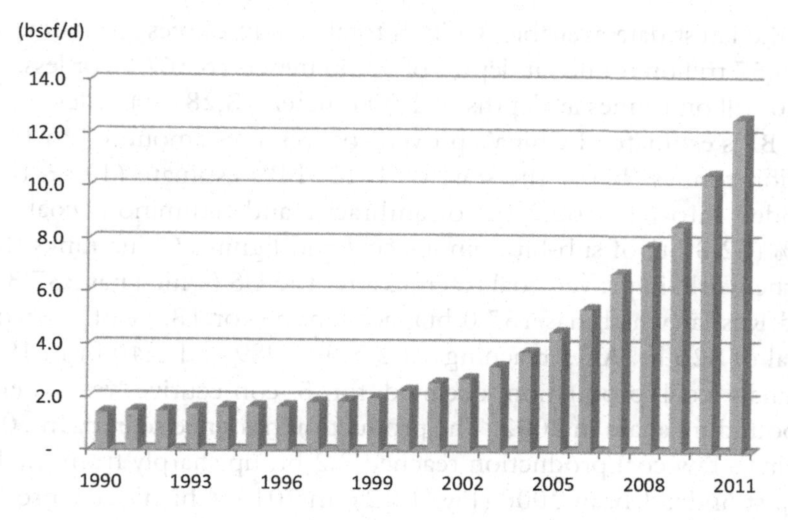

Fig. 1-11. China's Annual Natural Gas Consumption, 1990–2011.
Note: 2011 data are preliminary.

Over the next 10 to 15 years, natural gas production in China is expected to grow rapidly, at a much faster rate than the slow growth for oil. Under the base-case scenario, China's natural gas output is expected to increase to 17.7 bscf/d in 2020 and 25.7 bscf/d by 2030. During the same forecasted period, China's natural gas consumption is expected to rise to 29.1 bscf/d in 2020 and 43.2 bscf/d by 2030. The result is widening natural gas import requirements Indeed, China is set to import more LNG, while pipeline imports from Central Asia and possibly Russia are expected.

It is worth noting that China's unconventional gas business is emerging and is likely to impact the gas industry 5 to 10 years from now. We will provide detailed coverage of unconventional gas resources and production in Chapter 3, and the consumption in Chapter 6.

1.4. Coal Demand, Supply, and Future Growth

China has vast coal deposits and resource potential, but like oil and gas, the gap between resources and proven reserves is rather large. Based on the latest data available, China's total coal resources are claimed to be 5.57 trillion tonnes at depths of 2,000 meters (6,562 ft) or less, and 2.86 trillion tonnes at depths of 1,000 meters (3,281 ft) or less.

BP's estimate of China's proven coal reserves amounted to 114.5 billion tonnes (bt) at the start of 2011. BP's estimate (114.5 bt) is divided into 54% (62.2 bt) of anthracite and bituminous coal, and 46% (52.3 bt) of sub-bituminous coal and lignite. China ranks third in the world in proven coal reserves after the US (which has 237.3 bt) and Russia (which has 157.0 bt), accounting for 13.9% of the world total of 826 bt. After reaching 1.02 bt in 1989 and 1.40 bt in 1996, China's coal production declined for 5 consecutive years before rebounding again in 2002. The production has since soared. In 2010, China's raw coal production reached 3.2 bt, up sharply from the low of just under 1 bt in 2000 (Fig. 1-12). In 2011, China's coal production increased further to 3.5 bt.

Until 2009, China had been a net coal exporter for several decades. However, the imports have grown rapidly since 2001. In the meantime, coal exports have been declining. In 2010, China exported only 19 mmt of coal, down significantly from the peak level of 94 mmt in 2003. The country imported a whopping 182 mmt of coal in 2009, up sharply from the 2001 imports of 3 mmt (Fig. 1-13). In 2011, the imports went up further to 222 mmt while the exports dropped to 15 mmt.

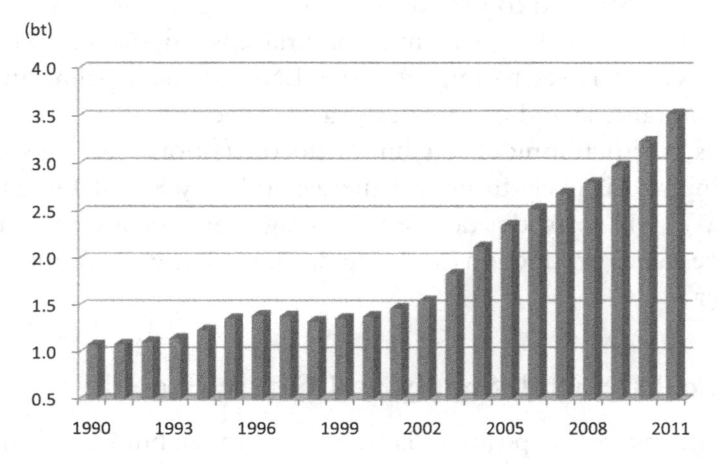

Fig. 1-12. China's Annual Coal Production, 1990–2011.

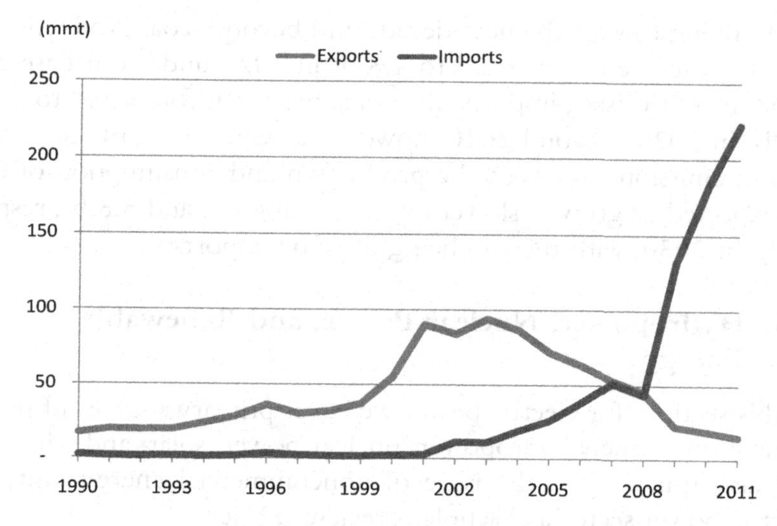

Fig. 1-13. China's Annual Coal Exports and Imports, 1990–2011.

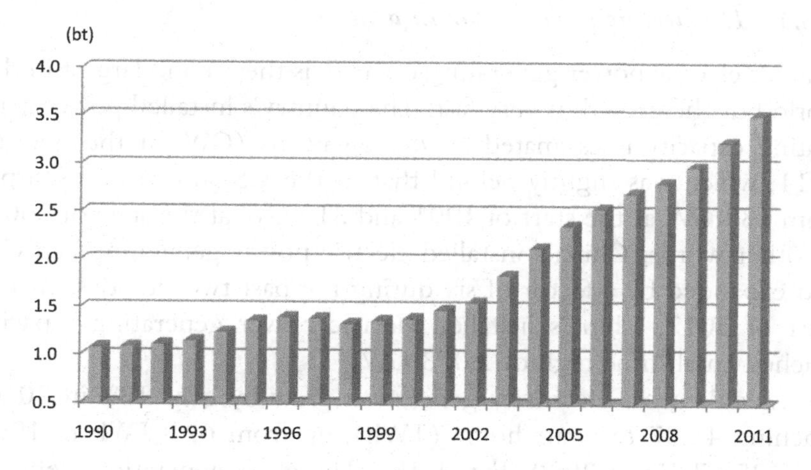

Fig. 1-14. China's Annual Coal Consumption, 1990–2011.

Note: 2011 data are preliminary.

China's coal consumption in 2010 is reached 3.4 bt, up from 1.0 bt in 1990 and 1.3 bt in 2000 (Fig. 1-14). During the 1990s, the AAGR of China's coal consumption was only 2.1%. However, the AAGR surged to 10.1% during the period of 2000–2010. In 2011, the coal use is estimated to reach at nearly 3.7 bt.

Looking toward the next decade and beyond, coal production in China is expected to increase to 4.3 bt in 2020 under our base-case scenario. With rising imports, the consumption is forecasted to reach 4.5 bt in 2020. Beyond 2020, however, as China's efforts to reduce carbon emissions intensify, the production and consumption of coal are expected to grow at slower rates, reaching 4.9 and 5.3 bt, respectively, in 2030, with the gap being filled by imports.

1.5. Hydropower, Nuclear Power, and Renewable Energy

In this section, for electric power we cover primary sources of power generation, namely hydropower, nuclear power, solar, and wind. We will also touch upon the issue of noncommercial energy. But, the electric power sector as a whole is reviewed briefly.

1.5.1. *The electric power sector in general*

China's electric power generating capacity is the second largest in the world but the growth is very fast. The country's installed power generating capacity is estimated at 983 gigawatts (GW) at the start of 2011, which was slightly behind that of the US and was up sharply from 138 GW at the start of 1991 and 319 GW at the start of 2001. In other words, China's installed electric power generating capacity had expanded by a factor of six during the past two decades. At the start of 2012, China's installed electric power generating capacity reached an all-time high of 1,073 GW.

China's gross electricity generation grew by over 13% in 2010, reaching 4,207 terawatt hours (TWh), up from 621 TWh in 1990 and 1356 TWh in 2000 (Fig. 1-15). The gross generation went up further to 4,700 TWh in 2011. This has placed China as the No. 1 electric power producer in the world. The annual growth of China's electric power generation averaged 7.6% per annum during the 1980s, 8.0% during the 1990s, but accelerated to 12.3% between 2000 and 2010.

Over the longer period of time, China will continue to need more power plants to meet the power requirements for economic

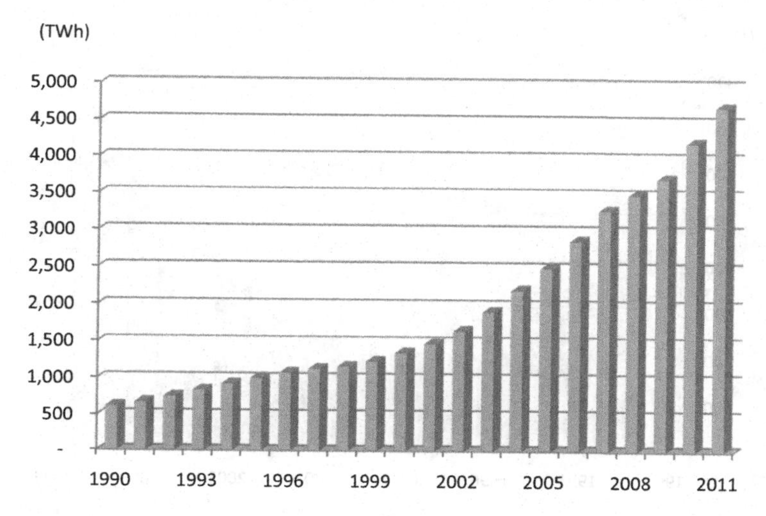

Fig. 1-15. China's Annual Gross Electric Power Generation, 1990–2011.

growth. Our projections show that China's installed electric power generation capacity is likely to reach 1,658 GW in 2020 and 2404 GW by 2030. As a result, the total electric power generation — as well as demand[2] — is expected to reach 8,336 TWh in 2020 and 12,384 TWh by 2030.

1.5.2. *Hydropower*

At the start of 2011, China's installed hydropower capacity was over 218 GW. China ranks No.1 in the world in terms of installed hydroelectricity capacity. The hydropower capacity at the start of 2011 accounted for 22% of China's total installed electric power generating capacity. In 2010, the output of hydroelectricity reached 722 TWh, up from 127 TWh in 2000 and 222 TWh in 2000 (Fig. 1-16). In 2011, however, China's hydroelectricity went down to some

[2] As China engages in only minor exports and imports of electricity as compared to the total electric power used, the gross electricity generation for the future is almost identical to electric power consumption for the country.

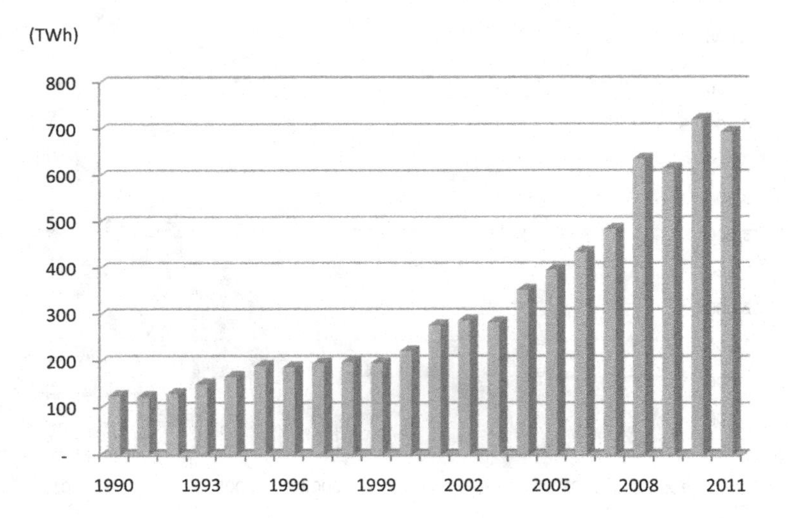

Fig. 1-16. China's Annual Gross Hydroelectricity Output, 1990–2011.

694 TWh, due to the drought in South and Southwest China, even though the installed hydroelectric generating capacity went up further to 231 GW at the start of 2012.

Overall, because hydroenergy is regarded as a relatively clean renewable energy with great potential in China, it has been given priority in the country's energy development planning. Over the next ten years and beyond, the Chinese government's target is to increase or at least maintain the hydropower share in the country's total installed power generating capacity.

Our base-case scenario shows that the share of hydroelectricity in China's total PEC is expected to increase to 8.5% by 2020 and 10.5% by 2030.

1.5.3. *Nuclear power*

China has reasonably large uranium resources. Overall, China's indigenous uranium resources are adequate for the needs of nuclear power expansion in the short term, and will be enough for the medium term. Over the long term, however, more exploration is needed to increase the proven uranium resources to meet the growing need as more nuclear power plants are built.

Until 1982, China did not elect to build any nuclear power plants in spite of the country's long-drawn development of indigenous nuclear technology. Between 1982 and 1993, nuclear power construction proceeded rather slowly. The country's first nuclear power plant has a capacity of 300 MW and was built at Qinshan in Zhejiang Province. It started commercial production in May 1993. China now has a total of 14 reactor generators from 6 nuclear power plants in operation with a total capacity of 11934 MW (Table 1-1). In 2010, power generation from the nuclear plants was 78 TWh, up from 17 TWh in 2000 (Fig. 1-17). In 2011, China's nuclear power generation reached 86 TWh.

Meanwhile, China has embarked on the path to massively expand its nuclear power capacity (Zhou and Zhang 2010, Zhou *et al.* 2011). Currently, 31 new reactor generators are under construction, totaling 34,210 MW in capacity (Table 1-2). Upon their completion, China's

Table 1-1. Status of China's Nuclear Powerplants in Operation as of January 2012.

		Reactor Generator			
Plant and Phase	Province	Series No.	Total	Capacity (MW)	Time Operational
Daya Bay NPP	Guangdong	1	1	984	Feb-94
Qinshan NPP Phase I	Zhejiang	1	2	300	Apr-94
Daya Bay NPP	Guangdong	2	3	984	May-94
Qinshan NPP Phase II	Zhejiang	1	4	650	Apr-02
Qinshan NPP Phase II	Zhejiang	2	5	650	May-02
Ling Ao NPP Phase I	Guangdong	1	6	990	Jan-03
Ling Ao NPP Phase I	Guangdong	2	7	990	Jan-03
Qinshan NPP Phase III	Zhejiang	1	8	728	Jul-03
Qinshan NPP Phase III	Zhejiang	2	9	728	Jul-03
Tianwan NPP Phase I	Jiangsu	1	10	1,060	May-07
Tianwan NPP Phase I	Jiangsu	2	11	1,060	Dec-07
Ling Ao NPP Phase II	Guangdong	1	12	1,080	Jul-10
Qinshan NPP Phase II	Zhejiang	3	13	650	Oct-10
Ling Ao NPP Phase II	Guangdong	2	14	1,080	Aug-11
Total				**11,934**	

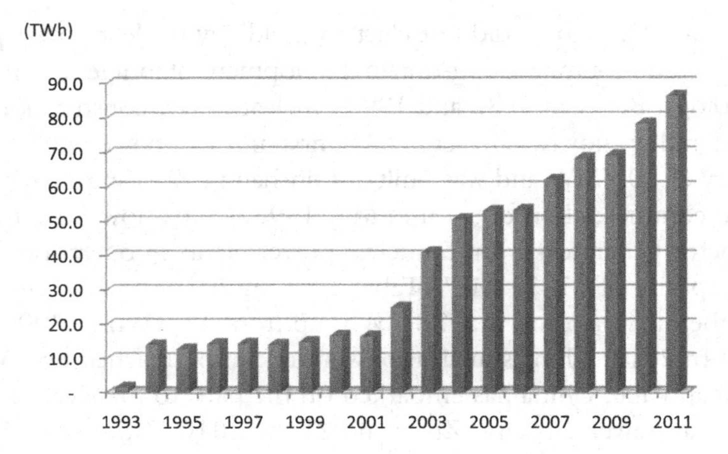

Fig. 1-17. China's Annual Nuclear Power Output, 1992–2011.

total installed nuclear power capacity will be raised to 44 GW. In addition, over 100 GW of new capacity are planned.

In the long run, China's ambitious program for nuclear power development has not been affected by the nuclear power problems faced by Japan as a result of the earthquake and tsunamis on March 11, 2011. Our base-case projection forecasts As such, the share of nuclear power in China's PEC is expected to increase notably, to 3.5% in 2020 and 5.9% by 2030.

1.5.4. *Solar, wind, and other commercially viable renewable energy resources*

The country has a huge renewable energy resource potential, ranging from small hydro and wind power, to biomass (bio-fuels) and industrial waste. Biofuels are classified as biomass. In terms of the overall use of renewable energy in China, the present amount is enormous. However, a significant portion of it is in the noncommercial use of biomass, particularly firewood and straw. The commercial utilization of renewable energy is at a low level but has been growing fast since the 1980s.

China has a promising future for its renewable energy by using commercial biomass, wind power, solar energy, geothermal energy,

Table 1-2. China's Nuclear Powerplants Under Construction.

Plant and Phase	Province	Reactor Generator Series No	Reactor Generator Total	Capacity (MW)
Qinshan NPS Phase II	Zhejiang	4	1	650
Hongyanhe NPP Phase I	Liaoning	1	2	1,080
Hongyanhe NPP Phase I	Liaoning	2	3	1,080
Hongyanhe NPP Phase I	Liaoning	3	4	1,080
Hongyanhe NPP Phase I	Liaoning	4	5	1,080
Hongyanhe NPP Phase II	Liaoning	5–6	7	2×1,080
Ningde NPP Phase I	Fujian	1–4	11	4×1,080
Sanmen NPP Phase I	Zhejiang	1	12	1,250
Sanmen NPP Phase I	Zhejiang	2	13	1,250
Haiyang NPP Phase I	Shandong	1–2	15	2×1,250
Taishan NPP Phase I	Guangdong	1	16	1,750
Taishan NPP Phase I	Guangdong	2	17	1,750
Fuqing NPP Phase I	Fujian	1	18	1,080
Fuqing NPP Phase I	Fujian	2	19	1,080
Fuqing NPP Phase II	Fujian	3–4	21	2×1,080
Yangjiang NPP Phase I	Guangdong	1–2	23	2×1,080
Yangjiang NPP Phase II	Guangdong	3–4	25	2×1,080
Fangjiashan NPP	Zhejiang	1	26	1,080
Fangjiashan NPP	Zhejiang	2	27	1,080
Changjiang NPP Phase I	Hainan	1	28	650
Changjiang NPP Phase I	Hainan	2	29	650
Fangchenggang Hongsha NPS Phase I	Guangxi	1	30	1,080
Fangchenggang Hongsha NPS Phase I	Guangxi	2	31	1,080
Total				**34,210**

*Qinshan expansion.

Note: NPS = Nuclear Power Station.

and other sources (Zhao *et al.*, 2011). However, the challenges facing their use are also tremendous. In a broad sense, renewable energy includes hydroelectricity, biomass, wind, geothermal, solar energy, ocean energy, combustible waste from industries and in urban cities, and alternative fuels for transportation (mainly originating from biomass). Conventional hydroelectric power is the most developed and leading renewable energy at present, where medium- to large-scale hydroelectric power plants are built throughout the world. As such, renewable energy is also narrowly defined to exclude conventional medium- to large-scale generation of hydroelectric power and instead concentrates on its small-scale generation. Moreover, the noncommercial use of biomass is widespread in many developing countries, including China. Thus, efforts are being made by governments of these countries to reduce the noncommercial use and expand the commercial use of biomass. In China the conversion from noncommercial to commercial biomass use is imperative because of the large potential.

Due to its size, China has an enormous potential for renewable energy resources. It has huge hydroenergy resources, which were discussed earlier. China is also suitable for developing solar energy and the potential for geothermal energy is high in the western parts of the country. China has a gigantic biomass resource base. The biomass energy potential in China is over 7 mmboe/d. At present, about two-thirds of that potential has been realized but the use is primarily in the rural area and often in traditional ways, forming a major part of the noncommercial use of energy in China. For the past 25 years, China has taken large strides to reduce the noncommercial use and increase commercial use of biomass, such as methane stoves. As China's economy continues to grow, the availability of biomass provides the basis for China to develop biofuels for transportation and other purposes (O'Kray and Wu, 2010). The increasing amounts of industrial and urban waste could be used for power generation. In addition to the above-mentioned renewable resources, the potential for ocean energy, geothermal, and other sources is also large. For all renewable energy resources, it is challenging to turn resource potential to proven resources and producing capacities. This is particularly the case for the modern use of renewable energy, where the competition from conventional nonrenewable energy is stiff.

Excluding hydroelectricity, which has been well developed, China's current use of renewable energy varies from one source to another, but the total volume is actually quite large, due in large part to biomass use. In 2010 China's use of solar, wind, and other commercially viable renewable energy sources amounted to over 500 kboe/d, accounting for 1.0% of the total PEC. But their growth rate of the past five years has been fast. In comparison, the consumption of traditional nonrenewable energy in the form of biomass, is estimated at 4.1 mmboe/d in 2010, accounting for 7.7% of the total PEC of 53.9 mmboe/d. In 1990, China's total PEC was only 17.4 mmboe/d but the share of noncommercial biomass was 23%. The decline in share was mainly from the noncommercial part of the renewable energy while the commercial part has been growing notably since the early 1980s. Meanwhile the growth of wind, solar, and other commercially viable renewable energy sources (including biomass power, methane stoves, and other commercial use of biomass) has been fast.

Prior to 2005, China had been slow in developing wind power; the development has since accelerated. At the start of 2011, China had nearly 47 GW of installed wind power, exceeding the US for the first time to be the world's largest, up sharply from 268 MW at the start of 2000 and 764 MW at the start of 2005 as well as 26 GW at the start of 2010. Moreover, China continues to be the fastest growing country for installed wind power as well, with total capacity rising further to 63 GW at the start of 2012.

China's installed solar photovoltaic power generation capacity reached 450 MW at the start of 2011. At the start of 2012, China's photovoltaic power generation capacity is estimated to have jumped to 2.1 GW. China is the leader of the world in their use of solar water heaters: over 60% of the world's solar water heaters are installed in China. At the start of 2011 the total area heated by solar energy in China is estimated to have exceeded 150 million cubic meters (mmcm), up from 130 mmcm at the start of 2009 and 80 mmcm at the start of 2006.

Renewable and new energy has been given a high priority since the new millennium, particularly after China committed to reduce the intensity of its carbon emissions by 40%–45% by 2020 from the 1990s levels. Under the 11th FYP (covering the period from 2006 to 2010), China promised to reduce its energy intensity by 20%. In December 2005, the National People's Congress (NPC) — in the Chinese Parliament — passed the first ever *Renewable Energy Law of the PRC*, which took effect on January 1, 2006. In December 2009, the Standing Committee of the NPC approved the revised *Renewable Energy Law of the PRC (Revised)*. The new law has become effective since April 1, 2010. It covers wind power, solar energy, hydropower, biomass, geothermal, ocean energy, and other nonfossil energy sources. Realizing the special nature of hydropower, which is well developed in China, the law separates hydroenergy from the rest of the renewable energy and requests a further review by the government on how the law may be applied to hydro. Also the law does not cover the noncommercial use of biomass, including straw, firewood, and animal dung. The main objective of the law is to promote the development of renewable energy.

In March 2010, China's latest *Mid- to Long-Term Development Program for Renewable Energy* was released. Based on this program, the Chinese government will soon announce specific targets for new energy developments by 2020, which are understood to include the following:

- **Hydropower:** Increased the installed hydroelectric power generating capacity to 300 GW, of which 75 GW will be small hydro.
- **Windpower:** Increased the installed capacity to 100–150 GW (the target under the 12th FYP is 110 GW by 2015).
- **Biomass power:** Increase the installed capacity to 30 GW.
- **Biomass methane:** Total area of methane stoves will reach 44 billion square meters.
- **Solar photovoltaic power:** Increase the installed capacity to 20 GW (the target under the 12th FYP is 5 GW by 2015).

- **Solar heating:** Increase the total area heated by solar energy to 300 million square meters.
- **Other renewable energy:** Develop geothermal, ocean energy, and other such resources.

Some of the above-mentioned targets, such as solar photovoltaic power, are too ambitious. For wind power, however, the 2020 target may be understated. Overall, it is estimated that at least 5 trillion yuan (US$736 billion) will be needed to achieve the set targets. Our forecasts show that China's solar, wind, and other commercially viable energy will increase its share in total PEC to 3.2% in 2020 and 4.9% by 2030.

1.6. Economic Development and Energy Intensity

As the population growth has been slowing down, rapid economic development is the single most important and formidable force supporting the strong demand growth of energy in China. Beyond that, as energy prices rise, demand may be affected. Many specific factors are also driving sectoral demand for energy. We will discuss the impact of rising prices and sector-specific factors for gas demand in future chapters. In this section, the focus is squarely on the growth of the Chinese economy, measured primarily by gross domestic product (GDP) as well as the impact of China's new carbon emission policies.

1.6.1. *Economic development: Foundation for the future growth of oil demand*

China's economic growth since the end of the 1970s has been spectacular. During the period of 1978–2010, China's officially reported real GDP growth registered 9.8% per annum on average. In 2009, despite the impact of the global financial crisis, China's real GDP growth reached 9.2%. For 2010 and 2011, the real GDP growth rates in China were 10.3% and 9.2% respectively.

In constant 2011 yuan, China's real GDP increased from 5.9 trillion yuan (US$915 billion in 2011 dollars) in 1990 to 15.9 trillion yuan (US$2.5 trillion) in 2000, and finally to 47.2 trillion yuan (US$7.3 trillion) in 2011. Meanwhile, the Chinese population increased from 1.16 billion at the end of 1990 to 1.28 billion at the end of 2000 and 1.35 billion at the end of 2011 (Table 1-3). As a result, the per-capita GDP in China (in constant 2011 US dollars) rose from $800 in 1990, to $1946 in 2000, and US$5,417 in 2011.

Measured by exchange-rate GDP in 2010, China overtook Japan to become the second-largest economy in the world after the US. In 2010, China accounted for 9.3% of the world's GDP based on conventional exchange rate, which was far below the share of 23.1% held by the US, but ahead of 8.5% by Japan.

The calculations are all based on the official GDP figures, and conversions to US dollars are based on official exchange rates. If purchasing power parity (PPP) is applied, total GDP, as well as

Table 1-3. China's Year end Population, 1980–2011.

Year	Population (Million)	Growth Rate	Year	Population (Million)	Growth Rate
1980	1,000.7	1.35%	1996	1,236.3	1.01%
1981	1,016.5	1.58%	1997	1,247.6	0.92%
1982	1,030.1	1.33%	1998	1,257.9	0.82%
1983	1,043.6	1.31%	1999	1,267.4	0.76%
1984	1,058.5	1.43%	2000	1,276.3	0.70%
1985	1,075.1	1.56%	2001	1,284.5	0.65%
1986	1,093.0	1.67%	2002	1,292.3	0.60%
1987	1,110.3	1.58%	2003	1,299.9	0.59%
1988	1,127.0	1.51%	2004	1,307.6	0.59%
1989	1,143.3	1.45%	2005	1,314.5	0.53%
1990	1,158.2	1.30%	2006	1,321.3	0.52%
1991	1,171.7	1.16%	2007	1,328.0	0.51%
1992	1,185.2	1.15%	2008	1,334.7	0.49%
1993	1,198.5	1.12%	2009	1,340.9	0.48%
1994	1,211.2	1.06%	2010	1,347.4	0.48%
1995	1,223.9	1.05%	2011	1,353.8	0.48%

per-capita GDP, turns out to be substantially higher in China. For instance, using a PPP-based measurement developed by the International Monetary Fund (IMF), China's GDP is estimated at US$12.6 trillion in 2011, implying a per-capita GDP of US$9329. The PPP-based GDP places China way ahead of Japan and ranks it as the second largest economy in the world after the United States.

Based on PPP, China accounted for 13.6% of the world GDP in 2010, while the US share was 19.5% (IMF, 2011a and 2011b). China's share thus exceeded the share of 5.9% for Japan by a large margin. China's 2010 per-capita GDP based on PPP was US$7, 563, but still below the world average of US$10, 793, and far below US$46,860 for the US and US$34,043 for Japan, though China was ahead of India's US$3,413.

In addition to the rapid economic growth, the past 25 years also witnessed booming foreign trade and foreign investment in China, both of which grew much faster than the real GDP in China. In 2008, China's total foreign trade reached US$2.6 trillion, up from merely US$115 billion in 1990 and US$474 billion in 2000. Due to the impact of the global financial crisis, China's foreign trade fell by as much as 34% in 2009 to US$2.2 trillion, the first time since 1998, which was when China's foreign trade last fell as a result of the Asian financial crisis. For 2010, however, China's exports and imports rose again sharply, with the total trade topping an all-time high of nearly US$3 trillion (Fig. 1.18). Then in 2011, the total volume of trade increased again to an all-time high of US$3.6 trillion.

The AAGR for total merchandise imported and exported during the 1980–2010 period was 17.6%, of which the exports had an AAGR of 17.7% while it was 17.6% for imports. Except for 1993, China has had a trade surplus since 1990. The trade surplus surged to US$296 billion in 2008 before dropping to US$196 in 2009. For 2010, China's trade surplus shrunk further to US$183 billion. For 2011, the trade surplus decline further to US$155 billion.

Foreign capital continues to move into China. The actual direct foreign investment (DFI) amounted to an all-time high of US$92.4 billion in 2008, before going down slightly to US$90 billion in 2009. This was up from US$3.5 billion in 1990 and US$40.7 billion in

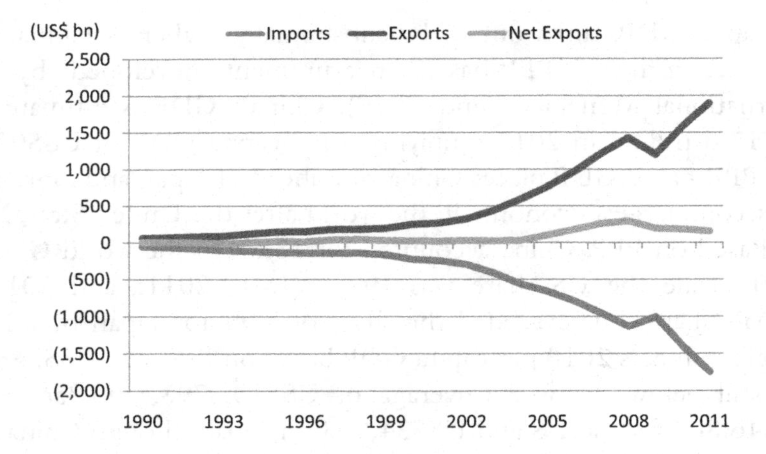

Fig. 1-18. China's Exports, Imports, and Trade Balance, 1990–2011.

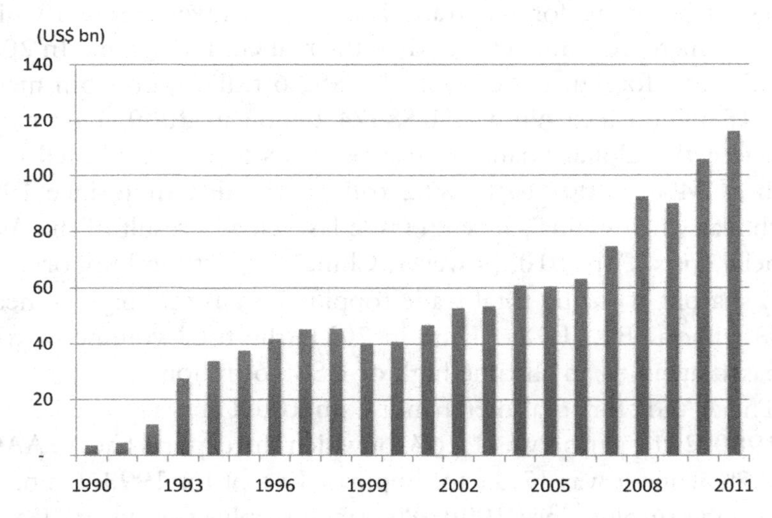

Fig. 1-19. China's Actual Direct Foreign Investment, 1990–2011.

2000 (Fig. 1-19). For 2010, the DFI rose again to US$106 billion and then to US$116 billion in 2011. From 1979 to end of 2011, over 750,000 foreign-funded companies were established. The cumulative actual DFI during the above-mentioned period was nearly US$1.2 trillion.

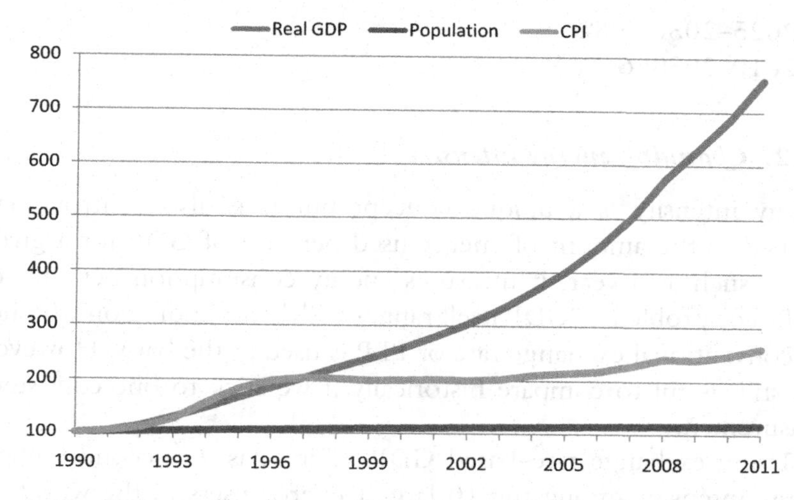

Fig. 1-20. Indexes of Population, Real GDP, and CPI in China 1990–2011 (1990 = 100).

Fig. 1-20 provides indexes for population, GDP, and retail prices from 1985 to 2011, setting 1990 as the base index equal to 100. By 2011, the population index reached 118, the real GDP index 759 and the consumer price index 261. The interactions of the last two indicators suggest that the income (GDP) effect on the energy demand may be somewhat moderated by the rising prices.

Economic growth in China has not been evenly distributed among the different provinces and regions. For the country as a whole, the real GDP growth rate is forecasted to be 7.1% during the forecast period of 2011–2030 under the base-case scenario, raising the total GDP to US$26 trillion (in constant 2011 US dollar). Under the high-case scenario, the AAGR of GDP between 2011 and 2030 can reach 7.4%, while it will be 3.9% for the low-case scenario.

More specifically, we assume the following AAGRs of GDP for the entire book under the Base-Case Scenario:

- 2011–2015: 7.9%
- 2015–2020: 7.4%
- 2020–2025: 6.7%

- 2025–2030: 5.8%
- 2010–2030: 6.9%

1.6.2. *Changing energy intensity*

Energy intensity is a unique concept but it is also controversial. Defined as the amount of energy used per unit of GDP for a given period such as a year, it measures energy consumption per unit of GDP. The problem is GDP itself ranges widely depending on whether the conventional exchange rate or PPP is used as the basis. However, it is still useful to compare historically if we stick to one consistent measurement.

Using exchange rate–based GDP, China has the second highest energy intensity among the 10 largest energy users in the world, at 3.3 boe per US$ (in thousands) of GDP (US$kGDP at current price) in 2010, and behind Russia. Its energy intensity in 2010 was nearly 5 times as high as that of Japan and 2.8 times that of the US.

If PPP-based GDP is used, China's energy intensity is reduced to 1.9 boe/US$kGDP, about 130% higher than Japan's and around 60% higher than that of the US. Despite the reduction, China has the second highest energy intensity among the top ten energy consuming countries, behind only Russia.

Comparing with its own history, China did demonstrate a substantial decline of energy intensity since 1980, down from 11.2 boe/US$kGDP (in constant 2011 dollar) all the way to 3.2 boe/US$kGDP in 2001 but went up to 3.3 boe/US$kGDP in 2004 before coming down again to 2.9 boe/US$kGDP in 2011 (Fig. 1-21). In other words, China's energy intensity had actually been reduced by over 75% between 1980 and 2011. This has reflected faster economic expansion coupled with reasonable growth of primary commercial energy use. (Zhang and Tian, 2010; Chu, Fesharaki, and Wu, 2006; Li *et al*, 2011; Zou and Chau, 2006; Yuan *et al*, 2008; Yuan *et al*, 2010)

For the 11th FYP (covering the 2006–2010 period), the Chinese government promised to reduce the energy consumption per unit of GDP by 20% by the end of 2010. Based on China's own data, it was

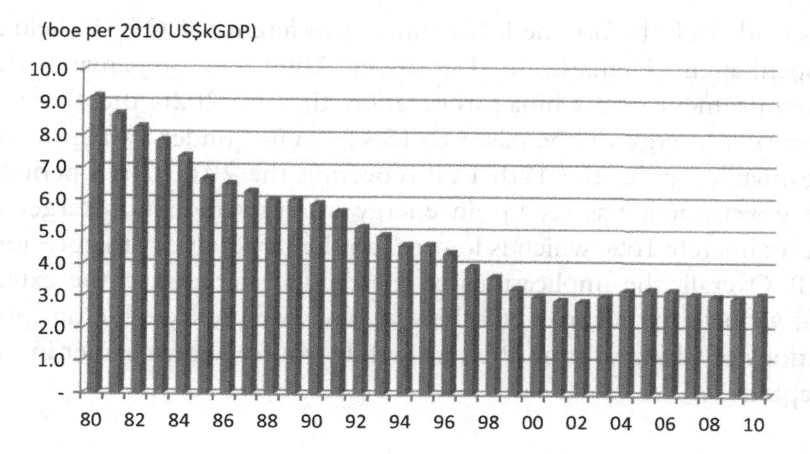

Fig. 1-21. China's Changing Energy Intensity (Exchange Rate-Based GDP), 1980–2010.

Note: Energy intensity is defined as PEC per unit of GDP.

claimed that the energy intensity was down by 15.61% from the end of 2005 to the end of 2009. However, the official data also shows that the energy intensity went up by 0.9% during the first half of 2010. As such, the government had made concerted efforts during the second half of 2010 to reduce the intensity. Still the government finally announced that the energy intensity actually dropped by 19.06% during the 11th FYP, short of the official target but that did not prevent the government from declaring a great achievement in this effort. It is quite clear that the Chinese government has done a lot as far as the energy intensity is concerned but the accuracy of official energy and economic growth data in China is often subject of doubt.

Looking ahead, the most relevant target concerning China's energy intensity set by the government was its announcement in late November 2009 that China would reduce its carbon emission intensity[3] by 40%–45% by 2020 from the 2005 levels. The announcement

[3] Carbon Emission Intensity is defined as the amount of CO_2 emitted from energy use per unit of GDP for a given period, such as a year.

was made right before the UN Climate Conference (COP 15) held in Copenhagen, Demark, in December 2009. Accompanying this announcement was China's reiteration that by 2020 the share of renewable energy will be raised to 15% from just under 9% at present. Meanwhile, under the 12th FYP (covering the 2011–2015 period), the government has set up an energy intensity reduction target of approximately 16%, which is lower than the target under the previous FYP. Overall, the implications of these policy targets, to the extent that we believe they may be achieved, have been reflected in our projections of China's future PEC growth by source shown earlier in this chapter.

chapter 2

Changing Structures of the Petroleum Industry and Energy Policies

After five decades of development, China has a large and well-established oil industry, which plays an important role in China's national economy and social development. China is one of the largest oil producers, refiners, and consumers in the world. Currently, it ranks fifth in total crude oil production after Saudi Arabia, Russia, US, and Iran, and it ranks second in both petroleum products consumption and distillation refining capacity after US. However, China still lags far behind in natural gas development and use. The country has been rapidly catching up in developing its gas sector, increasing imports, and expanding the market.

Combining oil and gas, the petroleum industry remains one of the most heavily protected industries in China. Despite many organizational changes and restructuring of the industry, the state, through the state-owned oil companies, has a huge influence on the petroleum industry, ranging from upstream exploration, development, and production to downstream refining, distribution, and marketing. The reform of the oil and gas industry has never stopped since the 1980s, but there is still a long way to go to achieve full liberalization of the industry and oil and gas markets. As of early 2012, China's first ever *Energy Law* is being reviewed and amended. If passed, the *Energy Law* will provide clearer directions of China's future institutional reform for the petroleum industry and the energy sector.

This chapter provide a brief review of the recent institutional changes in China's petroleum industry in Section 2.1. A presentation of who's who in China's oil industry is provided in Section 4.2, so as to have a better understanding of the regime governing the petroleum industry and markets in China. Finally, we review the evolving petroleum policies of China with a focus on the current situation.

2.1. Institutional Changes in the Petroleum Industry

China has a large and integrated petroleum industry with a history of indigenous technology development, especially in the 1960s and 1970s during the period of self-reliance. After the end of the 1970s, China started a massive opening of the petroleum industry to foreign technologies, investments, and trade.

2.1.1. *The 1990s and before*

Prior to the 1980s, the last organizational change of the Chinese oil and gas industry was the establishment of the Ministry of Petroleum Industry (MOPI) and the Ministry of Chemical Industry (MOCI) in 1978, from the defunct Ministry of Petroleum and Chemical Industries. MOPI was in charge of most of the upstream exploration and all of the development and production activities in China. The downstream refining industry was managed by MOCI, MOPI, and local governments.

In 1982, the China National Offshore Oil Corporation (CNOOC) was established. CNOOC's mandate was to conduct upstream offshore oil and gas business activities in China, including exploration, development, and production, as well as the opening of China's offshore oil and gas sector to foreign investments. China's offshore oil and gas sector was first opened in 1979 — the first-ever opening of China's petroleum industry since the 1960s — and has since grown to a large scale. At the time of its foundation, CNOOC was supervised by the now-defunct MOPI. In the downstream refining sector, China Petrochemical Corporation (Sinopec) was founded in 1983, taking over 90% of China's refineries from various government ministries and local governments. The downstream business of MOPI was therefore drastically reduced in the 1980s, and all refineries operated by MOCI were transferred to Sinopec.

In 1988, China went through a major change in its government structure. First, it abolished MOPI and established the China National Petroleum Corporation (CNPC) in an effort to separate government regulatory functions from business operations. In the meantime, CNOOC became independent and was placed directly under the State Planning Commission (SPC). Second, the government also abolished three other ministries: coal, electric power, and nuclear industry, and established three respective state corporations in their demise. Third, the Ministry of Energy (MOE) was established, assuming the responsibility of overall planning and policy coordination. The government functions of the former MOPI as well as Sinopec were transferred to MOE. The MOE existed for only five years and became defunct in 1993, and its governmental functions were largely reverted to CNPC and Sinopec. By then, China's upstream oil and gas business was largely divided between CNPC (onshore) and CNOOC (offshore). Sinopec dominated the downstream refining sector, although CNPC also possessed significant refineries, which grew vigorously in the 1990s. A minor player in the upstream sector was the exploratory arm of the Ministry of Geology and Mineral Resources (MGMR), which later became China National Star Petroleum Corporation (CNSPC) in 1996.

The oil industry had long been criticized for the separation of upstream oil production from downstream refining, the ambiguous state-enterprise relationship, and many other problems. In search of a better structure for the overstaffed and inefficient industry, the oil sector underwent another round of structural changes starting in March 1998. As a result, both CNPC and Sinopec were restructured into two integrated oil companies operating in divided geographical areas of China.

The reorganization, which was largely completed in July 1998, involved ownership transfers of enterprises between CNPC and Sinopec, and from the local governments and other companies to CNPC and Sinopec. With the reorganization, the interests and assets of CNPC and Sinopec were divided along geographical lines. CNPC's territory encompasses the entire Northeast, Northwest, West, and parts of the Southwest and the North, as defined in this book. Sinopec operates in the Middle and Lower Yangtze regions, the South, part of the Southwest, and part of the North. In addition to the reorganization of CNPC and Sinopec, MGMR and MOCI were abolished. In the meantime, SPC was renamed the State Development Planning Commission (SDPC). Upon the demise of MGMR, together with a number of other state administrations for oceanography, geological mapping, and land management, etc., the new Ministry of Land and Natural Resources (MLNR) was established in March 1998. For MOCI, the enterprises previously affiliated with it were either merged with CNPC and Sinopec (such as its refineries and ethylene plants) or became large independent state enterprises (such as the fertilizer plants). With the abolishment of MGMR, CNSPC was first placed under MLNR, and then under the newly established State Administration of Petroleum and Chemical Industries (SAPCI), before it was taken over by Sinopec in early 2000. The government functions of the now defunct MOCI, along with those of CNPC, Sinopec, and CNOOC, were transferred to SAPCI, which came under the State Economic and Trade Commission (SETC).

Since the 1998 reorganization, the two integrated companies, CNPC and Sinopec, have further consolidated their assets, while CNOOC has expanded its downstream petrochemical activities and the LNG business. During the 1999–2001 period, all three state oil companies also formed full-fledged stock companies and launched initial public offerings (IPOs). In the oil trading area, Unipec and Chinaoil were restructured in late 1998, thereafter ending Sinochem's equal status in the joint-venture oil trading companies and granting exclusive control over Unipec to Sinopec and exclusive control over Chinaoil to CNPC. Some of the major developments are summarized as follows.

2.1.2. *IPO and streamlining of state oil companies*

CNPC established PetroChina Company Limited (PetroChina) in November 1999, while Sinopec formed Sinopec Corp in February 2000. Prior to that, China National Offshore Oil Corporation Ltd. (CNOOC Ltd.) had been established by CNOOC in 1999. The three state oil companies have since transferred all their core businesses to their respective stock companies. They have kept other businesses — mostly the nonproducing ones — and also some debt-ridden production units, in the parent companies.

Upon its establishment in November 1999, PetroChina took from CNPC most of their upstream petroleum subsidiaries, refineries, sales companies, and pipeline companies as well as research institutions with focus on exploration and development, refineries and petrochemicals, sales, and pipelines. The parent company, CNPC, owns businesses in engineering and technical services, production services, overseas investments, manufacturing, property management, and social services. Sinopec Corp was established in February 2000, with Sinopec as its sole shareholder before the overseas stock listing in October 2000. Sinopec Corp also took the main upstream, refining, and petrochemical business from the parent company Sinopec.
Meantime, both CNPC and Sinopec have greatly enhanced their control over oil imports and exports. After the restructuring of Sinopec and CNPC in mid-1998, Sinochem, once the largest oil trader in China, was marginalized and forced to reduce its respective shares from 50% to 30% in both Chinaoil (a joint venture between CNPC and Sinochem) and Unipec (a joint venture between Sinopec and Sinochem). Sinochem has since lost management roles in both state oil trading companies. As of now, Sinochem still retains 30% stake in Chinaoil, but it has no share with Unipec. Although Sinochem has members who sit on the board of Chinaoil, Sinochem has no influence on the operations of Chinaoil.

CNPC/PetroChina and Sinopec have taken a series of other measures to consolidate their refining business by upgrading refineries, increasing investments for the production of higher quality products, products trading, and marketing. In addition to consolidation, the state oil companies have also made some efforts to streamline corporate structures and size.

2.1.3. *China's entry into the WTO and the 2000s*

Another important event for China's petroleum industry is the country's entry into the WTO. China's journey to join the General Agreement on Tariff and Trade (GATT), the predecessor of WTO, began in 1986. After 15 years of tortuous negotiations, setbacks, and progress, China finally became a full WTO member on December 11, 2001. Prior to then, the important breakthroughs were the China–US trade agreement signed in November 1999, the China–EU trade agreement signed in May 2000, and the passing of permanent normal trade relations (PNTR) for China by the US Congress at the same time.

The trade agreements with the US and the EU laid the foundation for much of the WTO concessions granted to China for its petroleum industry. The concessions were mainly in two areas: oil trade and marketing. For oil trade, China had agreed to lower tariffs on crude and products and gradually expand the imports of refined products by nonstate oil companies. For oil marketing, China promised to open up the retail oil business to foreign investments by the end of 2004 and the wholesale oil business by the end of 2006. These concessions have since been implemented to various extents. After existing for merely 3 years, the Chinese government abolished all 9 State Administrations affiliated with the State Economic and Trade Commission (SETC) in 2001. Governmental functions performed by these administrations were transferred to regular departments under SETC.

Among the agencies abolished were the State Administration of Petroleum and Chemical Industries (SAPCI). As mentioned earlier, SAPCI, along with other administrations, was established in March 1998 as part of the governmental restructuring. After SAPCI was done away with in February 2001, an industry association named China Petroleum and Chemical Industry Association (CPCIA) was established in April 2001. CPCIA has over 200 member companies including the three state oil companies. It mainly provides various services to its member companies but has limited governmental functions and management roles to play. As such, the three state oil companies (CNPC, Sinopec, and CNOOC) and their listed companies were placed under the State Council and guided directly by SETC (before its own demise in 2003) and SDPC (later renamed in 2003) for policy matters.

The last major reshuffle of the Chinese government cabinet and ministries occurred in 2003 during the 10th Assembly of the National People's Congress (NPC). Key terms for the government change, however, were determined back in November 2002 during the 16th Chinese Communist Party (CCP) Congress in Beijing, which produced a new CCP Central Committee and the CCP Central Committee Secretariat for the following five years ending in 2007. On November 15, 2002, the First Plenary Session of the 16th CCP Central Committee was held, leading to the formation of a 24-member CCP Politburo (plus one alternative member), 9-member Politburo Standing Committee, and the CCP Central Military Commission (CMC). Hu Jintao was elected the General Secretary of the CCP, replacing Jiang Zemin. As a result the fourth-generation Chinese top leadership, led by Hu Jintao and Wen Jiabao, finally came to the front stage and the so-called Hu–Wen regime began. Nearly two years later, Hu also took over the Chairmanship of the CMC from Jiang Zemin in September 2004.

China's 10th NPC wrapped up in March 2003. As expected, Hu Jintao as the CCP General Secretary was elected the President of China at the March 2003 NPC. The parliament also produced a new State Council — the Chinese Cabinet. Wen Jiabao, a former Vice Premier, was appointed as the new Premier. Later in March 2005, Hu Jintao replaced Jiang Zemin to become the Chairman of the People's Republic of China's CMC.

The major governmental changes under Premier Wen Jiabao in March 2003 can be summarized as follows:

- The SETC was abolished. This is one of the biggest changes in this round of reshuffling, ending five years of rivalry and overlapping responsibilities between SETC and the SDPC.

- The SDPC itself was renamed the National Development and Reform Commission (NDRC), taking over many of the functions from the now-defunct SETC.
- A new regulatory body, the State-Owned Assets Supervision and Administration Commission (SASAC) was formed. The establishment of SASAC is considered one of the most important developments in the government's reorganization. Now approximately 24.3 trillion yuan (US$3.6 trillion) of state assets, including those of the state oil companies, are under the supervision and management of this commission.
- A new regulatory body for banking business, the State Banking Management Commission (SBMC) was established. Both SASAC and SBMC are said to be semi-independent but supervised by the State Council. Their relationship, however, may evolve and change in the future.
- After decades in business, the Ministry of Foreign Trade and Economic Cooperation (MOFTEC) was abolished. A new Ministry of Commerce (MOFCOM) was established to be in charge of both domestic and foreign trade.

As far as the energy sector is concerned, soon after the NDRC was reorganized, the State Council decided at the end of March 2003 to establish the Energy Bureau within NDRC. Various departments and divisions related to energy, previously under SDPC and SETC, have since been transferred to the newly-established BOE. Backed by the NDRC, the BOE has since assumed the responsibility of coordinating planning, policy, and regulatory issues governing China's oil, gas, coal, power (thermal, hydro, and nuclear), and renewable energy.

For the two years since China's last reshuffling of the energy management and governing system in early 2003, the government had been mulling over ways to restructure the energy management system further. At the end of May 2005, the Chinese government decided to form the National Energy Leading Group (NELG) at a higher level within the State Council. The NELG was headed by Premier Wen Jiabao, the deputy heads were vice premiers, and the members include 12 ministers and an army general. In June 2005, the NELG established the National Energy Office (NEO) to represent it in the NDRC. The NEO was led by then NDRC Chairman Ma Kai; its Executive Vice Chairman was former CNPC President Ma Fucai.

The establishment of the NELG, known as "China's Energy Cabinet," indicates that the government could not settle the issue of whether it ought to establish a permanent governing body for energy at very senior levels. The debate over whether China needs a Ministry of Energy or a ministerial-level Energy Commission continued. The establishment of the NELG and the NEO at NDRC has put the Energy Bureau in an awkward position. For this reason, the government carefully defined the NELG as a coordinating council for discussions of critical energy issues at the highest level. The NEO served as the representative of NELG and handles its routine operations.

2.1.4. *Latest changes since 2008*

Five years after the last CCP Congress that established the Hu-Wen regime, the 17th CCP Congress was held in October 2007, which was again a prelude to the 11th NPC in March 2008. On October 22, 2007, the First Plenary Session of the 17th CCP Central Committee produced the new CCP Politburo (25 members), Politburo Standing Committee, and the CCP CMC. Hu Jintao's titles as the General Secretary of CCP and Chairman of CCP's CMC continued. The Politburo Standing Committee still has nine members of which five are new.

Prior to the assembly, there was an expectation that the new *Energy Law* would be discussed and passed, but it was not. In November 2008, the NDRC submitted the first draft to the State Council for review. As of early 2012, the *Energy Law* is still being reviewed and amended. Some major points of the draft energy law are worth noting:

- The draft law has 15 chapters, covering areas such as energy management, strategies, development, supply, conservation, reserves, emergency preparedness, rural energy, fiscal incentives, technologies, international cooperation, inspection, and supervision.

- China is eager to use the law to regulate various aspects of the energy industry, bolster energy efficiency, and promote energy conservation.
- The law may also lay ground for the establishment of an energy ministry in China.
- It also calls for the establishment of an energy price regime, where market-based prices are to be combined with government regulations to determine energy prices, but the market will play a more important role.
- An entry regime may be established for various energy sectors, including wholesale, retail, imports, and exports, where the government can set the minimum conditions for doing business in these areas. During the process, both public interest and national security will be taken into consideration.
- The law calls for a diversified ownership system for the energy industry, but for key areas, the government is called upon to have controlling share of any ventures or business.
- Finally, the law calls for the establishment of an energy reserves system, which includes strategic reserves of energy products and resources. Businesses and companies are called upon to contribute the state energy reserves along with government-owned reserves.

During the 11th NPC, the National Energy Administration (NEA) was established. Although the NEA is still attached to the NDRC — reflected by the fact that the Administrator is also a vice chairman of the National Development Reform Commission (NDRC) — it is now a semi-ministerial ranking government agency. Furthermore, the NPC approved the creation of the National Energy Commission (NEC) and the NEC was formally established in February 2010.

The NEC consists of the following members at present:

- Chairman: Wen Jiabao (Premier)
- Vice Chairman: Li Keqiang (Vice Premier)
- Commissioners:
  - You Quan (Deputy Secretary General, State Council)

- Zhu Zhixin (Director, Office of General Affairs, Chinese Communist Party Central Committee Task Force for Finance)
- Yang Jiechi (Minister of Foreign Affairs)
- Zhang Ping (NDRC Chairman)
- Wan Gang (Minister of Science and Technology)
- Miao Yu (Minister of Industry and Information Technology)
- Geng Huichang (Minister of National Security)
- Xie Xuren (Minister of Finance)
- Xu Shaoshi (Minister of Land and Natural Resources)
- Zhou Shengxian (Minister of Environmental Protection)
- Li Shenglin (Minister of Transportation and Communications)
- Chen Lei (Minister of Water Resources)
- Chen Deming (Minister of MOFCOM)
- Zhou Xiaochuan (President, People's Bank of China)
- Wang Yong (Chairman, SASAC, who replaced Li Rongrong in August 2010)
- Xiao Jie (Administrator, State Administration of Taxation)
- Luo Lin (Administrator, State Administration for Work Safety)
- Shang Fulin (Chairman, China Banking Supervision Committee)
- Wu Xinxiong (Chairman, China Electric Power Supervision Committee)
- Zhang Qinsheng (Deputy General Chief of Staff, People's Liberation Army)
- Liu Tienan (NDRC Vice Chairman and Administrator of NEA)

The NEC office is headed by the NDRC Chairman Zhang Ping. The Deputy Director is now Mr. Liu Tienan, who is also one of the nine NDRC vice chairmen as well as the head of the NEA. The major responsibilities of the NEC are (1) studying and formulating the national energy development strategies; (2) reviewing major issues related to energy security and developments; and (3) coordinating important tasks for domestic energy developments and international energy cooperation.

The latest establishment of NEC is nothing new. China did have a NEC in 1980 for two years and Ministry of Energy (MOE) in 1988 for five years, and had the similar high-ranking National Energy Leading Group (NELG), which established the National Energy Office (NEO) to represent it in the NDRC, in 2005 for three years. While the NEO did do some work in helping formulate energy policies and drafting China's first ever *Energy Law*, which has not been formally passed yet, the NELG had achieved little during the period of its existence between 2005 and 2008. Moreover, the establishment of the NEC was actually approved in March 2008 at the 11th NPC. At the time it was rumored to be headed by Vice Premier Zhang Dejiang, who is in charge of industrial activities in Premier Wen Jiabao's cabinet. The latest NEC debut in early 2010 was thus just an implementation of a decision made two year ago though it clearly has had a facelift. Not only is it headed by the premier himself, Vice Chairman Li Keqiang is also a powerful person. Li is considered a successor to Wen barring unexpected developments. The appointment of NDRC Chairman Zhang Ping as the Director of the NEC Office may also have brought NEC closer to the functional agency NEA.

Still the question is: will the NEC work? We certainly have our doubts. First, being such a high-level organization with commissioners from almost all ministries and the PLA, can it really be a functional commission to deal with even broad-based energy issues? In our view, that is very difficult though not impossible. When most ministers are involved, conflicts of interest may arise to slow down any decision making on some of the major energy issues.

Second, what is the difference between the now-defunct NELG and this NEC? When the NELG was established in 2005, it was also chaired by Premier Wen Jiabao and known as "China's Energy Cabinet." At that time, the very existence of the NELG and NEO had once put the Energy Bureau (within NDRC) in an awkward position. In 2008, NELG and NEO were done away with. Will NEC be any better? Of course, the NEA is now a higher level organization compared with the Energy Bureau within the NDRC, but the same problems facing the latter several years ago are still here for the NEA.

Finally, NEC (and for that matter NELG of several years ago) is often regarded as a transitional arrangement toward the formation of a more formal Ministry of Energy (MOE). If that is true, it proves the point that the NEC is not a permanent layer of governance and its role can be limited and transitional over the long run.

However, we also believe that if efforts are made to ensure that the NEC is more functional than the now-defunct NELG, and if NEC's office is better organized than the previous NEO, the structure just established is still the best for China at the present. The reason is simply that, under the current circumstances, there is hardly a better way. The establishment of NEC and the structure of the commission imply that energy issues in China have been given the highest priority in the government. The high level of governance does mean, in theory, there will be better coordination of all energy types, including particularly renewables and new energy. The key, however, is that NEC and its office must be actively functional and play a meaningful role rather than be just for show.

Another reason for the creation of the NEC is that China may not be ready for an MOE. Does China really need a super MOE? In the end, yes, but given the facts, the energy sector is vast and individual energies are dominated by large and powerful state companies, and we do not believe that a super MOE will work for China. Many of the same problems that doomed the MOE the last time (1988–1993) still exist. The MOE will only be useful if the Chinese energy industry is fully opened up. Recently, Mr. Li Rongrong, former chairman of SASAC, indicated that for a sector where markets are fully developed, the state-owned enterprises should be de-monopolized or even privatized. That is a good policy direction. For the energy sector, however, the problem is that the progress for moving in this direction (de-monopolization and privatization) has been minimal and the environment for a fully functional MOE is far from being there yet. It is still too early to determine the ultimate impact of the new energy governance on China's energy sector developments and markets. However, in several areas, the possible implications — assuming that NEC functions effectively — can still be assessed as follows.

- **China's Overseas Energy Investments:** Since coordinating international cooperation and addressing the issue of energy security are among the main responsibilities assigned to the NEC, we expect that stronger government support for the overseas oil, gas, and other energy investments by Chinese state oil companies will be forthcoming. In the past, the Chinese state oil companies often competed with each other for overseas energy assets acquisitions. This has eased up a bit in the recent past and is expected to receive better government coordination under the new management regime.
- **Oil and Gas Price Reforms:** Since the NEC Office is headed by the NDRC Chairman, Zhang Ping, formulation and implementation of future oil and gas price reforms may proceed at a higher level more effectively. On the downside, however, the oil and gas price regime may also be used by the government as a leverage to combat inflation and achieve other policy goals of the State Council. Under those circumstances, the government may tighten rather than ease up on the control of prices.
- **Pipeline Gas and LNG (Liquefied Natural Gas) Imports:** Better government coordination regarding LNG terminal projects, prices, pipeline routes, and sources of imports may be expected from the new energy management regime.
- **Development of Renewables and New Energy:** This is widely considered to be one of the major areas to benefit from the new energy regime with a high-level and central NEC in place. In the past, the management of wind, solar, small hydro, geothermal, shale gas, coal-bed methane (CBM), biomass, biofuels, and other renewables as well as new energy was scattered amongst different government departments and agencies. With the new NEC, faster development of these areas can be achieved at a higher level with the highest possible government support.

In short, the present institutional structure governing the petroleum industry in China is rooted in decades of changes in the 1980s and 1990s, particularly the March 1998 reorganization as outlined earlier. It was further reshaped following the NPC in March 2003 when Wen

Jiabao became the new Premier of the State Council and then in March 2008 when Wen was re-elected to another five-year term. None of these changes in 2003, 2008, and later years were as massive as that of the 1998 reorganization, when the number of ministries was slashed from 41 to 29.

2.2. Who's Who in the Petroleum Industry

China has a large and integrated petroleum industry with a history of indigenous technology development, especially in the 1960s and 1970s during the period of self-reliance. After the end of the 1970s, China started a massive opening of the petroleum industry to foreign technologies, investments, and trade.

For the energy sector as a whole, the major governing bodies are the following:

- **State Council (Chinese Cabinet):** The highest government body in charge of all economic activities in China including those of the state oil companies. The current premier of the State Council is Wen Jiabao, who was re-elected to a five-year term by the NPC in March 2008 and has been in the position since March 2003.
- **National Energy Commission (NEC):** Formally established in February 2010. The purpose of establishing the NEC is: (1) to study and formulate the national energy development strategies; (2) to review major issues related to energy security and developments; and (3) to coordinate important tasks for domestic energy developments and international energy cooperation.
- **National Energy Administration (NEA):** The newly established NEA in March 2008 is now at a level just a half step lower than a full ministry and is now headed by Mr. Liu Tienan, who is a Vice Chairman of the NDRC. All functions of the former Energy Bureau and the NEO have been transferred to the NEA, which will be larger in size and staff than the former Energy Bureau and NEO combined. Most of the responsibilities of the former Energy Bureau are assumed by the NEA. These responsibilities include

but are not limited to (1) conducting research on domestic and overseas energy research; (2) initiating proposals for energy development strategies and important energy policies; (3) drafting energy development plans and provide advice on related reform on economic structures; (4) managing oil, gas, coal, and electric power sectors; (5) managing the SPR; and (6) initiating proposals for energy conservation and the development of new energy. In addition, some of the assigned tasks of the now defunct NEO are assumed by the NEA as well: tracking the development and status of energy security, forecasting and issuing warnings on strategic energy problems, organizing relevant departments and institutions to conduct research on energy strategies and planning, and studying important policies with regard to energy development and conservation, energy security, and emergency responses as well as international cooperation on energy.

- **NDRC:** The NDRC was last expanded in March 2003 and put in charge of socio-economic strategies, long-term planning, large projects, improvement of industrial structures, and price monitoring, among many other areas. Its status was reconfirmed at the March 2008 session of the NPC. The new mandate for the NDRC is to focus more on major social and economic issues. The commission chairman was Ma Kai — who has now assumed the position of a State Councilor — between 2003 and March 2008 and the current Chairman is Mr. Zhang Ping. For energy in particular, NDRC is responsible for national planning for oil, gas, coal, and electric power, as well as other industries.
- **State Assets Supervision and Administrative Commission (SASAC):** The SASAC is a special, ministerial-level agency under the State Council. The major responsibilities of SASAC are to regulate the huge state assets held by numerous state-owned enterprises (SOEs), to serve as the state shareholder in SOEs, to promote the restructuring of state assets and the establishment of modern enterprises, to improve the corporate structures of SOEs, and to improve the overall structure of the state economy. SASAC manages 123 large state-owned enterprises (SOEs) with total assets of some 21 trillion yuan (US$3.1 trillion). Through mergers, the number of

large SOEs is down from 196 at the beginning when SASAC was established but the total assets have tripled. Until recently, the chairman of SASAC had been Mr. Li Rongrong since April 2003. Mr. Li is the former chairman of the now defunct SETC. In August 2010, Li was replaced by Mr. Wang Yong, who was the Administrator of the China General Administration for Quality Supervision, Inspection, and Quarantine. One of the important powers held by SASAC is the ability to hire or fire SOEs' management; though for large and extra-large SOEs, the final say lies with the State Council and the CCP Ministry of Central Organization.

- **Ministry of Commerce (MOFCOM):** This ministry was established in 2003 combining both foreign and domestic trade. MOFCOM is in charge of the management of foreign and domestic trade. For oil trading, MOFCOM issues licenses and quotas for imports and exports of crude and major refined products. The minister of commerce is currently Mr. Chen Deming, who replaced Bo Xilai in December 2007.
- **Ministry of Land and Natural Resources (MLNR):** MLNR was established in March 1998. It is in charge of the licensing of acreage and blocks for upstream exploration and mining. The current minister of MLNR is Mr. Xu Shaoshi, who assumed the position in April 2007.

In addition, the Environmental Protection Administration, the Ministry of Public Security, the State Administration for Quality Control, Inspection, and Quarantine (SAQCIQ), and provincial and local governments are involved in the management of the downstream oil industry and oil markets in various degrees. For the petroleum (oil and gas) industry in particular, the structure of the state petroleum industry is shown in Fig. 2-1.

As a result of recent developments, China now has three state oil companies:

- **CNPC and its Publicly Listed Company PetroChina:** The giant CNPC is headed by Jiang Jiemin as the Chairman, who also serves as the Chairman of PetroChina. President of CNPC as well

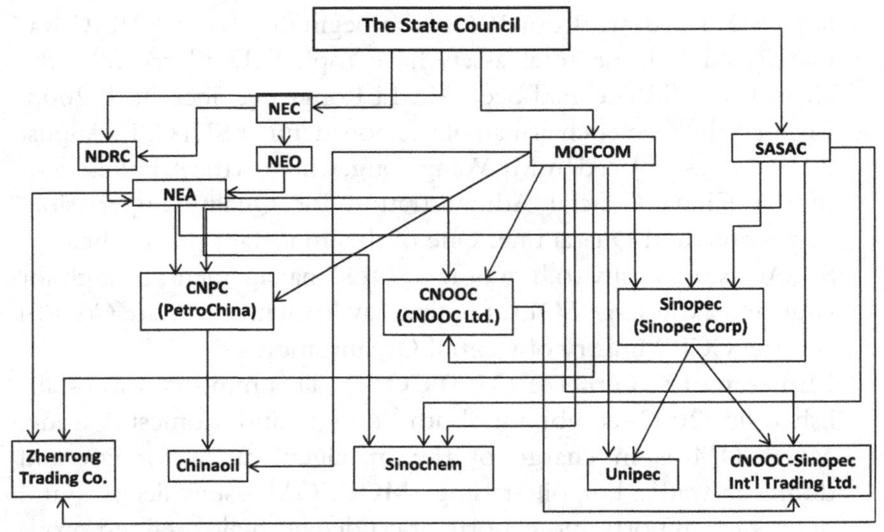

NEC: National Energy Commission. NEA: National Energy Administration. NEO: National Energy Office.
NDRC: National Development and Reform Commission. MOFCOM: Ministry of Commerce.
SASAC: State-Owned Assets Supervision and Administration Commission
CNPC: China National Petroleum Corporation. PetroChina: PetroChina Company Limited.
Sinopec: China Petrochemical Corporation. Sinopec Corp: China Petroleum and Chemical Corporation
Unipec: United International Petroleum & Chemicals Co., Ltd. Chinaoil: PetroChina International Co., Ltd.
CNOOC: China National Offshore Oil Corp.

Fig. 2-1. Organizational Chart of the Chinese Petroleum Industry (State), 2011.

as PetroChina is Zhou Jiping, who is also Vice Chairman of PetroChina.

- **Sinopec and its Publicly Listed Company Sinopec Corp:** Sinopec's current Chairman is Mr. Fu Chengyu and President is Mr. Wang Tianpu. Mr. Fu and Mr. Wang are also Chairman and President of Sinopec Corp., respectively.
- **CNOOC and its Publicly Listed Company CNOOC Ltd.:** The Chairman of CNOOC is now Mr. Wang Yilin and the President if Mr. Yang Hua.

China currently has five designated state oil trading companies:

- **Sinochem:** One of the oldest trading companies in China established in the 1950s. Until 1993, Sinochem had exclusive import and export rights for crude oil and refined products. That role was reduced following the establishment of Chinaoil and Unipec, and has been further curtailed after the 1998 reorganization. The current president of Sinochem is Mr. Liu Deshu.

- **Chinaoil:** Established in January 1993, a 50/50 joint venture (JV) between Sinochem and CNPC. CNPC has increased its share to 70% and assumed sole management of the company since 1998. Currently Chinaoil is active in China's limited crude and product exports, and engages in limited crude imports, and imports of fuel oil. Chinaoil's president is Wang Lihua.
- **Unipec:** Established in January 1993, a 50/50 JV between Sinochem and Sinopec. Sinopec has increased its share to 70% and assumed sole management of the company in 1998. At the moment, Sinopec has 100% ownership in Unipec. Currently Unipec is active in imports of crude and refined products and limited exports of products. Currently, Dai Zhaoming heads Unipec.
- **Zhuhai Zhenrong Oil Trading Company:** It was established in the mid-1990s by the military and has exclusive rights to import crude oil from Iran. Zhenrong's linkage with the military has been severed since 1999 but it is still a very unique state oil trading company. Zhenrong has recently entered the fuel oil import business and is actively exploring investment opportunities in other areas. After the step down of Yang Qinglong, who had been the president of Zhenrong since its establishment, Zhang Dongchuan is now the president of the company.
- **CNOOC-Sinopec United International Trading Ltd.:** Established in March 2004, this is a joint venture between CNOOC (60%) and Sinopec (40%) and is the most recently designated state oil trading company. Its trading rights as a state-designated oil trading company include both crude oil and major refined products.

In addition to the above-designated state oil trading companies, China has many other oil trading companies, particularly for fuel oil imports. Since the end of 2001, each year China allocates certain amounts of crude oil and refined product import quotas to oil trading companies other than above-mentioned five companies. In the upstream oil sector, crude oil production is still dominated by CNPC/PetroChina. In 2010, CNPC/PetroChina accounted for 51.7% of China's crude oil production, followed by Sinopec at 21.0%, CNOOC/its foreign partners at 20.5%, and Yanchang at 6.8% (Fig. 2-2) (FGE, 2011).

The refining sector is now dominated by Sinopec and CNPC/PetroChina. At the end of 2010, Sinopec owned 44.9% of China's total capacity of 11.4 mmb/d of refining, while CNPC/PetroChina had 31.5% (Fig. 2-3). CNOOC and its joint-venture partners owned

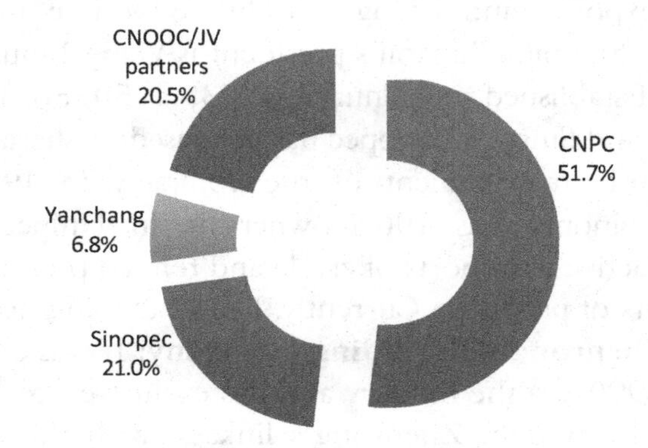

Fig. 2-2. China's Crude Oil Production by Company, 2010.

Note: Total output was 4.06 mmb/d.

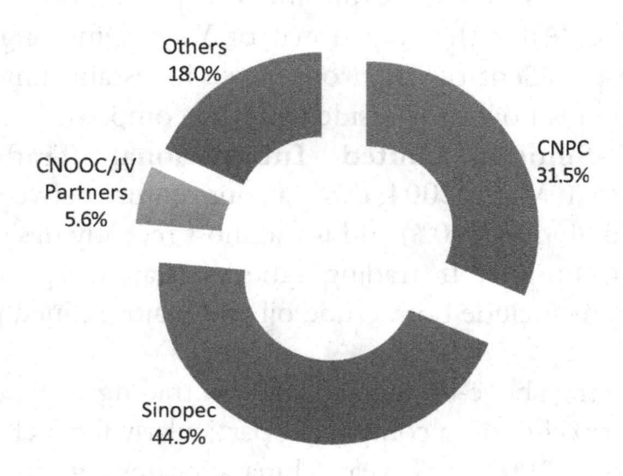

Fig. 2-3. China's CDU Capacity by Company, End 2010.

Note: Total capacity was 11.4 mmb/d.

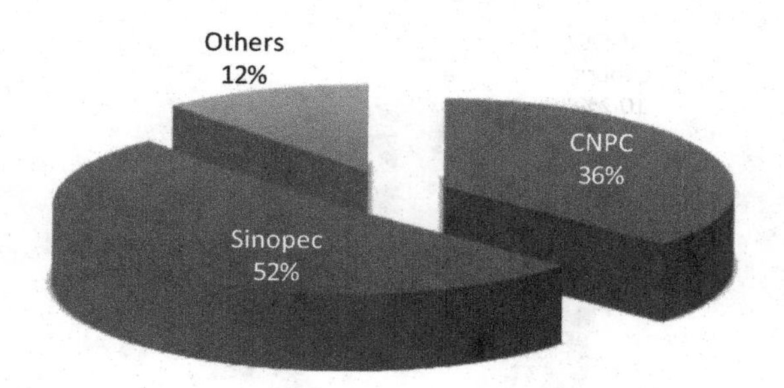

Fig. 2-4. China's Crude Runs by Company, 2010.

Note: Total refining throughput was 8.46 mmb/d.

5.6% and the remaining 18.0% is owned by local governments and private Chinese companies. The crude runs by companies in 2010 are illustrated in Fig. 2-4 (FGE, 2011).

The five designated state oil trading companies still monopolize China's crude oil trade and most of the trade for gasoline, diesel, jet fuel, and naphtha. Trade of fuel oil is more liberalized than these four products while the imports and exports of LPG, lubricants, and some other petroleum products have long been open.

At present, Chinaoil and Sinochem are in charge of China's onshore crude oil exports, but Chinaoil has a larger share. CNOOC and its foreign partners market their crudes both in China and in the international markets. For crude oil imports, Unipec is the major player, although Chinaoil also imports crude for PetroChina's West Pacific Petrochemical Co. Ltd. (WEPEC) Dalian refinery and from Central Asia to Xinjiang. Another state oil trading company, Zhuhai Zhenrong Trading, is importing mainly Iranian oil on a basis of barter trade. Both Chinaoil and Unipec are major players of refined product exports for China. For product imports, Unipec is the dominant player. Through the allocation of MOFCOM, Sinochem also imports refined products for the Chinese oil market. In addition to the state oil trading companies, China has also over 100 nonstate oil trading companies for fuel oil imports, and a number of nonstate oil trading companies for the imports of other main products.

For natural gas, the production dominated by CNPC/PetroChina. In 2009, CNPC/PetroChina accounted for 77% of China's natural

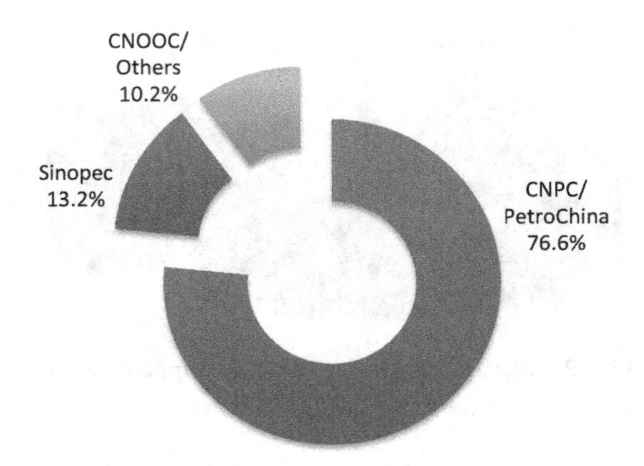

Fig. 2-5. China's Natural Gas Production by Company, 2010.
Note: Total output was 9.1 bscf/d.

gas production, followed by Sinopec at 13% and CNOOC/others at 10% (Fig. 2-5) (FGE, 2011). Prior to 1998, Sinopec had no upstream presence.

2.3. China's Evolving Energy Policies: An Overview

Before the "open-door" policy was introduced by the Chinese government in 1978, energy policy was part of China's overall planning economy. The formation of the energy policy was heavily rooted in the Soviet-style central planning system, which was adopted in the early 1950s, and the "self-reliant" development system, which lasted from 1960 to the late 1970s.

Since the late 1970s, China has begun its sweeping economic reforms and has since achieved rapid economic growth. The huge energy requirements for China to realize its ambitious economic targets led the government to officially recognize that energy is one of the most critical issues in the development of the Chinese economy, and to begin energy sector reforms in the early 1980s.

Since the reform era of the 1980s and 1990s, the Chinese government's term for the economy has evolved from a "socialist commodity economy" to a "socialist market economy" today. The latter term assumes that state corporations can act as profit-making entities under loose government guidelines. Since the mid-1980s, this policy has led to the transformation of state energy corporations from pure government plan implementers to active market participants. This process has been accelerated by China's entry into the WTO at the end of 2001.

China's energy planning and policies are reflected in its five-year plans and long-term social and economic development plans. The year of 2011 was the first year of China's 12th five-year program (covering the 2011–2015 period). In March 2011, the NPC passed a resolution on *The 12th Five-Year Program for China's National Economic and Social Developments.* Under this national program, promotion of energy development and changes was once again selected as a key area important enough to have a national plan. China's energy policies have long been dominated by policies for individual energy sectors, i.e., coal, oil and gas, petrochemicals, power, as well as energy conservation. The 11th FYP (covering the 2006–2010 period) as well as 12th FYP are similar in that regard. However, for the 11th FYP, there were two important changes. First, the Chinese government changed the title from a five-year *plan* to a five-year *program.* The government's intention was to reduce the mandatory nature of the five-year program while increasing the portion under government guidance. While we use the same abbreviation FYP to refer to the five-year program, the difference should not be discounted. Second, starting from the 11th FYP, the government has made the five-year program a rolling one with frequent assessments and long-term linkage with future years. The 11th FYP has ended in end of 2010, and most of the policies have achieved their goals. Mostly notably, China successfully achieved its 20% energy intensity reduction target during the 11th FYP period, although it scrambled to cut power production in the last quarter of 2010 in order to meet the target, which caused power shortage in many parts of the country.

The 12th FYP provides national development guidelines, strategies and policies for 2011–2015. Some of the major social, economic, and energy goals that are set by the 12th FYP for 2015 are:

- Population: Increases from 1.34 billion in 2010 to 1.39 billion.
- GDP growth from 39.8 trillion yuan (US$5.9 trillion) in 2010 to 55.8 trillion yuan (US$8.2 trillion in constant 2010 US dollar) with an AAGR of 7%.

- Raise the urbanization rate from 47.5% in 2010 to 51.5%.
- Reduce carbon intensity by 17% and energy intensity by 16%;
- Increase the share of nonfossil fuels in China's primary energy mix from 8.3% to 11.4% of China's total energy mix;
- Reduce sulfur emissions by 8% and NO_x emissions by 10%.

For the energy sector as a whole, the principles for energy development over the next five years set under the 12th FYP are:

- Promote the use of clean energy and develop multiple types of energy.
  - o For oil and gas in particular, the FYP calls for further exploration of domestic oil and gas, stabilizing domestic oil production, increasing natural gas production rapidly, and speeding up the exploration and development of unconventional gas.
- Optimize the regional distribution of energy development.
  - o Concerning oil and gas, FYP stipulates that the strategic petroleum reserves system needs to be improved, natural gas storages expanded, and the capability of emergency preparedness elevated.
- Enhance the transportation network of energy.
  - o For oil and gas, the FYP calls for the speed-up of broadening the channels of imports and enhance the domestic trunk line system. It also stipulates that pipeline gas imports, LNG terminals, and interregional gas pipelines and distributional networks be better coordinated. The target is to have a distributional system that incorporates not only natural gas, but also CBM and gas manufactured from coal.

chapter 3

Upstream Oil and Gas Sector Developments

China became self-sufficient in oil supply after the discovery and development of the Daqing oil field in the late 1950s and 1960s. The self-sufficiency ended in the early 1990s, when China became a net oil importer. In 2011, imported oil — crude oil and products combined — is estimated to account for 27% of China's apparent oil consumption, up from merely 7% in 1995 and 34% in 2000.

Until the mid-1990s, the development of natural gas in China was long neglected. Production did not pass 1 billion standard cubic feet per day (bscf/d) until 1977. It took another 20 years for the natural gas output to reach over 2 bscf/d in 1997. Since then, the production has accelerated, doubling to 4.8 bscf/d in 2005 and more than tripling to 8.3 bscf/d in 2009, thanks to the greater efforts made by Chinese oil companies — primarily CNPC/PetroChina — to explore and develop gas fields in Tarim, Ordos, and Sichuan basins (Fridley, 2008). In 2010, China produced 9.3 bscf/d of natural gas, up by 12.5% from 2009. For 2011, China's natural gas output went up again to be 10.0 bscf/d.

In this chapter, we will discuss the current situation and future prospects of oil and gas natural gas exploration, development, and production in China. The rest of the chapter is organized as follows: Section 3.1 briefly reviews the upstream oil developments, including production by field and the quality of major crudes; Section 3.2 focuses on the upstream natural gas sector including the future growth. In Section 3.3, we discuss the development of unconventional gas in China.

3.1. An Overview of Upstream Oil Developments

China is Asia's largest crude oil producer at present. Like US, however, China's domestic crude oil output accounts for less than half of its consumption. In this section, we first briefly discuss the history of China's upstream oil sector developments, review the status of main oil fields in the country, and end with a discussion of the future growth of the oil sector.

3.1.1. *History of the upstream oil sector developments*

We divide the upstream oil sector in the People's Republic of China into five phases. Each phase is characterized by some unique development issues, which are discussed briefly. To provide an overall picture of the five decades of crude oil production, Table 3-1 shows the annual output from 1950 to 2011.

Phase I: The Early Stage of China's Petroleum Industry (1949–1959)

China had never been a significant oil producer or consumer and hardly established any modern refineries until the 1950s. In the mid-1950s, China discovered the Karamay oil field in the Xinjiang Autonomous Region, Fuyu oil field in Jilin Province, and other new oil and gas fields in Qinghai and Sichuan Provinces. In the meantime, the government started to move exploration to the eastern part of the country with a primary focus on Northeast China. From 1952 to 1959, oil production increased eightfold, reaching 74.6 kb/d in 1959, of which 19.4 kb/d was shale oil. China was one of the largest shale oil producers at that time. However, the country was still a net oil importer for the entire period of Phase I.

Phase II: Historical Moment: Discovery of the Daqing Oil Field (1960–1965)

Perhaps the most important event during this period was the discovery of Daqing in 1959. From September 1959, when the first

Table 3-1. China's Crude Oil Production and Growth, 1950–2011.

Year	Output (kb/d)	Growth (%)	Year	Output (kb/d)	Growth (%)
1950	4	—	1981	2,024	−2.7
1951	6	55.0	1982	2,042	0.9
1952	9	41.9	1983	2,121	3.9
1953	12	40.9	1984	2,292	8.1
1954	16	27.4	1985	2,498	9.0
1955	19	22.8	1986	2,614	4.6
1956	23	19.6	1987	2,683	2.6
1957	29	25.9	1988	2,741	2.2
1958	45	54.8	1989	2,753	0.4
1959	75	65.0	1990	2,766	0.5
1960	104	39.4	1991	2,820	1.9
1961	106	2.1	1992	2,834	0.5
1962	115	8.3	1993	2,905	2.5
1963	130	12.7	1994	2,922	0.6
1964	170	30.9	1995	3,001	2.7
1965	226	33.4	1996	3,138	4.6
1966	291	28.6	1997	3,215	2.4
1967	278	−4.6	1998	3,220	0.2
1968	320	15.2	1999	3,200	−0.6
1969	435	36.0	2000	3,251	1.6
1970	613	41.0	2001	3,279	0.9
1971	788	28.6	2002	3,340	1.9
1972	913	15.9	2003	3,392	1.6
1973	1,072	17.4	2004	3,508	3.4
1974	1,297	21.0	2005	3,627	3.4
1975	1,541	18.8	2006	3,695	1.9
1976	1,743	13.1	2007	3,726	0.8
1977	1,873	7.4	2008	3,798	1.9
1978	2,081	11.1	2009	3,790	−0.2
1979	2,123	2.0	2010	4,060	7.1
1980	2,119	−0.2	2011	4,073	0.3

successful exploratory well was constructed, to 1963 production capacity in the Daqing field reached 120 kb/d. In 1963, Daqing crude output was 88 kb/d, about 68% of the total national crude production of about 130 kb/d. It is very obvious that Daqing has become the dominant oil-producing field in China since the early 1960s.

Immediately after Daqing was found, exploration activities started in the onshore area around Bohai Bay, including the provinces of Liaoning, Hebei, Shandong, and Henan. By 1965, a number of oil fields were discovered in these areas, including Dagang near Tianjin and Dongying (part of the Shengli oil fields) in Shandong Province. The exploration in Shandong paved the way for the further development of the Shengli oil fields later.

Phase III: A Giant Oil Producer in Asia (1966–1978)

The third phase coincided with the chaotic Cultural Revolution, which lasted from 1966 to 1976. In this period, the "self-reliance" policy continued, although China's isolation was eased in the beginning in the early 1970s, following the improvement in relations with the United States. China's trade with Japan and Western Europe, including imports of advanced equipment, flourished in the 1970s, greatly strengthening China's technological capabilities in its petroleum industry. Ironically, although the Cultural Revolution created a lot of problems and interruptions to the production of oil, the demand for oil also increased dramatically during this period. One of the main reasons was the burning of crude oil for power generation, heating, and other purposes, which is now considered to be an erroneous policy of the leaders at that time. From 1966 to 1970, direct burning of crude increased from 46.8 kb/d to 215 kb/d, and further increased to a high level of more than 400 kb/d during the period of 1975–1979.

To meet the growing demand for oil, a full-scale development of Daqing was carried out, along with the development of Shengli and Dagang. By 1975, Daqing oil production reached 1 mmb/d and has since been maintained at that level. Meanwhile, the development and production at Karamay in Xinjiang and Fuyu (part of the Jilin oil fields) in Jilin Province continued. During this period, further oil and gas exploration activities were conducted in Sichuan Province, in the middle Yangtze River area, and in North China, Liaoning, Shaanxi, and Gansu Provinces, and in the Ningxia Autonomous Region. Since 1963, a number of oil fields have been found in the Liaoning Province. Liaohe, the third largest oil producing fields in China, was discovered. The exploration activities in Hebei Province led to the discovery of Renqiu oil field, which is the most important of the Huabei oil fields.

By 1978, China's oil production reached more than 2 mmb/d, nearly six times the crude production of 291 kb/d in 1966. China became the largest oil producer in the Asia-Pacific region and was the eighth largest crude producer in the world. Of the total production in 1978, 1 mmb/d was produced by Daqing, 557 kb/d was produced by the Shengli, Dagang, Karamay, and Jilin oil fields, 245 kb/d was produced by the Huabei oil fields, 71 kb/d was produced by Liaohe, and the rest was provided by other fields. During the same period, China's refining capacity increased by a factor of five.

Phase IV: Fueling Two Decades of Economic Growth (1979–1999)

Since the early 1980s, almost all major onshore oil fields in the eastern part of the country had been discovered and developed. In sharp contrast to the rapid oil production increase in the late 1960s and 1970s, oil production growth in the 1980s and 1990s was moderate. Since 1979, the Chinese economy achieved a spectacular growth rate. Between 1979 and 1999, the real GDP growth increased by 9.8% per annum on average, making the Chinese economy 5.5 times bigger in 1999 than in 1979. Instead of a rigid Soviet-style planned economy, the petroleum industry now had to fuel a dynamic economy in which the appetite of the consumers was constantly increasing. Although oil use had become more efficient, rapid economic growth required large volumes of high-quality oil products. In this phase, China's crude oil production growth started to level off. The output increased from 2.1 mmb/d in 1979 to 2.8 mmb/d in 1990 and then 3.2 mmb/d in 1999. The average annual growth rate (AAGR) of the crude output was 2.7% during the 1980s and declined to 1.6% during the 1990s. In comparison, the growth was an impressive 13.2% per year on average in the 1970s.

After the crude exports peaked at 601 kb/d in 1985, they started to decline. The year 1989 marked the beginning of the era for China to import meaningful amounts of crude oil when the imports jumped from 17 kb/d in 1988 to 65 kb/d in 1989. However, it was the 1990s that saw a surge in oil imports for China, as the country moved steadily from being a net oil exporter to a net importer, and the net imports have been growing rapidly. By 1999, China already had 1.4 mmb/d of total oil imports (crude and products combined) and 1.0 mmb/d of net imports.

Phase V: Quest for Energy Security in the 21st Century (Since 2000)

In the 21st century, energy security has emerged as an important issue for China. In the past, the country managed to produce nearly all the energy it needed. However, China's energy imports, primarily oil, have increased significantly since the late 1980s, while exports have been declining. Currently, China is not only a net oil importer but also a net natural gas importer since 2007 and a net coal importer since 2009. Among all three fossil energy sources, oil is still the main driver of China's growing demand for imported energy.

Since 2000, China's economic growth has continued to rise. The real GDP achieved an unprecedented average annual growth of 10.5% during the 2000–2010 period and real GDP growth in 2011 is also estimated to be 9.3%. The actual GDP reached US$5.9 trillion in 2010, nearly tripling the GDP of US$1.9 trillion in 2000 (in 2010 US dollar). During this period, China was able to increase its oil production and continues to do so. The output increased from 3.24 mmb/d in 2000 to 4.06 mmb/d in 2010, with an AAGR of 2.2%, which was almost the same as the growth rate of 2.1% during the 1979–1999 period. High oil prices since 2005 further provided stimulus to the upstream exploration and production (E&P) activities in China. China's crude exports were 208 kb/d in 2000 and it declined to 61 kb/d in 2010. During the same period, the crude imports more than tripled from 1.40 mmb/d to 4.79 mmb/d. In the meantime, China's imports of refined products also increased while product exports fluctuated. On a net basis, China's net import of crude oil and refined products combined was more than triple from 1.5 mmb/d in 2000 to 5.1 mmb/d in 2010 and further to 5.5 mmb/d in 2011.

China's upstream oil production is likely to remain stagnant although there may be a more-than-expected increase in offshore crude production. This will be discussed further in Section 3.2, after a review of the major crudes produced in China.

3.1.2. *Production by Company and field*

China's major oil fields are located in the eastern part of the country, particularly in Northeast and North China. However, oil fields in the eastern part have matured since the late 1970s, while nearly all of China's crude oil production increase in the 1980s and 1990s came from the offshore area and the western part of China, particularly Xinjiang (Tarim Basin) and the Shaan-Gan-Ning region (Ordos Basin). In 1991, the eastern part of China still accounted for 89% of the country's total crude production, while Western/Northwestern China plus offshore fields combined accounted for 10% of the national total. In 2010, the share of East China declined to 50%, while production from the Northwest/West and offshore fields in China increased to 25% and 21%, respectively (Table 3-2).

CNPC has always been a major player in the upstream sector, but the 1998 reorganization has reduced its share. Prior to 1998, CNPC owned nearly all of the onshore oil and gas fields. After the 1998 reorganization, CNPC transferred Shengli, Zhongyuan, Henan, Jiangsu, and other small fields to Sinopec (Table 3-3), making it the second largest crude oil producer. In 2010, China produced 4.07 mmb/d of crude oil, up by 7.3% over 2009. The high crude production growth in 2010 was mainly because of the early start-up of several small fields and ramp-up production of the Penglai 19-3 in the offshore areas. Of the total growth, offshore production increase accounted for 77% of the growth.

As shown in Table 3-3 and Fig. 3-1, of the total output for 2010, CNPC/PetroChina, produced 2.10 mmb/d (51.6%), followed by Sinopec/Sinopec Corp at 849 kb/d (20.9%), CNOOC Limited and

Table 3-2. Crude Oil Production by Area, 1991–2010.

Area	1991	1993	1995	1997	1999	2001	2003	2005	2007	2008	2009	2010
Output (kb/d)												
East	2,526	2,509	2,467	2,440	2,339	2,270	2,210	2,143	2,139	2,109	2,043	2,025
Northwest/West	217	274	329	424	497	558	673	805	911	973	959	1,010
Offshore	48	93	168	326	323	364	437	553	554	566	625	837
Others*	29	30	37	25	46	106	89	116	125	141	163	195
TOTAL	2,820	2,905	3,001	3,215	3,205	3,299	3,409	3,617	3,729	3,790	3,790	4,067
Share (%)												
East	89.6	86.4	82.2	75.9	73.0	68.8	64.8	59.3	57.4	55.7	53.9	49.8
Northwest/West	7.7	9.4	11.0	13.2	15.5	16.9	19.7	22.3	24.4	25.7	25.3	24.8
Offshore	1.7	3.2	5.6	10.1	10.1	11.0	12.8	15.3	14.9	14.9	16.5	20.6
Others*	1.0	1.0	1.2	0.8	1.4	3.2	2.6	3.2	3.4	3.7	4.3	4.8
TOTAL	100.0	100.0	100.0	100.0	100.0	100.0	100.0	100.0	100.0	100.0	100.0	100.0

*Others include production from SSPC and its predecessors and local companies.

Table 3-3. Crude Oil Production by Field and Company, 1998–2010 (kb/d).

Field/Company	Region	1998	2000	2002	2004	2006	2008	2009	2010
CNPC-owned									
Daqing	Northeast	1,114	1,057	1,003	925	868	802	800	797
Huabei	North	95	91	88	86	88	89	85	85
Liaohe	Northeast	290	279	270	256	240	239	200	189
Dagang	North	86	80	79	97	106	102	97	95
Xinjiang	West	174	183	201	222	238	244	218	219
Jilin	Northeast	79	75	89	85	98	132	118	123
Changqing	Northwest	80	93	122	162	212	275	314	361
Yumen	Northwest	8	9	12	15	16	14	8	10
Sichuan	Southwest	4	3	3	3	3	3	3	3
Jidong	North	13	12	13	20	34	40	35	35
Tarim	West	77	87	100	107	121	130	111	110
Tu-Ha	West	59	57	50	45	41	42	32	33
Qinghai	West	35	40	43	44	45	44	37	37
CNPC Subtotal		2,115	2,066	2,072	2,068	2,111	2,156	2,057	2,097

(*Continued*)

Table 3-3. (*Continued*)

Field/Company	Region	1998	2000	2002	2004	2006	2008	2009	2010
Sinopec-owned									
Shengli	North	546	534	534	533	548	553	557	546
Henan	North	37	37	38	38	36	36	38	45
Zhongyuan	North	80	75	76	67	62	60	58	55
Jianghan	Mid Yangtze	15	17	19	19	19	19	19	19
Jiangsu	Lower Yangtze	25	31	31	32	33	34	34	34
Dian-Qian-Gui	Southwest/South	1	1	1	1	1			
Anhui	Lower Yangtze	2							
Shanghai Ocean									
SSPC[a]			48	59	78	102	130	142	150
Sinopec Subtotal		706	743	758	768	802	833	848	849
CNOOC		326	350	420	493	552	566	625	837
Yanchang	Northwest	33	49	76	130	187	224	239	239
Others	Lower Yangtze	30	35	80	26	21			
Others[b]		63	84	156	156	208	235	260	284
TOTAL		**3,210**	**3,244**	**3,406**	**3,485**	**3,674**	**3,790**	**3,790**	**4,067**

[a]SSPC was renamed from CNSPC in early 2000, which is now part of Sinopec.

[b]Includes local and other oil producers.

Note: 2011 output is estimate.

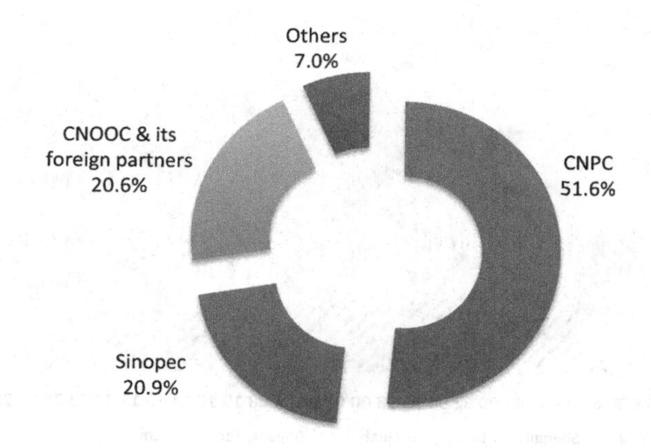

Fig. 3-1. China's Crude Oil Production by Company, 2010.
Note: Total ouput was 4.06 million b/d in 2010.

its foreign partners at 837 kb/d (20.6%), and others 523 kb/d (7.0%). Among others, the biggest local company is Yanchang Petrochemical Company, which produced 239 kb/d of crude in 2010.

3.1.3. *Future prospects of oil production in China till 2030*

In summary, over the next 20 years, China's crude oil production is expected to rise moderately to 4.2 mmb/d in 2020 and just under 4.3 mmb/d by 2030 under our base-case scenario (Fig. 3-2). But under the high-case scenario, China has the potential to produce 4.6 mmb/d of crude oil by 2020 and 4.8 mmb/d by 2030. Similarly, China's oil production may also decline to 4.0 mmb/d by 2020 and 3.8 mmb/d by 2030 under the low-case scenario (Fig. 3-3).

3.2. Natural Gas Exploration and Production

Field development often leads to the production of natural gas, and therefore the volume of natural gas produced by a particular field often reflects the degree of development of the field. Because of the close relationship between development and production, planning is

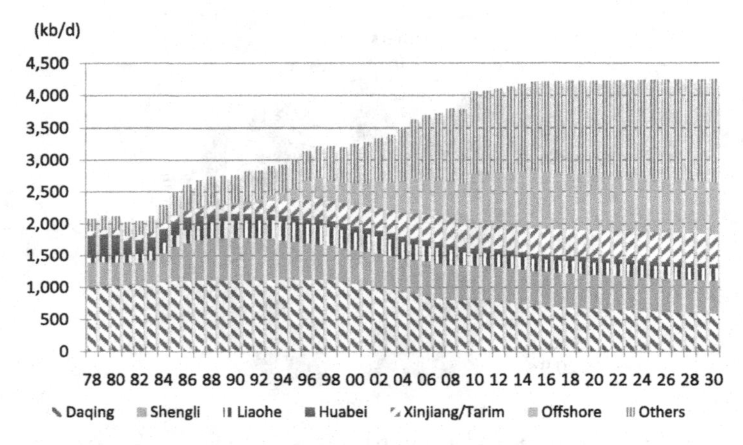

Fig. 3-2. Historical and Projected Crude Production by Field Base-Case Scenario, 1978–2030.

Note: Data for 2012–2030 are projections.

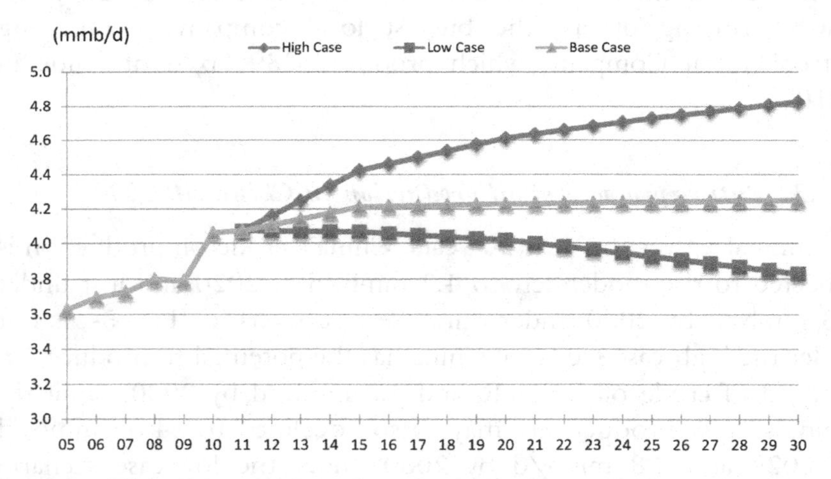

Fig. 3-3. High, Low, and Base-Case Crude Production Forecasts for China to 2030.

Note: Data for 2012–2030 are projections.

more important in this stage. While a number of factors determine the efforts of natural gas exploration and development, including funding, technologies, and geographic and geological conditions, additional factors have to be considered for development alone. These additional factors include transportation, storage, distribution, and marketing, which are related to the actual production and disposition of natural gas.

Until the mid-1990s, China's natural gas output — an indicator and result of natural gas development — fluctuated along with oil production since the majority of China's natural gas was associated gas. In fact, gas development and production was not given a high priority by the Chinese oil producers. Since the mid-1990s, however, China has stepped up the efforts to develop nonassociated gas. The natural gas sector has since embarked on a path of high growth in development and production.

3.2.1. *Overall development and production*

Discovery and utilization of natural gas started in Sichuan over 2000 years ago. Massive exploration and development of the Sichuan fields began in the late 1950s. The exploration was first aimed at oil, but soon turned to natural gas. Starting at 28 million scf/d (mmscf/d) in 1959, natural gas production in China increased during the 1960s, from 100 mmscf/d in 1960 to 190 mmscf/d in 1969, as a result of the development of the Sichuan gas fields (Table 3-4). Production went up rapidly in the 1970s, because of the increased production from the Sichuan fields and the rapid growth of associated natural gas from the eastern oil fields (mainly from the Songliao Basin). In 1979, total natural gas production reached 1.4 bscf/d, up from 278 mmscf/d in 1970. During the 1980s, although associated gas output continued to grow, production from the Sichuan fields declined, resulting in an overall stagnation in natural gas production in China. For instance, the output in 1988 was about the same as the production in 1980. Since the late 1980s, the efforts by the government and Chinese state oil companies to search for oil and gas in west China (Chen, Li and Wu, 2010; Huang, Todd and Zhang, 2011) have resulted in discoveries of natural gas in the Tarim Basin. Subsequently, more gas was also found in the Qaidam and Ordos basins, leading to a shift of strategy by the Chinese government to speed up the development of natural gas, which had been neglected for decades.

Table 3-4. China's Natural Gas Production, 1952–2011 (mmscf/d).

Year	Output	Growth (%)	Year	Output	Growth (%)
1952	0.8	—	1982	1,154.6	(6.3)
1953	1.1	37.9	1983	1,181.6	2.3
1954	1.5	36.4	1984	1,199.4	1.5
1955	1.6	13.3	1985	1,251.0	4.3
1956	2.5	52.5	1986	1,331.3	6.4
1957	6.8	170.0	1987	1,343.9	0.9
1958	10.6	57.1	1988	1,375.9	2.4
1959	28.1	163.6	1989	1,456.1	5.8
1960	100.3	257.6	1990	1,480.1	1.6
1961	142.2	41.7	1991	1,555.1	5.1
1962	117.1	(17.7)	1992	1,523.4	(2.0)
1963	98.7	(15.7)	1993	1,622.1	6.5
1964	102.3	3.6	1994	1,698.9	4.7
1965	107.4	5.0	1995	1,736.4	2.2
1966	129.6	20.7	1996	1,940.8	11.8
1967	141.3	9.0	1997	2,196.6	13.2
1968	135.1	(4.4)	1998	2,252.3	2.5
1969	189.6	40.4	1999	2,438.0	8.2
1970	277.7	46.4	2000	2,624.5	7.7
1971	361.9	30.3	2001	2,934.4	11.8
1972	467.0	29.1	2002	3,160.1	7.7
1973	578.6	23.9	2003	3,387.8	7.2
1974	728.6	25.9	2004	4,000.4	18.1
1975	856.3	17.5	2005	4,771.9	19.3
1976	974.5	13.8	2006	5,665.2	18.7
1977	1,172.7	20.3	2007	6,699.2	18.3
1978	1,328.4	13.3	2008	7,748.0	15.7
1979	1,404.9	5.8	2009	8,250.1	6.5
1980	1,376.9	(2.0)	2010	9,279.9	12.5
1981	1,232.7	(10.5)	2011	9,971.4	7.5

Natural gas production had begun to accelerate since the mid-1990s. Total output was 1.7 bscf/d in 1995, 2.6 bscf/d in 2000, and 4.8 bscf/d in 2005 before surging further to 9.3 bscf/d in 2010 and 10.0 bscf/d in 2011 (see Table 3-4). The average annual growth of 11.5% during the 1995–2011 period contrasted drastically with an AAGR of merely 1.5% for the 1980–1994 period.

3.2.2. *Production by company and field*

Prior to the 1998 reorganization of the Chinese petroleum industry, CNPC was virtually the exclusive producer of onshore natural gas in China, accounting for over three-quarters of China's total gas output. Sinopec became a player in the upstream oil and gas sector after the 1998 reorganization, but its role in natural gas production is still minor (Table 3.5). In 2010, Sinopec's share in total natural gas production was 13.2%. Since 2009, Sinopec has reorganized its natural gas division and has been targeting to rapidly develop its natural gas business and expand its natural gas presence in the country.

However, between 1998 and 2010, natural gas output from offshore China had grown slowly while production from CNPC/PetroChina had gone up quickly. In fact, between 1998 and 2010, the AAGR of natural gas production by CNPC/PetroChina was 14.0%; it was 15.0% for Sinopec and only 4.9% for CNOOC. As a result, CNPC/PetroChina's share of total natural gas output increased to 76% in 2010 from 64% in 1998, while the share of CNOOC (offshore China) declined to 7% from 17%.

China currently has four natural gas producing centers. These four centers refer to onshore East, onshore Southwest, Northwest & West, and Offshore.

- **Onshore East:** This part encompasses the Daqing, Zhongyuan, Shengli, Liaohe, Jilin, Huabei, Dagang, Jianghan, Jidong, Henan, and Jiangsu oil and gas fields, where associated gas plays a major role, while nonassociated gas accounts for a much smaller share. In this area, which has mainly associated gas fields, CNPC owns the fields in the northeast, whereas Sinopec owns most of the rest. In 2010, natural gas output from the eastern area accounted for 13% of the national total, down sharply from 47% in 1991 (Fig 3-4).
- **Onshore Middle:** The middle part of China, which includes the Changqing gas fields in Northwest China and Sichuan gas fields in Southwest China, predominantly produces nonassociated gas. All fields in the central area are largely owned by CNPC, but

Table 3-5. Natural Gas Production by Field and Company, 2000–2010 (mmscf/d).

Field/Company	Region	2000	2002	2003	2004	2005
CNPC/PetroChina-owned						
Daqing	Northeast	222	196	197	196	237
Huabei	North	42	52	56	56	55
Liaohe	North	111	109	102	97	89
Dagang	North	39	38	35	33	32
Xinjiang	Northwest	156	195	214	247	280
Jilin	Northeast	19	21	22	24	26
Changqing	Northwest	199	379	502	719	729
Yumen	Northeast	2	6	2	2	8
Sichuan	Southwest	771	848	889	943	1,145
Jidong	North	6	4	4	5	7
Tarim	West	72	105	105	131	549
Tu-Ha	West	89	111	119	129	148
Qinghai	West	38	111	149	173	205
South/Others	South	0	5	11	12	37
Subtotal		**1,766**	**2,175**	**2,407**	**2,768**	**3,548**
Sinopec-owned						
Shengli	North	66	73	78	86	85
Henan	North	5	11	10	10	10
Zhongyuan	North	129	157	165	169	161
Jianghan	Mid Yangtze	9	11	10	10	12
Jiangsu	Lower Yangtze	2	2	3	4	6
Dian-Qian-Gui	Southwest	8	7	9	10	8
Shanghai Ocean	Offshore	0	0	0	16	18
Sinopec Star	Nationwide	159	218	228	257	309
Subtotal		**379**	**478**	**502**	**563**	**608**
CNOOC/CNOOC Ltd.		**382**	**360**	**315**	**472**	**492**
Others		**98**	**142**	**164**	**198**	**123**
TOTAL		**2,625**	**3,155**	**3,388**	**4,000**	**4,772**

(*Continued*)

Table 3-5. (*Continued*)

Field/Company	Region	2006	2007	2008	2009	2010
CNPC/PetroChina-owned						
Daqing	Northeast	237	248	270	292	290
Huabei	North	53	56	55	60	79
Liaohe	North	86	85	84	78	77
Dagang	North	31	41	43	43	36
Xinjiang	Northwest	279	282	331	349	368
Jilin	Northeast	27	37	53	115	136
Changqing	Northwest	776	1,065	1,386	1,834	2,043
Yumen	Northeast	8	6	5	3	2
Sichuan	Southwest	1,288	1,401	1,431	1,455	1,487
Jidong	North	9	15	30	44	42
Tarim	West	1,066	1,491	1,677	1,750	1,777
Tu-Ha	West	160	168	147	146	122
Qinghai	West	237	329	426	418	543
South/Others	South	20	0	0	0	0
Subtotal		**4,278**	**5,223**	**5,938**	**6,589**	**7,001**
Sinopec-owned						
Shengli	North	77	76	74	68	49
Henan	North	8	7	6	5	6
Zhongyuan	North	159	147	102	90	456
Jianghan	Mid Yangtze	12	12	13	15	16
Jiangsu	Lower Yangtze	6	5	6	6	5
Dian-Qian-Gui	Southwest	6	2	0	0	0
Shanghai Ocean	Offshore	70	25	17	14	14
Sinopec Star	Nationwide	416	508	583	622	664
Subtotal		**754**	**781**	**802**	**819**	**1,209**
CNOOC/CNOOC Ltd.		**601**	**661**	**666**	**601**	**661**
Others		**33**	**34**	**343**	**241**	**306**
TOTAL		**5,665**	**6,699**	**7,748**	**8,250**	**9,177**

Sinopec's SSPC also operates in the Sichuan Basin. At 38% of the national total in 2010, the share of the central area was down from 41% in 1991 (see Fig 3-4). We expect that gas production from this region will grow rapidly in the coming years, mainly

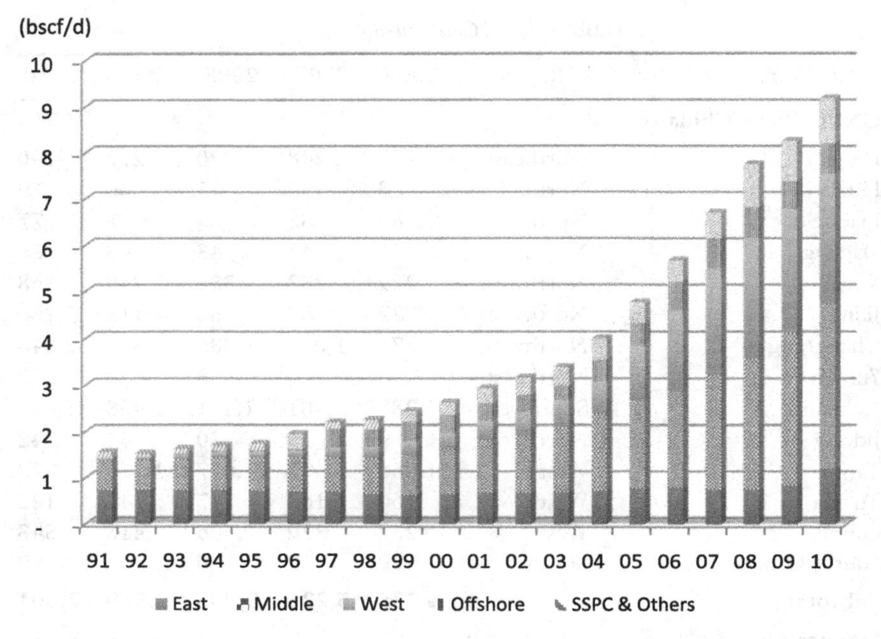

Fig. 3-4. Natural Gas Production by Area, 1991–2010.

driven by increase in production in the Sinopec Puguang and PetroChina Changqing gas fields. Sinopec has just started production from its Puguang gas field in Sichuan since the end of 2009. Puguang and Yuanba gas fields in Sichuan and the new finds are a further guarantee of gas supply to the Puguang-Shanghai gas pipeline linking provinces and cities in East China. The firm is planning another pipeline from Sichuan to supply markets in South China, such as the Guangdong Province, Hong Kong, and Macau. Besides the production expansion in the Puguang gas field, PetroChina is also increasing its Changqing gas field production.

- **Onshore West:** The western part produces both associated and nonassociated gas, especially in the Tarim, Tu-Ha, and Qaidam basins. However, only associated gas is produced from the Junggar Basin. While the Qaidam Basin belongs to the Qinghai Province, there are two definitions for Xinjiang fields. The narrow definition refers to those that are in the Junggar Basin only, especially the Karamay oil and gas field. The Junggar

Basin's oil and gas fields are managed by CNPC Xinjiang Petroleum Administration. In a broad definition, all fields in the Junggar, Tarim, and Tu-Ha basins belong to the Xinjiang Urgur Autonomous Region. The majority of the fields in the western area belong to PetroChina, although the SSPC of Sinopec also has a presence in the Tarim Basin. The western area accounted for 31% of the total national gas output in 2010, up dramatically from 4% in 1991 (Fig. 3-17). Gas production from the Tarim and Junggar Basin is also expected to increase rapidly in the future.

- **Offshore:** Nonassociated gas forms the bulk of China's offshore natural gas production, from the South China Sea, East China Sea, and Bohai Bay. Except for small operations of Sinopec's SSPC in the East China Sea, all offshore gas fields are operated by CNOOC and its partners. In 1991, no natural gas was produced in the offshore area. The production reached 392 mmscf/d in 1999, accounting for 18% of the national total (Fig. 3-17). However, with approximately 661 mmscf/d of natural gas produced in 2010, the share of offshore gas fields in China in the national total declined to 7%.

On an overall basis, nonassociated gas consistently accounted for more than 70% of China's total natural gas output during most of the 1950s and 1960s, and at one time, this share was as high as 98%. The share of nonassociated gas began to decline in the 1970s. In 1981, for the first time, the production of associated gas exceeded that of nonassociated gas. For most of the 1980s and the first half of the 1990s, nonassociated gas accounted for roughly about 40%–45% of the total national output. Since the late 1990s, nonassociated gas output has exceeded associated gas output again and is leading China's natural gas production at present and in the future.

3.2.3. *Future prospects for gas production till 2030*

Looking ahead, China still has the potential to increase its natural gas production substantially, though uncertainty also looms large. The

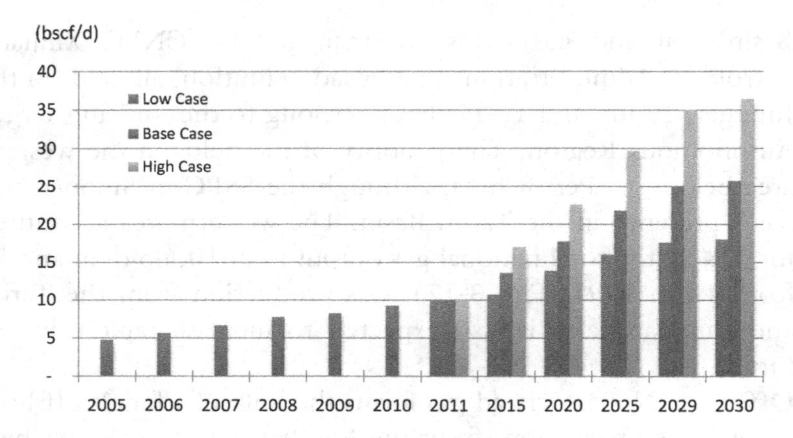

Fig. 3-5. Outlook for Natural Gas Production in China.
Note: Data for 2015–2030 are Projections.

major sources of additional gas production will be in the Tarim Basin, Jungar Basin, Ordos Basin, Puguang gas field, and offshore China.

- Base Case: Our base-case scenario shows that China's natural gas output is projected to increase to 17.7 bscf/d in 2020 and 25.7 bscf/d in 2030 (Fig. 3-5).
- High Case: Our high-case scenario assumes that production in the Ordos, Tarim, Puguang, and offshore fields are higher than expected. Under the high-case scenario, a breakthrough is expected in natural gas E&P in the Tarim Basin, Ordos Basin, and offshore areas. Under this scenario, natural gas output is expected to be 22.6 bscf/d by 2020 and 36.4 bscf/d in 2030 (see Fig. 3-7).
- Low Case: Our low-case scenario assumes that gas development in the Tarim and Ordos basins are hampered by slower pipeline construction and less exploration success. In that case, natural gas output in China could be as low as 13.9 bscf/d in 2020 and 18.0 bscf/d in 2030 (see Fig. 3-4).

3.3. Unconventional Gas Developments

There are three major unconventional gas reservoir types:

- **Tight Gas:** Produced from low-permeability sandstone and carbonate reservoirs.
- **Coalbed Methane (CBM):** Held in and produced from coal seams. CBM wells often need to be "dewatered." In addition, CBM is a cleaner energy source, lowering the mine explosion risks due to methane build-ups in coal mining is an added benefit for extracting and using CBM. Moreover, extraction of CBM can also reduce emissions of methane, a major type of greenhouse gas.
- **Shale Gas:** Produced from shale. Shale gas reservoirs also have low permeability.

China has been producing tight gas since the late 1990s. At present, tight gas accounts for a little less than 20% of China's natural gas production, which has been included in the total discussed throughout this book.

The focus of this chapter is on CBM and shale gas in China. Topics covered include unconventional gas resources and reserves; CBM production; shale gas exploration; major players and participants in China's unconventional gas industry as well as policy issues; and challenges the country is facing, with a look at the prospects of future unconventional gas developments and its role in China's total gas supply.

China began exploring for and utilizing CBM in the 1990s. At present, the CBM industry in China is at the early stage of development. Given the rich resource potential and government support with a series of preferential policies and foreign participation, the CBM industry in China will have a very promising future. Yet it is also facing challenges such as investment barriers, infrastructure constraints, and pricing issues. China should do more to deal with these challenges. As for shale gas, China began researching into this unconventional gas in the early 2000s. However, the actual exploration activities did not start until the end of 2009. As such, the history of shale gas development in China is much shorter and it is full of uncertainties as well as experiencing a faster take-off versus CBM development.

3.3.1. *Resources and production*

CBM

Based on China's latest survey, its CBM resources are massive. However, depending on the definitions and proven degrees, the resources and reserves have different layers as follows:

- An estimated 1,300 trillion cubic feet (tcf) (36.8 trillion m^3) resides within the depth of 2,000 m beneath the surface, the third largest amount in the world, next to Russia (3,991 tcf) and Canada (2,684 tcf), and ahead of the US (742 tcf).
- Of the total, the CBM resources between the depths of 1,500 and 2,000 m (4,921–6,562 ft) account for 374 tcf (28.8%) and resources at a depth less than 1,000 m account for 504 tcf (38.8%).
- Recoverable CBM resources are estimated at around 385 tcf (10.9 trillion m^3).
- Despite these resources, the cumulative proven geological reserves at the start of 2010 were only 7.1 tcf (200 billion m^3), while recoverable reserves, which is equivalent to proven reserves of the international standard, stood at 2.2 tcf (62 billion m^3) at the start of 2009.

Region-wise, North China holds the largest amount of CBM resources in the country, followed by the Northwest and the South (Fig. 3-6). China currently has 8 basins that each contains more than 35.3 tcf (1 trillion m^3) of CBM resources (Fig. 3-7).

Around half of China's coal mines have a high concentration of methane. Methane extraction in China started as early as the 1950s. In the 1950s and 1960s, the purpose of extracting CBM from the coal mines was mainly to reduce the risk of gas explosions and other

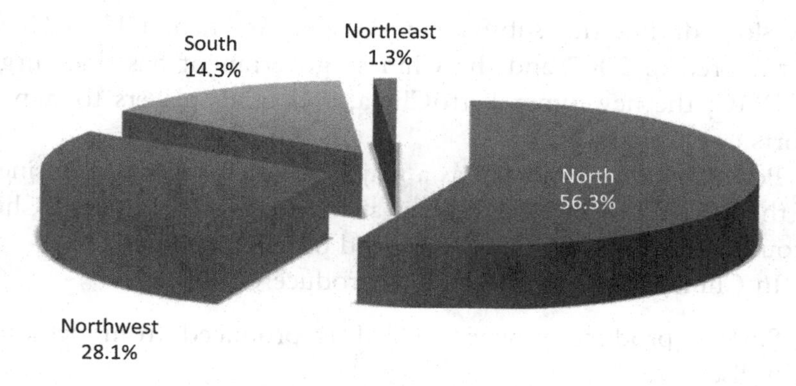

Fig. 3-6. CBM Resources by Region.

Note: Total resources: 1,300 tcf.

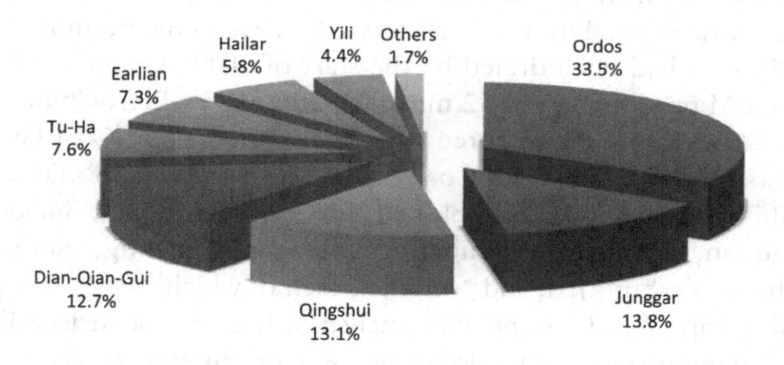

Fig. 3-7. CBM Resources by Basins.

Note: Total resources: 1,300 tcf.

potential dangers for coal miners. In the 1970s and 1980s, China conducted only very limited experiments on the extraction of CBM in several regions. The nationwide appraisal of the CBM resources began only in the 1990s.

Since the 1990s, China has been exploring for and utilizing CBM. The extraction and utilization of CBM entered a new stage of development after the establishment of the state-owned CUCMC (China United Coal-bed Methane Corporation) in 1996. Overall, however, the progress for CBM production and commercialization in China was slow during the subsequent decade. As such, CUCMC was restructured in 2007 and the Chinese government has since urged CUCMC, the newcomer PetroChina, and other players to step up efforts to develop CBM.

PetroChina has emerged as a major player in the CBM business. Of the 10.2 tcf of proven reserves at the start of 2011, PetroChina accounted for 65%, CUCMC 17%, and other companies 18%.

In China, there are two ways to produce CBM:

- Surface production where CBM is produced from dedicated wells, and
- Where CBM is extracted from coal mines.

In 2010, China produced 863 mmcf/d of CBM, of which 152 mmcf/d was from surface wells and 711 mmcf/d was from coal mine extractions. For the surface CBM development, more than 4,000 wells had been drilled by the start of 2011. Of the total surface CBM production of 152 mmcf/d, 20% was by PetroChina, 16% by CUCBMCC, 58% by three large coal mines — Jin Coal Group, Lu Coal Group, and Yang Coal Group, 6% by others. So far CBM capabilities have been established for 10 coal mines, including Yangquan, Huainan, Huaibei, Shuicheng, Panjiang, Songzao, Jincheng, Fushun, Jixi, and Ningmei, each of which has a CBM production capacity of around 10 mmcf/d or higher. For surface E&P, CBM demonstration, development, and production projects have been established at the Qinshui Basin of Shanxi Province, Fuxin Basin of Lianning Province, and Hancheng in the Ordos Basin of Shaanxi Province.

As the above-mentioned data show, only 18% of China's CBM production in 2010 came from CBM wells and a whopping 82% of the total comes from CBM extractions in coal mines in 2009. This is one of the challenges China is facing, where the surface production levels are very low. Given the fact that each year some 2 bcf/d of CBM is emitted from coal mines, the extracted CBM accounts to less than one-third of the total. Each year, China emits and thus wastes as much as 1.3 bcf/d of CBM. The waste is actually higher considering a large portion of the produced CBM is not utilized.

Shale gas

Compared to CBM, the exploration of shale gas in China began at a much later stage. Current estimates for shale gas resources vary from source to source, ranging from 918 to 1,589 tcf. China has not yet established proven reserves. In April 2011, US Energy Information Administration (EIA 2011) released a report assessing shale gas resources of 14 regions outside the US. The report has put China's risked gas in-place at a whopping 5,101 tcf and technicially recoverable resources of shale gas at 1,275 tcf.

China has not yet established proven reserves. Areas where potential proven reserves are located include: North China, Northest China's Songliao Basin, Tarim Basin in the west, Sichuan Basin in the southwest, and Ordos Basin in the northwest. The latest developments of shale gas exploration and other activities are:

- Research activities began in the early 1990s.
- First joint-research agreement was signed in 2007.
- In 2009, the governments of US and China signed the Memorandum of Cooperation for Shale Gas Development. The Chinese government has since made development of shale gas an important area to consider.
- First shale gas well, Wei 201, was drilled in December 2009 by the PetroChina–Shell joint venture.
- In September 2009, the Research Center for Resource Strategies of the Ministry of Land and Natural Resources (MLNR) completed a survey well to determine China's shale gas-rich areas.
- Gas exploration of Sinopec in northeast Sichuan Province has been going on for years, which include shale gas. Yuanba-9 well is a shale gas exploration well in that area. Sinopec also has shale gas exploration activities in Jiangsu and Huizhou provinces with Yuanye-1 well and Huangye-1 well; in the Municipality of Chongqing with Jianye-1 well and Jianye HF-1 well; and in Hubei and Henan provinces. HF-1 is the first horizontal well by Sinopec and the drilling has begun since late 2011.

- Yanchang Petroleum Group began exploration activities for first shale gas well, Liuping 177. The well is located in the county of Ganquan of Yan'an in Shaanxi Province. First bidding round for shale gas exploration, which was intended for 2010 initially, was held on June 27, 2011 by the MLNR. It includes two blocks: a larger one is the Nanchuan block in Hunan and Guizhou provinces and the smaller one is the Xiushan block in Chongqing, Guizhou, and Hunan provinces. The bidding was open to five Chinese companies only: PetroChina, Sinopec, China United CBM Corp. (CUCBMC), Henan CBM Corp., and Yanchang Petroleum Co. of Shaanxi Province. The winner of the larger block was Sinopec and that of the smaller one is Henan CBM Corp. Sinopec planned to spend 590 million yuan to drill one well to obtain reference data and 11 pre-exploratory wells. Henan CBM Corp. will spend 250 million yuan to drill two wells to obtain reference data and 8 pre-exploratory wells.

Since September 2011, MLNR has been preparing for the launch of the second round of shale gas bidding. The actual bidding, originally scheduled for the end of 2011, is expected to occur in 2012.

China has not produced shale gas so far. The future production potential is discussed later in this chapter.

3.3.2. *Policy issues and challenges*

With tightening pressures on promoting coal mine safety, alleviating greenhouse gas emissions, and supplying more clean energy, the Chinese government has increasingly paid more attention to the development and production of CBM. Since 2005, a series of development plans and preferential policies have been issued by the government to encourage the development and use of CBM, including tax reductions and financial and other support, which reflects the government's strong desire to develop CBM.

Currently, these preferential policies and incentives — most recent of which were issued in February 2007 by the Ministry of Finance and General Administration of Taxation — can be summarized as the following:

- *Value-Added Tax (VAT)*: For CBM extraction and production companies, a VAT is set at a reduced 13%; it will be first levied and then the VAT will be reimbursed to the company. If the reimbursed tax is used for future investment, no income tax will be levied as well. The normal VAT is 13% for conventional gas and 17% for other activities in China.
- *Accelerated Depreciation*: CBM extraction companies can accelerate depreciation of its special CBM equipment purchased, such as pump, monitoring devices, and generators. The specific accelerated depreciation method can be decided by the companies themselves.
- *Income Tax*: Profits are exempted from the tax for the first two years and are taxed at 50% of the rate for the next three years.
- *New Equipment Investment*: Any such investment can be deducted from the increment tax of the current year over the previous year.
- *Subsidy*: There is a subsidy on CBM production of 0.2 yuan per cubic meter.
- CBM for power generation: A subsidy if 0.25 yuan (4 US¢)/kWh is provided. *Resources Tax*: For CBM production companies, resource taxes on surface CBM production are waived for now.
- *Import Duties*: Imported materials, equipment, and ancillaries needed for CBM exploration and development are exempted from duty.
- *CBM Price*: The government will not interfere in the setting of CBM prices. The price will be determined by sellers and buyers based on market conditions.

However, to further develop the CBM industry, China is facing many challenges such as cost issues, infrastructure bottlenecks, institutional constraints, and other investment barriers. The same challenges have impeded China's CBM development of the past 5 to 10 years. In order to develop the CBM industry, China needs to overcome these challenges and take further specific and favorable measures and policies.

1. China needs to make greater efforts to expand CBM exploration activities in order to significantly increase the proven part of the resources. Lack of funding for CBM development was one of the major obstacles in the past.

2. To overcome the unique and often difficult geological conditions for CBM E&P and to massively produce CBM, the Chinese have to introduce advanced technologies and develop technologies of their own to achieve their targets.
3. As in the case of natural gas, the E&P of CBM have to be accompanied by the construction of pipelines to transport CBM to consuming centers. China should expand to construct more pipelines in the future.
4. China has to establish the market-based regulatory framework and institutions for the healthy development of the CBM industry. For instance, giving more quality domestic companies the cooperation right with foreign companies and dealing with the disputes over the duplicate mine rights and CBM exploration rights in some important mines.
5. China has to solve the problem of overlapping rights of CBM development versus coal mining by various players, particularly among local coal mining companies. In Shanxi Province, 35 companies have CBM permits. However, 28 of them have overlapping claims with coal mining companies for a total area of 3,448 sq km (1,332 sq miles).
6. Finally, although a series of promotional policies have been issued, they are generally inadequate, vague, and temporary. The Chinese government should further specify preferential tax and financial policies and make the support long term, transparent, and stable. For instance, the government should set a longer period, such as 20 or 25 years, for exempting CBM E&P from paying the resource tax. It should also increase the number of years where zero income tax is applied to CBM operations.

At present, China does not have separate policy incentives for shale gas. However, same or similar policy measures and incentives on CBM are expected to apply to shale gas as well.

3.3.3. *Future growth*

CBM

Although exploration, development, and utilization of CBM remain at low levels at present, the potential for China's CBM industry is still

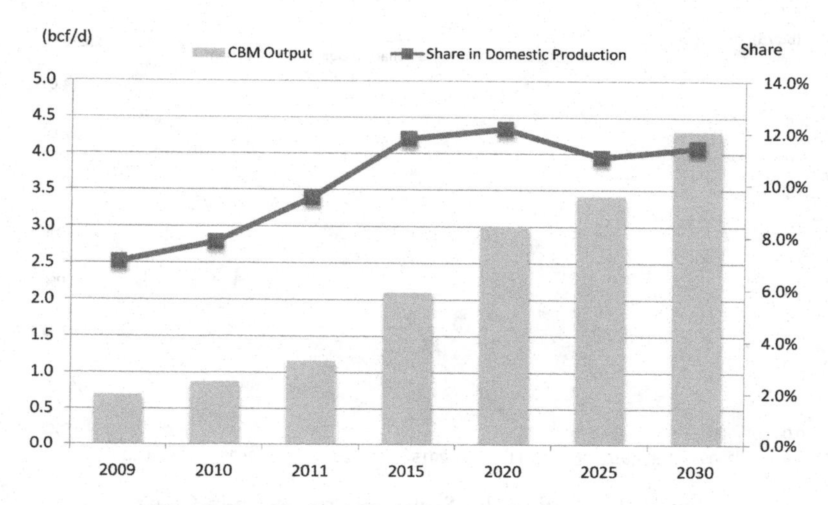

Fig. 3-8. Outlook for CBM Production in China.

big due to its rich resources, solid government support with a series of preferential policies, and foreign participation.

China's plan for future CBM exploration, development, and production is ambitious. As it stands now, China has failed to reach most of the targets set out under the 11th Five-Year Program (FYP), covering the 2006–2010 period.

All factors considered, we expect that China will produce 3.0 bcf/d by 2020 and 4.3 bcf/d by 2030 under our base-case scenario (Fig. 3-8). Under this scenario, CBM production will account for 12% of total gas (natural gas and unconventional gas — inclusive of CBM and shale gas — combined) production in 2020 but go down to 11% in 2030.

Shale gas

For shale gas, we expect China to produce:

1.8 bcf/d by 2020 and 4.4 bcf/d in 2030 under our base-case scenario (Fig. 3-9). Under this scenario, shale gas production will account for 8% of total gas (natural gas and unconventional gas — inclusive of CBM and shale gas — combined) production in 2020, and 13% in 2030.

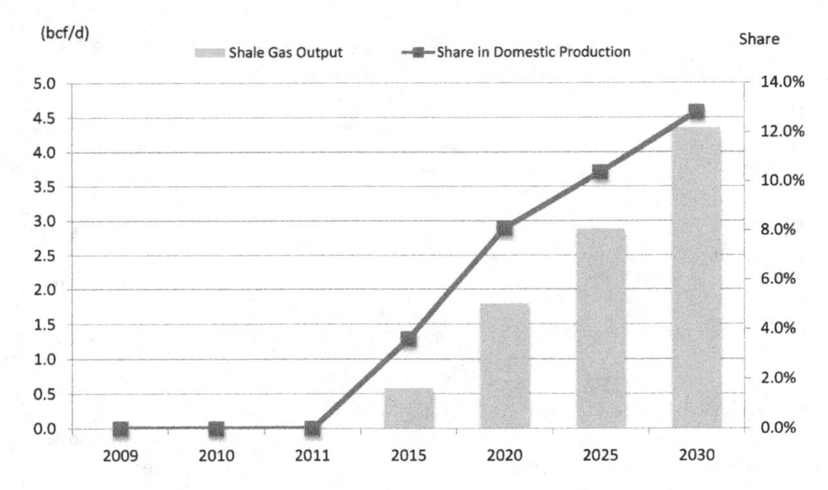

Fig. 3-9. Outlook for Shale Gas Production in China.

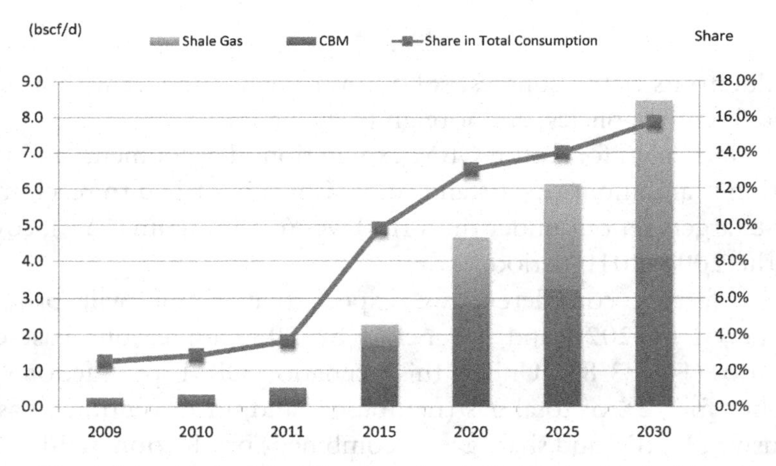

Fig. 3-10. Outlook for Unconventional Gas Production in China.

CBM and shale gas combined

On a comparable basis and if we add up CBM and conventional natural gas, unconventional gas production is forecast to reach 4.5 bcf/d by 2020 and 8.2 bcf/d by 2030. It will thus account for 20% of total gas (natural gas plus unconventional gas) production by 2020 and 24% in 2030 (Fig. 3-10).

chapter 4

China's Downstream Refining Industry: Current Situation and Future Prospects

China currently has the world's second largest refining sector, behind US. After decades of development, China's refining industry has expanded spectacularly, with the capacity of crude distillation units (CDUs) rising from 2.1 million b/d (mmb/d) in 1985 to 7.1 mmb/d in 2005, and finally exceeding 11 million b/d since mid-2010. In this chapter, the current situation and future prospects of China's refining industry are discussed.

This chapter is divided into five sections. A brief discussion of the history of China's refining sector developments is featured in Section 4.1. Sections 4.2 and 4.4 examine a number of issues concerning China's oil refining industry, including its capability, the processing configuration (where a discussion of China's handling of sour crudes is featured), crude runs and utilization rates. Section 4.5 assesses China's long-term plan to expand its refining capacity.

4.1. Historical Developments

From the very beginning, the development of the People's Republic of China's refining industry was tied-in with the development of the upstream oil sector. In 1949, China's refining capacity was only 3.4 kb/d. After a decade of restoration, expansion, and new construction, the capacity reached 116 kb/d in 1959. After the Daqing oil field was discovered, China's refining capability was boosted in the 1960s. Discoveries of other oil fields had further spurred the growth of China's refining capacity. As a result, the CDU capacity jumped to 880 kb/d in 1970, 1.35 mmb/d in 1975, and 1.86 mmb/d in 1978.

Following the extensive expansion during the 1970s, the refining sector seemed to be hesitant to grow again. This was largely due to the stagnation of crude oil production in the country, as well as the government's policy of maximizing crude oil exports in the early 1980s. As a result, crude refining capacity showed little increase between 1979 and 1985, rising from 1.9 mmb/d to only 2.1 mmb/d. One of the most important events in the early 1980s was the establishment of the China Petrochemical Corp., or Sinopec, in 1983. Upon its establishment, Sinopec controlled 31 refineries with a combined distillation capacity of about 1.9 mmb/d, and therefore accounted for 91% of the country's total refining capacity.

Beginning in 1986, China's crude exports started to decline gradually. A few years later, crude imports began, and they have been increasing in volume. Between 1985 and 1989, China entered another round of refining capacity expansion, which went up to 2.6 mmb/d from 2.1 mmb/d in 1985. Throughout the 1980s, Sinopec managed to own and operate 90% of China's refining capacity. Since the early 1990s, the refining industry in China has undergone dramatic changes. During the 1990–1997 period, leading up to the 1998 reorganization, Chinese state and local oil companies moved fast to add new refining capacity, although Sinopec also expanded its capacity. However, the pace of capacity slowed down between 1997 and 2000 due to the government cracking down on small refineries. Since the early 2000s, the refinery expansion, upgrading, and revamping, as well as refining industry restructuring have continued. Between the start of 1990 to the start of 2011, China added a total of 8.2 mmb/d of refining capacity, averaging around 400 kb/d each year (Fig. 4-1).

China currently has the world's second largest refining sector behind the US. After decades of development, its refining industry has expanded spectacularly, with crude distillation capacity rising to 7.1 million b/d in 2005 from 2.1 million b/d in 1985 and has finally

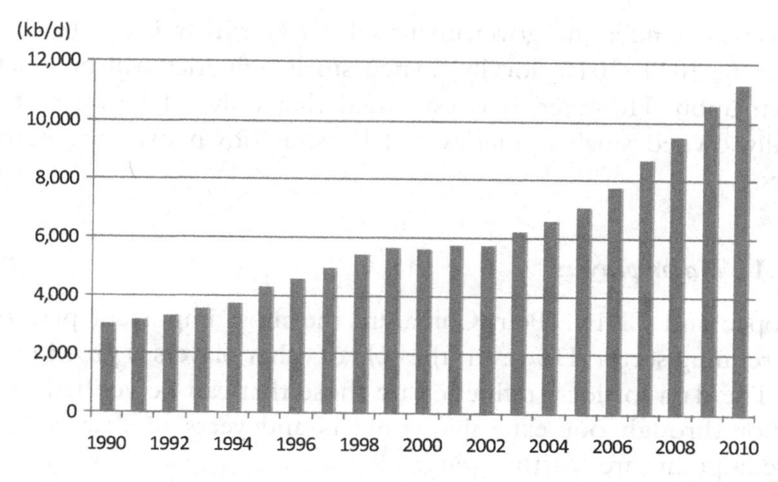

Fig. 4-1. China's End of the Year Refining Capacity, 1990–2010.

exceeded 11 million b/d since mid-2010, reaching 11.3 mmb/d in end 2010.

4.2. Refining Capacity Capability and Players

China's total refining capacity data are not all reliable. The main reason is the thorny issue of locally owned refineries, which are dubbed "teapot refineries," although this term is not entirely accurate as some of these refineries are relatively large. While China's CDU capacity has been expanded substantially since the late 1990s, small refineries were shut down as well through the government crackdown on locally owned refineries as well as adjustments made by Sinopec and CNPC/PetroChina. Since 1999, nearly 1.1 mmb/d of Sinopec, CNPC/PetroChina, and most importantly, locally owned refineries have been shut down and scaled back.

Since 2003, however, locally owned refineries have staged a comeback when oil markets have become tight with booming oil demand in China. As of today, total refining capacity of locally owned refineries — some of which have already formed alliances or joint ventures with state oil companies such as CNOOC or Sinochem — is estimated at over 2.4 mmb/d. The future of these small refineries is uncertain. Under the government's 12th Five-Year Program (FYP), covering 2011–2015, locally owned small refineries will be cracked down upon. However, it is estimated that only a fraction of these locally owned small refineries will be shut down over the coming years.

4.2.1. *Major players*

Sinopec and CNPC/PetroChina are the most important players in the refining sector. However, the role of other players is growing too.

The data for local refineries are those that can be verified by the author through our extensive contacts and years of data research. Several points are worth noting:

- Sinopec and CNPC/PetroChina are the two dominant refiners in China and they have been expanding their CDU capacity at a fast pace. CNOOC has also recently expanded into the market with its fully owned 240 kb/d Huizhou refinery. Data for these three national oil companies (NOCs) are the most reliable.
- Sinopec has the largest capacity in China. At end of 2010, Sinopec had nearly 5.1 mmb/d of crude distillation unit capacity, accounting for 45% of the national total. This was up from 2.9 mmb/d in end 2000. Sinopec's refineries are located mainly in the Middle and Lower Yangtze regions, the South, part of the North but with little presence elsewhere (Table 4-1). In other words, they concentrate in the more affluent coastal cities in the country.
- CNPC/PetroChina had 3.5 million b/d of CDU capacity in end 2010, 31% of the national total. This was up from 2.2 mmb/d from 2000. Before the major restructuring of the Chinese petroleum industry in 1998, CNPC's total CDU capacity was under 800 kb/d. CNPC/PetroChina's assets are located mainly in the Northeast, the Northwest, the West, the Southwest, and part of the North. However, CNPC/PetroChina has been aggressive in penetrating into areas under Sinopec's control. The recently started up 200 kb/d Qinzhou refinery in Guangxi is a good example.

Table 4-1. Distribution of Refining Capacity by Region, as of End 2010 (kb/d).

Region	Sinopec	CNPC/ PetroChina	CNOOC	Local	Total	Share
Northeast	—	1,975	—	229	2,204	19.5%
North	1,692	254	240	1,276	3,462	30.7%
Mid Yangtze	570	—	—	—	570	5.1%
Lower Yangtze	1,658	—	160	33	1,851	16.4%
South	1,046	220	240	109	1,615	14.3%
Southwest	—	22	—	22	44	0.4%
Northwest	5	495	—	376	921	8.2%
West	100	506	—	3	609	5.4%
TOTAL	**5,116**	**3,472**	640	**2,048**	**11,276**	**100.0%**

- Other national oil companies, CNOOC and Sinochem, are also aggressively expanding their refining business. Prior to the 1998 reorganization, the now-defunct MOCI owned the 106 kb/d Jilin Chemical Co. in Jilin Province. The refinery has since become part of CNPC/PetroChina. CNOOC started its wholly owned 240 kb/d Huizhou refinery in Guangdong, which is designed to process low-sulfur crudes with high TAN (total acid number) in 2009. Both CNOOC and Sinochem have joint ventures with local refineries. The total capacity of CNOOC, Sinochem, and their associated local refineries amounts to some 800 kb/d at present, accounting for 7% of the nation's total CDU capacity in end 2010.
- Regarding locally owned refineries that have nothing to do with any state oil company, the size in end 2010 is estimated at 1.9 mmb/d, accounting for 16% of the national total.

China has many individual refineries, depending on how refineries are defined and how accurate the data for local refineries are. As shown in Fig. 4-2, at the start of 2010, China had:

- 2 refineries with individual capacities not less than 400 kb/d;
- 18 refineries that have individual capacities between 200 and 399 kb/d;

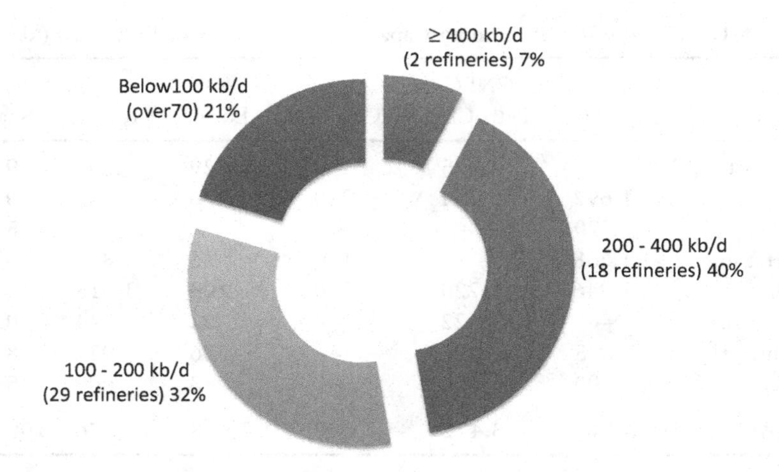

Fig. 4-2. Chinese Refineries of Different Sizes, End 2010.

Note: Total CDU capacity was 11.3 mmb/d.

- 29 refineries with individual capacities between 100 and 199 kb/d;
- Over 70 refineries with individual capacities less than 100 kb/d.

At the beginning of 2011, China has 49 refineries that have capacities of at least 100 kb/d, and their combined capacity is 8.6 mmb/d (76% of the total). At least 70 refineries have an individual capacity lower than 100 kb/d, of which are mostly local refineries.

4.2.2. *Role of locally owned refineries*

Chinese small refineries have the following commonalities:

1. They are mainly located in areas around oil fields or near ports, with particularly high concentrations in provinces such as Shandong, Shaanxi, Guangdong, Liaoning, Hebei, and Henan.
2. Some of the local refineries are not small at all. A good example is refineries owned by the local company Yanchang Group in Shaanxi Province, where their combined crude distillation capacity is

306 kb/d. Yanchang is indeed the largest local company in China for both upstream oil production and downstream oil refining.

3. Except for the Yanchang Group, which has its own oil fields, crude supply to locally owned refineries is limited.
4. Most of these refineries rely on fuel oil as feedstock.
5. Facing continuous cracking down of the government, many of these local refineries that are unwilling to be shut down have chosen to team up with one of the state oil companies or expand their size aggressively so as not to be "small" anymore.

As mentioned, China's refining industry has long been dominated by two major players, Sinopec and CNPC/PetroChina, while locally owned small refineries are subject to restrictions by the government due to their scale, environmental impact, and other reasons. China's local refineries are mostly located in areas surrounding oil fields or near ports, with particularly high concentrations in provinces such as Shandong, Shaanxi, Guangdong, Liaoning, Hebei, and Henan.

Currently, China's total CDU capacity of locally owned refineries is estimated at 1.8 mmb/d, for the following reasons, our data may not capture the whole picture:

- **Under-reporting:** This is still the major problem in getting precise data about local refineries.
- **Definitional issue:** Some topping plants are still too simple to be qualified as refineries.
- **Use of fuel oil:** As mentioned later, many local refineries use fuel oil as feedstock, making any calculation, ranging from crude runs to output of refined products, difficult.
- **Relationship with the state oil companies:** This can be part of the definitional issues. Some refineries are really just local as they formed alliances with the state oil companies, particularly Sinopec and CNPC/PetroChina. Some local refineries are not really small. A good example is the giant 160 kb/d refinery owned by the local company Yanchang Group in Shaanxi Province. Yanchang is indeed the largest local company in China for both upstream oil production and downstream oil refining.

There are three main sources of crude supply to local refineries:

- **Quota Crude:** Sinopec and PetroChina provide limited crude oil to local refineries under the quota by the central government. In recent years, the total crude quota for Shandong's local refineries was less than 50 kb/d.
- **Heavy Oil:** The local refineries also use heavy oil as feedstock, which come from the oil fields of Yanchang, CNOOC, Xinjiang, Liaohe, as well as some wasted oil from oil fields. Since the heavy oil is rich in sulfur and coke, and may cause more corrosion on equipment, state-owned refineries do not use this oil as raw material.
- **Imported Fuel Oil:** The local refineries use fuel oil as feedstock to produce gasoline and diesel. They usually choose the imported 180 CST and M100 fuel oil.

Refined products produced by local refineries have the following characteristics:

- Local refineries sell their gasoline and diesel to private service stations. In general, these products meet the national standard of oil products.
- In 2008, some local refineries received commissioned crudes from Sinopec and PetroChina to process crude oil when domestic oil product supplies were tight. The two state-owned companies provided crude oil to the local refineries, paid them a processing fee, and bought back their oil products — gasoline and diesel. The gasoline and diesel were provided to the service stations under Sinopec and PetroChina. However, that arrangement has since stopped.
- Local refineries also produce some off-spec diesel for farming, fishing, as well as industrial users (including ceramic, glassware, dying, plastic, and chemical factories). These diesel consumers do not need high quality diesel and prefer to choose cheaper off-spec diesel, which can be provided by local refineries.

There are numerous challenges facing the local refineries. The biggest problem facing the local refineries is the lack of a stable supply of crude oil. Domestic crude oil resources are in the hands of the three NOCs (Sinopec, PetroChina, and CNOOC). With the expansion of these three NOCs' refining capacity, the resources available to local refineries are becoming squeezed and unstable.

At present, fuel oil (particularly, imported fuel oil) is the main raw material for local refineries. However, as fuel oil prices fluctuate with crude oil prices, it is difficult to guarantee profits. In recent years, consumption tax and increased customs duties have raised the production cost for the local refineries. A consumption tax has been levied on fuel oil since April 1, 2006 and the local refineries which that import fuel oil have to pay a consumption tax. Since January 1, 2009, the fuel oil consumption tax soared from 101.5 yuan/tonne (US$2.3/b) to 812 yuan/tonne (US$18.4/b). Since January 1, 2010, China raised the import customs duty for #5–7 fuel oil from 1% to 3%. As a result, processing of fuel oil for local refineries has become difficult to remain profitable. However, Sinopec and PetroChina do not need to pay a consumption tax due to the fact that they use crude oil as feedstock. So the production cost for the local refineries are much higher than the production cost for the two state oil companies.

The local refineries are often forced to cut their utilization rates or stop running due to fluctuating prices of imported fuel oil as well as high taxes. In 2009, the average utilization rate of Shandong's local refineries was 31%, down 2% from 2008. The utilization rate was 10%–20% for Guangdong's local refineries. For 2010, the utilization rates improved across the board for all refineries in China, including local ones. The average profit of Shandong's local refineries was –436 yuan/tonne (–US$9.9/b), and –152 yuan/tonne (–US$3.4/b) for Guangdong's local refineries. The situation was worse than 2008. For 2010, the refining economics for local refineries continued to remain bad. It is expected that the refining margin for local refineries will worsen in the future as the Chinese government will control the domestic gasoline and diesel price with higher international crude prices.

In 2009, China's NDRC announced their planning objectives of eliminating inefficient production capacity in the next three years, which clearly states: by 2011, the backward and inefficient refining units with capacity lower than 20 kb/d will be eliminated; the units with capacity between 20 and 40 kb/d will be shut down or restructured under the government guidance; and the new refinery projects under the name of processing heavy oil and for the production of asphalt are prohibited. China currently has at least 32 local refineries that have a CDU capacity of 20 kb/d or higher. The total capacity amounted to 1.7 mmb/d in end 2010. With a lack of crude sources and high taxes, the local refineries will continue operating at a low rate of utilization or stop running altogether. However, the local refineries have been looking for ways to survive. Many plan to expand their capacity. In Shandong Province, 120 kb/d of new CDU and another 120 kb/d of upgrading units were added during the first half of 2010. On the other hand, the local refineries have been expanding their retail network. Currently there is a total of 9,000 service stations in Shandong Province, consisting of Sinopec's 2,600, PetroChina's 738, and 5,547 by private companies.

China has been using local refineries as a supplementary source for refined oil. Whenever the refined oil market is tight, it will increase crude oil supply or even authorize them to produce for the major players. But as the refining capability is sufficient in the future, local refineries, especially the small and inefficient ones, will face pressure to mothball. Ever since the Chinese government cracked down on local refineries in 1998 and did it repeatedly after that, the relationships between local refineries and the state oil companies, particularly Sinopec and CNPC/PetroChina have been complicated. With the strong support of the central government, the state oil companies often have an upper hand in competing with local refineries and take them over. However, local refineries do get support from local governments. Furthermore, local refineries prefer to continue their business independently, even though facing constraints of oil sources and sales channels. Nonetheless, many local refiners do see the benefits of forming business alliances with or even becoming a subsidiary of the state oil companies. A quick review of how each state oil company deals with local refineries (shown in the following) is worthwhile.

Sinopec and local refineries

Sinopec has refineries all over in China, including a 200 kb/d Qingdao and a 280 kb/d Qilu refinery in Shandong Province. Therefore, Sinopec has no plans to purchase any local refineries but rather wishes to maintain sound collaborating relationships to avoid unnecessary competition. On January 28, 2008, the Shandong Fuel Oil Association officially established, as one of its key agendas, to import fuel oil from overseas through wholesale negotiation at a relatively lower price. Fuel oil is a crucial oil source for the production of local refineries. Therefore, almost all local refineries joined the association with no hesitation. One thing that needs to be pointed out is that the founder of this association, Shandong Zhonglian Petroleum and Chemical Corporation Limited, is completely controlled by Sinopec, which owns an 84% stake. Therefore, it seems that Sinopec intends to maintain its conventional advantage as the biggest player in the province by controlling the local refineries through the local fuel oil association.

CNPC/PetroChina and local refineries

CNPC/PetroChina supplies crude oil to local refineries in several Northeast provinces and in Shandong Province, as well as authorizing some of them to produce refined oil for them. PetroChina began cooperating with Shandong Dongming Petrochemical in 2009. They set up a joint venture, PetroChina Shandong Oil Transportation Company, in August 2009, with a total investment of 762 million yuan (US$115 million), consisting of 70% from PetroChina and 30% from Dongming. On July 28, 2010, the two sides signed an agreement to build an oil pipeline from Rizhao to Dongming. Under the agreement, PetroChina will provide crude oil to Dongming through the pipeline. In addition, PetroChina plans to build a new CDU with a designed capacity of 100 kb/d for Dongming.

CNOOC and local refineries

With the advantage of crude oil control, CNOOC plans to further strengthen its refinery business by purchasing local refineries in

Shandong Province. Since 2002, CNOOC has bought four local refineries: Daxie Petrochemical (160 kb/d), Zhongjie Petrochemical (60 kb/d), Shandong Haihua (also called Zhonghai Chemical, 60 kb/d), and CNOOC Asphalt Co. Ltd. (64 kb/d). In addition, CNOOC discussed combining or cooperating with five local refineries in Shandong Province, but they have not reached any agreement so far. They are: Fuhai Group (32 kb/d), Kenli Petrochemical (30 kb/d), Haike Petrochemical (30 kb/d), Shandong Shida Technology (30 kb/d), and Lijin Petrochemical (130 kb/d).

In short, due to constraints of oil sources, some of the local refineries in Shandong Province are likely to be fully or partially purchased by CNOOC. Sinopec and CNPC/PetroChina will focus mainly on establishing and expanding their own refineries, while at the same time cooperating with local refineries.

4.3. Processing Configurations

4.3.1. *Unique characteristics of refining configurations*

China's refining configuration has several distinguishing characteristics (Wu and Fesharaki, 2005a; Wu, 2011):

- First, it has a huge amount of cracking capacity. In comparison, China's ratio of combined cat cracking, hydrocracking, visbreaking, coking, and thermal cracking to CDU was 48%. That is nearly twice the share in Japan, much higher than the Asia-Pacific's average, and only slightly lower than the share in US (Table 4-2). The high cracking/CDU ratio is attributable to the country's long history of using mainly domestic crudes, which are heavy and waxy with high pour points, as refinery feedstock. Of the cracking plants, however, fluid catalytic cracking and resid catalytic cracking (FCC/RCC) outweigh the others. At the end of 2010, China had 2.7 mmb/d of FCC/RCC capacity, up from 1.8 mmb/d at the end of 2000. In addition to FCC/RCC, China's coking and hydrocracking capacity are also large. Coking capacity has been expanded at a rapid pace since 2004, reaching 1.4 mmb/d at the end of 2010. Hydrocracking capacity is even more dramatic.

Table 4-2. Comparison of Cracking Capacities, End 2010 (kb/d).

	China	Japan	India	Asia Pacific	USA
CDU	11,275.6	4,200.1	3,847.3	29,405.9	17,869.2
FCC/RCC	2,672.6	972.3	764.5	5,567.8	5,727.9
HDC[a]	1,131.2	134.4	335.8	2,254.8	1,668.7
VBR/TC[b]	260.5	—	173.6	806.0	34.0
Coking	1,432.9	150.6	433.2	2,158.4	2,474.1
Cat Reforming	879.2	798.0	281.8	3,214.5	3,543.8
HDT[c] & hydrorefining	3,496.0	2,029.2	1,387.0	9,423.2	14,062.3
FCC/RCC-to-CDU Ratio	24%	23%	20%	19%	32%
HDC-to-CDU Ratio	10%	3%	9%	8%	9%
Cracking-to-CDU Ratio[d]	49%	30%	44%	37%	55%
Reforming-to-CDU Ratio	8%	19%	7%	11%	20%
HDT to CDU Ratio	31%	48%	36%	32%	79%

[a]HDC = hydrocracking
[b]VBR = visbreaking; TC = thermal cracking
[c]HDT = hydrotreating
[d]Cracking includes all of those listed in this table.
Note: In China, HDT & hydrorefining includes gasoline, kerosene, and middle distillate hydrorefining.

Before 2004, China only had 270 kb/d of hydrocracking capacity. By end 2010, China's hydrocracking capacity has 1.1 mmb/d.

- The second characteristic of China's refinery configuration is that its cat reforming capacity (879 kb/d at the start of 2011, or 8% of CDU capacity) is still lower than the shares of cat reformers in Japan (19%) and the US (20%). China's reformer/CDU ratio is also less than the average ratio of 11% for the Asia–Pacific region. This difference is again partly due to China's historical crude slate, of which the naphtha yield is low and insufficient to support a large reformer capacity. However, cat reforming capacity in China at present is already more than double the capacity of 316 kb/d at the end of 2010.
- Third, China has sharply increased its hydrotreating/hydrorefining capacity in recent years to address the tightening specification for gasoil and to a lesser extent, gasoline. At the end of 2010, China had 3.5 mmb/d of hydrotreating/hydrorefining capacity,

a jump from less than 800 kb/d at the end of 2000. One issue of caution is that since Chinese data does not separate treating of gasoline, kerosene, and diesel/middle distillates, the capacity number reported here appears to be inflated in comparison with hydrotreating capacities of other countries.

- Fourth, China's capability for handling sour and acidic crudes has increased substantially since the mid-1990s, especially for Sinopec. China has increased its capability to handle heavy oil as well as fuel oil as feedstock. This is an area that is penetrated deeply by locally owned refineries, new ventures of state oil companies other than Sinopec and CNPC/PetroChina, such as CNOOC and Sinochem, and to a lesser extent, by CNPC/PetroChina itself whose crudes produced in aging fields in the northeast have become increasingly heavy.
- Finally, the utilization rate of China's refining capacity was historically low but has increased since the early 2000s. Before 1986, the government's policy of maximizing oil exports reduced the availability of feedstock to the domestic refining industry. Although more crude oil was diverted to domestic refineries thereafter, declining crude production, rapid expansion of the refining capacity, and the continued existence of small and very small refineries had kept utilization rates low during most of the 1990s. The situation has improved since the 2000s, more on which will be discussed later.

4.3.2. *Handling of sour crudes*

China's capability and experience in handing sour crudes deserves a special note. With some exceptions, such as crudes from Oman, Yemen, part of Abu Dhabi, as well as Arab Extra Light from Saudi Arabia, Middle East crudes all have high sulfur content, while many Chinese refineries, until the mid-1990s, were unable to process such crudes. China has since moved to raise its sour-crude handling capability.

In the mid-1990s, in anticipation of rising Middle East oil imports, Sinopec started revamping, upgrading, and expanding its refineries to add sour-crude processing capabilities. These efforts have produced some notable results. At the end of 2010, Sinopec and CNPC/PetroChina together had 3.2 mmb/d of processing capacity for imported sour crudes, which are dominated by Sinopec. This also means China has at least 7 mmb/d of refining capacity that can process only sweet crudes, a fact that severely limits China's choice of imported crudes and prompts China to seek sweet crudes from sources such as those from Africa and Latin America.

The plans for further expanding the sour crude handling capacity by 2010 will be discussed in Section 4.4. While the hydrogen-aided process is chosen as the main secondary unit to handle sour crudes, vacuum resid desulfurization (VRDS) has not been vigorously pursued in China. One reason is that China has a huge cracking capability, and the overall fuel oil production is low. Another reason is that there is still a lack of stringent standards for producing and using low sulfur fuel oil in China.

China has 7 VRDS units totaling 273 kb/d in end 2010, up from about 100 kb/d in 2007. The recent expansion of the VRDS capacities is mainly to meet the requirement to process more sour crudes. China also plans to add 141 kb/d by 2015 and another 120 kb/d by 2020. Nonetheless, comparing to the expansion of the primary and other secondary units in China, the resid desulfurization capacity and future buildup are relatively low. This is mainly because of China's slow pace in tightening fuel oil specs at home.

4.4. Refining Throughput and Utilization Rates

Crude runs have been growing vigorously but also unevenly from year to year. For instance, the growth of crude runs reached more than 750 kb/d in 2004, but it was negative in 1994 and 1998, or as little as 31 kb/d in 2001. In 2010, crude runs reached 8.5 mmb/d, up from 2.2 mmb/d in 1990 and 4.1 mmb/d in 2000 (Fig. 4-3). In other words, in a decade, China's refining crude runs quadrupled. In fact, 2010 was the year of historical significance where the increment of 1 mmb/d in crude runs was the highest ever for the country.

With stagnated domestic production, accompanying the fast growth of refining crude runs are rapidly rising crude imports

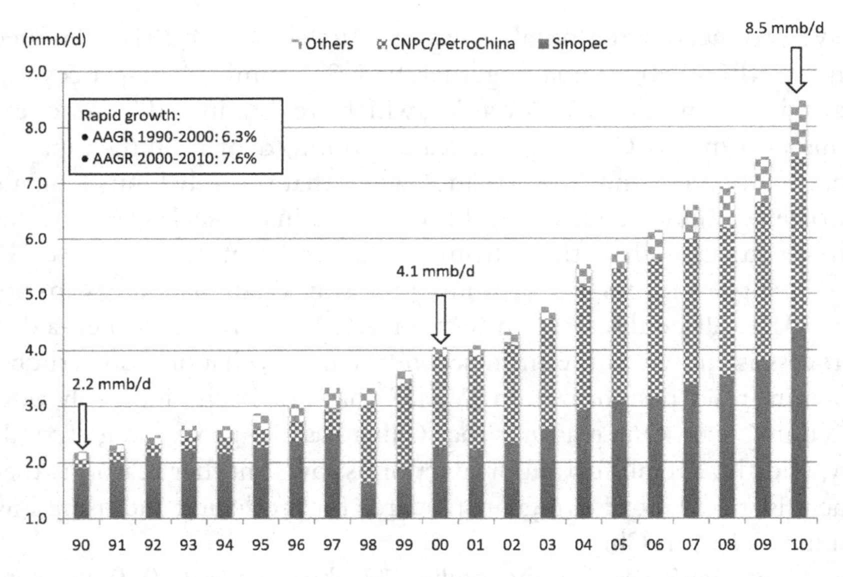

Fig. 4-3. China's Crude Runs by Company, 1990–2010.

(Fig. 4-4). In 2010, China imported 4.8 mmb/d of crude oil, 710 kb/d higher than imports of 2009, which set another record for growth. Compared to 2000, China's crude imports in 2010 were more than 2.5 times higher. Of the 4.8 mmb/d of crude oil imports in 2010 by China, African supplies accounted for 30%, or 1.4 mmb/d. This reflects the strong appetite of the Chinese refineries for heavy sweet crudes.

Based on the national crude runs and refining capacity reported here, Fig. 4-5 shows the changing utilization rate for Chinese refineries. Both overestimation and underestimation may occur in the numbers. On the one hand, because certain small refineries are not included in the capacity, the calculated rate might have been slightly inflated. On the other hand, since we use crude runs for comparison with the year-end capacity, the yearly rates tend to be underestimated. Moreover, the ratio is heavily affected by how a refinery's actual capacity is treated.

Historically, changes in refining throughput in China have been closely linked to the growth of crude oil production in the country

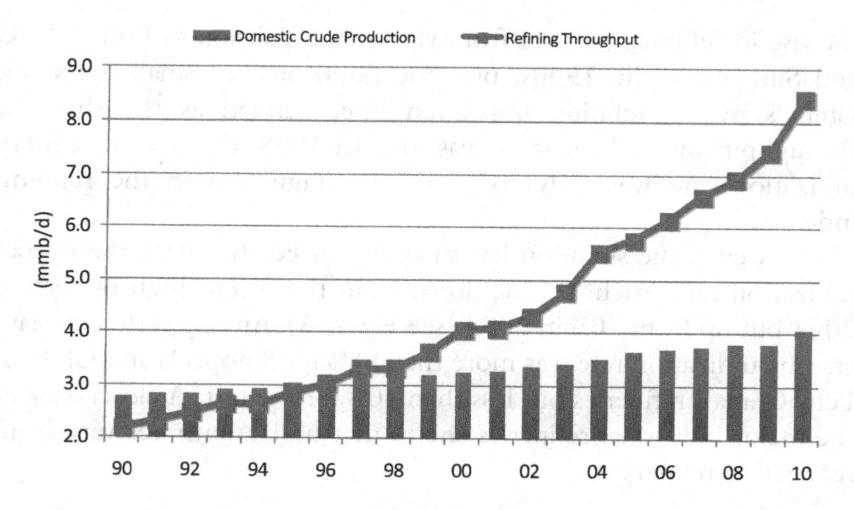

Fig. 4-4. China's Refining Throughout versus Domestic Crude Production, 1990–2010.

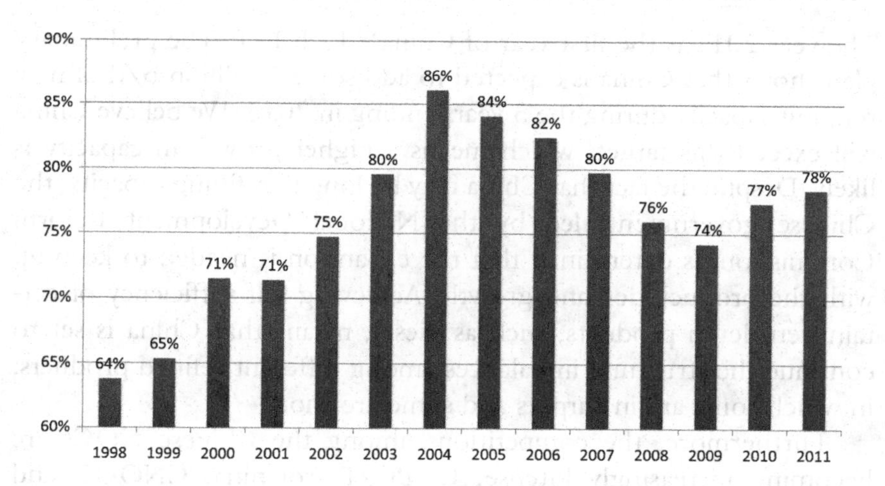

Fig. 4-5. Refining Utilization Rate in China, 1998–2011.

Note: 2011 data is an estimate.

and, understandably, to the expansion of its refining capacity. Since China became a net importer of oil overall in 1993, the refining throughput has experienced vigorous growth, and its relationship with domestic crude production also started to change. Because of the rise in refining capacity from vigorous expansion of both CNPC and Sinopec in the 1990s, plus the flourishing of small refineries, China's overall refining utilization rate, defined as the share of throughput in total capacity, was low. In 1998, the overall refinery utilization rate was only 61%, due to stagnation in the refining industry.

However, the situation has since improved. In 2010, the overall utilization rate reached 75%, down from the recent high of 83% in 2004 but up from 70% in 2009 (see Fig. 4-5). Among different players, the utilization rate was more than 88% for Sinopec's and CNPC/PetroChina's refineries but less than 40% for the rest. A closer look at the major individual refineries shows that utilization rates vary from refinery to refinery.

4.5. Outlook for Capacity Additions and Crude Runs

The year 2011 is the first year of China's 12th FYP. The preliminary plan shows that China is expected to add some 2 million b/d of new refining capacity during the 5 years ending in 2015. We believe China will exceed this target, which means a higher growth in capacity is likely. Despite the fact that China may be long in refining capacity, the Chinese government, led by the National Development Reform Commission, is determined that the expansion is needed to keep up with the product–demand growth. Achieving self-sufficiency of certain petroleum products, such as diesel, means that China is set to continue the structural imbalances among different refined products, in which some are in surplus and some are short.

Furthermore, the competitions among the Chinese NOCs are becoming increasingly intense. CNPC/PetroChina, CNOOC and Sinochem are keen to use their resources to expand into Sinopec's territories and business turfs in a bid to become "bigger and more powerful" while Sinopec is trying its best to protect its business in the coastal cities. Therefore, we expect that the Chinese national oil companies (Sinopec, PetroChina, CNOOC, Sinochem, and others) have intentions to overbuild in order to have a greater presence in the refining sector. Simply put, the larger the company, the more easily it can justify its importance and argue "what is good for it is good for the country."

Nonetheless, the Chinese government still holds the self-sufficient policy but has no intention to become a large petroleum products exporter. We believe that the National Development Reform Commission (NDRC) will pace the country's future refining build-up with its product demand growth to maintain the position of self-sufficiency in refined products, especially in diesel.

China's CDU capacity is expected to increase by about 2.6 mmb/d between end 2010 and end of 2015 and it is likely to add another 2.2 mmb/d of new CDU capacity between end 2015 and 2020. This refining expansion is about at the same rate as the demand growth.

Beyond the firm and likely projects, there are a dozen possible additions (a total of 2.7 mmb/d of refining capacity). Many of these projects have an uncertain future and their detailed plans are unknown. Under this category, more than half are unlikely to take off and most of the rest may be delayed indefinitely. However, there are a few that may be elected to be upgraded to the list of likely projects. Meanwhile, it is also possible that some likely projects for 2015–2020 may drop off the list as well.

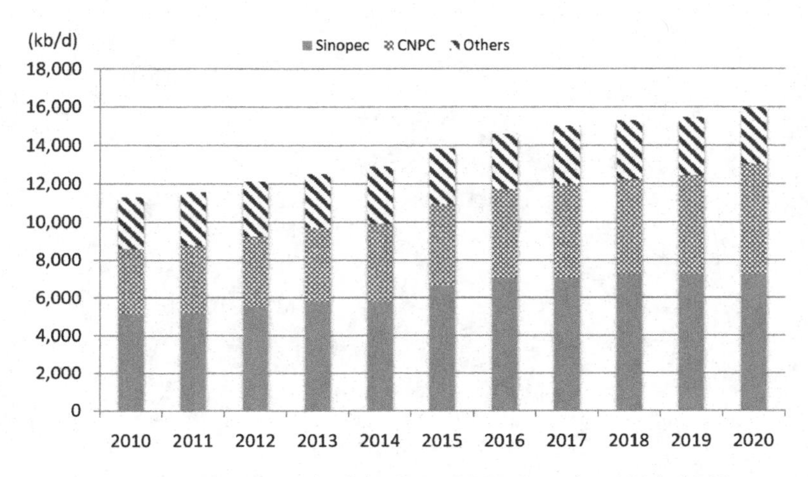

Fig. 4-6. China's End of the Year CDU Capacity, 2010–2020.

Toward 2020, we expect that Sinopec will remain the largest refiner in China, with 6.6 mmb/d of refining capacity (51% of the total) in end 2015 and 7.3 mmb/d (64% of the total) in end 2020. CNPC/PetroChina will have 4.3 mmb/d of refining capacity (38% of the total) in end 2015 and 5.2 mmb/d (46%) in 2020 (Fig. 4-6). Competition in the coastal provinces such as Guangdong and Fujian will be much more intense as all Chinese oil majors will build their refineries in those regions. China's sour crude processing capacity will also increase by 2.1 mmb/d in the next five years to reach 5.3 mmb/d. The crude runs are forecast to increase to 11.0 mmb/d in 2015, 13.2 mmb/d in 2020 and 15.2 mmb/d in 2030.

chapter 5

Oil Market Dynamics and Outlook for Demand, Supply, and Trade

This chapter reviews the developments of the Chinese oil markets of the recent past and presents an outlook on China's oil demand, supply, and trade. Petroleum price mechanism and reforms and regulations governing China's oil imports are first discussed. The chapter continues with a general review and analysis of the current situation and future prospects of petroleum product demand, supply, trade, and balances. Further discussions of individual refined products, including liquefied petroleum gas (LPG), gasoline, kerosene, and jet fuel (kero/jet), diesel or gasoil, and fuel oil are elucidated. Among the other products, the demand and supply of petrochemical feedstock (chemfeed) — where the primary emphasis is on naphtha — are examined. Finally, the overall demand and supply of petroleum products are discussed at the end of the chapter, where the future prospects for crude oil as well as refined products toward 2020 and 2030 will be presented.

5.1. China's Oil Market Dynamics

Deregulation of China's oil market has been continuing for over two decades. During the 1980s and early 1990s, the oil market moved gradually away from tight government control under the rigid centrally planned economy. The government, however, tightened the market toward the mid-1990s. In the late 1990s and early part of this decade, China attempted to deregulate the oil market again to a certain extent in preparation of joining the World Trade Organization (WTO).

During the following years after its joining the WTO in late 2001, China was busy in fulfilling its obligations and concessions it committed to the WTO, however, with mixed results. Since the Second Gulf War in 2003, when Saddam Hussein was toppled by the US-led forces and international oil prices started escalating in 2004, China's oil market regime had entered a stage where the government's move to regulate oil prices again and the further liberalization of other parts of the oil market coexist. After the outbreak of the global financial crisis in September 2008 and the collapse of oil prices during the second half of the year, the Chinese government introduced a new regime for main petroleum products. This regime has remained in effect to date.

Meanwhile, two important milestones of the further liberalization of the oil markets were the opening up of the retail market in December 2004 and the wholesale market in December 2006, which were part of China's concessions made for joining the WTO. We will discuss the two policy moves separately in the following section.

5.1.1. *Wholesale and retail trading of oil products*

In China, there are two types of wholesalers:

> The provincial, municipal, and local petroleum companies: These companies are local affiliates of Sinopec, CNPC/PetroChina, or CNOOC since June 1998.
>
> Independent wholesalers/oil traders: In China, independent wholesalers/oil traders refer to those who do not belong to either Sinopec or PetroChina — two major state oil companies in China. They may be owned either by local governments or private Chinese individuals.

From the early 1980s to the end of the 1990s, there were more than 8,500 wholesale enterprises of oil products and nearly 100,000 service stations in China. This period witnessed the rapid growth of locally owned and private wholesale as well as retail businesses in China. At the height of their presence, independent businesses accounted for 85% of the oil product market in China. The independent wholesale companies once reached 3,340 and service stations 56,300.

In 1998 and particularly 1999, the government started consolidating (reorganizing) the domestic oil products market. As part of the consolidation, the Chinese government drastically restructured the wholesale and retail oil product businesses by transferring crude oil exploration, development, and refining to Sinopec and PetroChina, and allowed the two state oil companies to merge not only independent refineries but also independent wholesale and retail businesses. After the consolidation, the number of oil product wholesale enterprises was reduced to 2,500 from the previous 8,500. Of the 2,500 wholesalers, over 1,700 enterprises were the subsidiaries of the two oil giants, and the other 700 were affiliated with the two oil giants. Since then, Sinopec and PetroChina have controlled the entire oil products wholesale market in China.

As of now, the number of independent wholesalers has declined to 663 — of which one-third are inactive — and independent service stations down to 45,000, where 40% of them are on the brink of closing down. In the meantime, Sinopec and PetroChina have expanded aggressively.

China currently has 2,519 petroleum product wholesalers, with the following structure:

Those that are owned or controlled by Sinopec and CNPC/PetroChina: 1,657

Other Chinese national oil companies (NOCs): 279

Independent wholesalers: 572

Foreign-funded wholesalers: 11

Currently, China has nearly 96,000 gas service stations. More specifically, the ownership structure for China's retail service stations is the following:

Stations owned or controlled by Sinopec: Over 28,800

Stations and CNPC/PetroChina: Nearly 18,250

Independent stations: Nearly 46,000 (not all are fully operational)

Other stations (including foreign funded): Around 3,000

Total: Nearly 96,000

In China, retail product prices for service and diesel are regulated by the government. For many years, the regulated retail prices have been below the comparable international prices, leading to a unique phenomenon of a "reverse" price regime in China. As such, the wholesale and retail businesses are very competitive in China and profit margins are thin or negative. This has made it hard for independent retailers and wholesalers to survive, while those under Sinopec and CNPC/PetroChina may be compensated by the parent companies from the huge profits reaped upstream. Some independent stations have no choice but to raise pump prices, thus breaking the Chinese price law.

Under these circumstances, business losses from wholesale and retail have increased rapidly. As mentioned earlier, about one-third of the independent wholesalers have largely stopped doing business, and as many as 40% of the independent retailers are in the process of closing down or going bankrupt.

Independent wholesalers and retailers in China are struggling to find a way to survive, including securing product supply from local refineries. Until China's domestic prices are pegged or fully linked with the international market, independent oil marketers in China will continue to have a hard time operating a sound and functional business.

5.1.2. *China's opening-up of wholesale and retail markets*

A separate section has been dedicated to discuss the opening up of retail and wholesale markets because this has been an important commitment made by the Chinese government as part of their concessions to join the WTO. The concessions and commitments made by China were the following: China would have to open up its retail market (including gasoline and diesel) in three years after China's entry into the WTO. The deadline for the retail market opening was December 11, 2004. By then, any foreign company would be allowed to operate service stations in China. The wholesale market for oil products would be opened within five years of China's entry into the WTO. The deadline of the wholesale market was December 11, 2006. By then, any foreign company will be allowed to build oil depots, wharfs, and sales network and operate the oil products wholesale business in China.

In December 2004, the Chinese government announced that its retail market has been opened up. Then in December 2006, a similar announcement was made with regard to the wholesale market. The Ministry of Commerce issued the Provisional Regulation on the Oil Products Market Management on December 2, 2004, which was the official document for the opening of the retail market obligated by China for entering the WTO. However, the interesting thing is that the new regulation covered the wholesale business as well. Effective on January 1, 2005, the main elements of the new regulation are listed as follows:

> Regarding oil products wholesalers, new companies are required to have stable supply channels of oil products. In previous regulations, only PetroChina and Sinopec could be allowed to operate the wholesale business.
>
> Oil products retail enterprises are required to sign a supply contract with an authorized oil products wholesale enterprise, as stable supply channels of oil products. In addition, new service stations must meet the development planning in this area.
>
> Regarding oil products storage enterprises, they must meet the local and national development planning.
>
> More specifically, the interpretation of the new regulation is as follow:
>
> The wholesale market for oil products has been opened up to domestic enterprises. Either companies or individuals may operate

oil products wholesale business by law, so long as they have a stable oil supply channel.

The retail market of oil products has been opened up for foreign enterprises. Foreign enterprises may operate an oil products retail business in China by law, only if they sign an oil supply agreement with an authorized oil products wholesale enterprise as a stable oil supply channel. In addition, any new service station should meet the development planning in this area.

By law, companies or individuals may build oil depots, only if the oil depots meet the national or local development planning and relevant construction conditions.

China issued a revised regulation in December 2006 as a way to signal its commitment under the WTO concession to open up the wholesale market. On December 6, 2006, the Ministry of Commerce issued the Regulation on the Crude Oil Market Management and Provisional Regulation on the Oil Products Market Management. These two documents overwrote the 2004 regulations and have become the latest regulations governing the oil marketing in China. It was China's move to officially open up the wholesale market to foreign and private Chinese investments as obligated for entering the WTO.

Compared to the policy issued in December 2004, which actually covered both retail and wholesale businesses, the December 2006 regulation formalized all the elements with specific implementation processes which were more practical. In fact, it has lowered the threshold for independent wholesalers.

5.1.3. *Oil trade: Rules and Regulations*

Oil trade discussed here covers crude oil imports and exports and product imports and exports. The situations differ from one area to another. China became a WTO member on December 11, 2001. The oil market and the associated rules, regulations, and policies have since changed and evolved to the current state.

China's oil trading companies are divided into state oil trading and non-state oil trading. For crude and refined product imports, five companies are designated as state oil trading companies: Unipec, Chinaoil, Sinochem, Zhenrong Trading Co., and the latecomer CNOOC through its joint venture with Sinopec. For crude and refined product exports, Unipec, Chinaoil, and Sinochem are the designated state oil companies, while CNOOC has long been granted permits to market its offshore oil at international market prices. Any company and trader other than the above-mentioned are all classified as non-state oil companies.

Crude imports

Since 2001, China has allocated a portion of the crude oil import quota for so-called non-state oil trading companies, while the majority of the crude imports are conducted exclusively by four state oil trading companies Unipec, Chinaoil, Sinochem, and Zhenrong Trading Co. In May 2004, CNOOC obtained its permit to be an authorized state crude importer. The joint-venture trading company CNOOC set up with Sinopec has thus become the fifth state oil trading company.

Crude Imports (Tariff): Effective January 1, 2002, the import tariff was reduced from 16 yuan (US$1.93) per metric ton (tonne) to zero.

Crude Imports (Import Quota): Starting in 2002, China agreed to increase the volume of the crude import quota by 15% for 10 years and renegotiate thereafter. A minimum of 20% of the crude oil import quota needs to be allocated to non-state oil companies.

China has since issued the following import quota of crude oil to non-state oil trading companies:

2002: 165 kb/d
2003: 190 kb/d
2004: 219 kb/d
2005: 252 kb/d
2006: 289 kb/d
2007: 333 kb/d
2008: 383 kb/d
2009: 440 kb/d

2010: 506 kb/d
2011: 582 kb/d

Crude exports

The exports are largely monopolized by Chinaoil, Sinochem, and CNOOC. Since China is exporting only Daqing and offshore crudes, Unipec has little business in this area. With tight supply, China has imposed a tax on exports of four energy products, including crude oil and coal since December 2006. The export tax for crude oil is 5%, which is still effective as of today.

Refined product imports

Imports of gasoline, naphtha, diesel, and jet fuel are largely monopolized by Unipec, Chinaoil, Sinochem, and Zhenrong as the allocated quota for so-called non-state oil trading companies is small. Fuel oil is more open. LPG and many specialized products have long been liberalized.

Product Imports (Tariff): Import tariff rates have been adjusted numerous times, mostly downward, since January 2002. Since January 2012 the tariff rates are:

LPG: 1%

Naphtha: 0%

Gasoline: 0%

Kerosene and jet fuel: 0%

Diesel: 0%

Fuel oil: 0%

Product Imports (Import Quota/Licensing and Regulations): Under the concession for entering the WTO, China promised to assign a minimum of 20% of the import quota of refined products to non-state oil trading companies and increase the volume by 15% each year, starting in 2002. Quotas for state oil trading companies were abolished at the beginning of 2004, while those for non-state oil trading companies remained. After the quota was abolished for state oil trading companies, licenses, and other forms of control are now in place.

China has since issued the following import quotas of refined products (predominantly fuel oil though) to non-state oil trading companies:

2002: 92 kb/d
2003: 106 kb/d
2004: 122 kb/d
2005: 140 kb/d
2006: 157 kb/d
2007: 185 kb/d
2008: 213 kb/d
2009: 245 kb/d
2010: 282 kb/d
2011: 324 kb/d

Refined product exports

Similarly, exports of gasoline, naphtha, diesel, and jet fuel are in the hands of Unipec, Chinaoil, and Sinochem. Exports of certain specialized products are also subject to government control. Direct export of gasoline and diesel are subject to the consumption taxes (US$24/b for gasoline and US$19/b for diesel) and value-added tax (17%).

In short, China's oil market has changed steadily since its entry into the WTO. It is clear that the government is playing a vital role in shaping the development of markets. On an overall basis, however, China is moving in the right direction, gradually opening up the market. However, as shown in the following, for refined product prices, the government has somewhat moved backward since 2004 in the name of ensuring the order of the market.

5.2. Crude and Product Price Reforms

Before 1983, the prices for both crude oil and refined products were firmly controlled by the government under the centrally planned economic management system and were artificially kept low. In the early 1980s, a two-tier pricing system was introduced in the petroleum sector, which gave markets an enhanced role in guiding oil production and oil demand. Although a number of other price reform measures have been implemented since the early 1980s, the two-tier price system remained intact until 1994.

The May 1994 reform raised prices for crudes but kept the two-tier pricing system. It also fixed the ex-refinery, wholesale, and retail prices for refined products. The government started linking domestic oil prices with the international markets in June 1998. The June 1998 reform resulted in an immediate lowering of domestic crude prices. To protect the interests of Sinopec, however, the announced reforms (for adjusting refined product prices monthly in parity with Singapore markets) were not implemented until November 1999, when international oil prices surged to unprecedented levels. Starting in July 2000, the SDPC (renamed NDRC since March 2003) formally announced that prices of refined products, such as crude oil, would also be adjusted monthly using Singapore prices as the base. In October 2001, the government went further to expand the linkage to Singapore, Rotterdam, and New York markets for domestic refined products through a formula that only the government could determine.

However, since mid-2003, the NDRC stopped moving (not raising) domestic prices of gasoline, diesel, jet fuel, and kerosene based on their own formulas. Instead, the government has chosen to adjust (increase) domestic prices only when they feel the time is "right" and gap is too big. In late 2006 and early 2007, when the international oil prices fell, the Chinese government in theory adopted a new price formula linking domestic product prices with the international crude oil market. However, the Chinese government had never had a chance to implement the new formula before the international oil prices escalated again in early to mid-2007. As such, the government's practice of capping, regulating, and restricting domestic prices for main products has continued to date. More details are discussed separately for crude oil and refined products in the following.

5.2.1. *Crude oil pricing*

As mentioned earlier, crude oil prices have historically been low in China. The reform measures in the 1980s and early 1990s resulted in the increase of planned prices. Under the May 1994 reform, new and generally higher two-tier prices were established for crude oil. The crudes were divided into four groups, and each group had two tiers.

In May 1998, following the reorganization of the two state oil companies, the SDPC decided to start the program that links domestic oil prices with international markets, effective as of June 1, 1998 for crude oil and June 5, 1998 for refined products.

The new price regime for crude oil that is still effective has the following key features:

Onshore crudes in China are divided into four categories:

Light crudes: including Daqing and some Liaohe crudes.
Medium I crudes: including Jianghan, Tarim Basin, Zhongyuan, and some Huabei crudes.
Medium II crudes: including Dagang, Shengli (excluding Gudao), and Yanchang crudes.
Heavy crudes: including Gudao and some Liaohe and Huabei crudes.

Onshore oil prices in the domestic market consist of two parts: baseline prices and premiums/discounts.

Prior to March 2001, the baseline prices were determined by the government based on average daily Singapore FOB (free on board) prices for a calendar month plus import tariffs. Tapis, Minas, Cinta, and Duri FOB prices in Singapore were used in various ways to serve this purpose. The baseline prices were announced by the SDPC on a monthly basis. At the end of each month, the SDPC published the baseline prices for all four categories of crudes, based on that month's average Singapore FOB prices and import tariffs. These baseline prices became effective on the first day of the next month. Premiums were determined by buyers and sellers within or between CNPC and Sinopec based on the cost of transportation, quality

> differentials, and market conditions. Discounts would apply if the international crude (such as Tapis) is superior in quality. In order to encourage refineries to use domestic crudes, baseline prices for domestic crudes were set at levels that are equal to or slightly lower than the baseline prices for imported crudes on a comparable quality basis.
>
> After March 2001, SDPC stopped publishing the baseline prices and the prices had to be negotiated between CNPC/PetroChina (the largest domestic crude supplier) and Sinopec (the largest domestic crude buyer) based on the international linkages outlined earlier.
>
> China's offshore crudes have already been priced in the international oil market and are treated as imported crudes by the Chinese domestic refineries. The price system for offshore crudes will therefore remain unchanged.

As of today, China's price regime for crude oil can be summarized as follows:

> Crude oil supplied by Sinopec and CNPC/PetroChina: prices are set by buyers and sellers based on the cost of imported crudes and freight for transporting crudes to the refineries.
>
> Crude oil supplied by Sinopec and CNPC/PetroChina to local refineries: prices are determined according to the prices set between the two state oil companies.
>
> Crude oil from CNOOC and other producing companies: prices are set based on the international oil market.

The link between domestic and international crude prices has been followed faithfully since June 1998, although the same cannot be said for refined products (to be discussed next). Fig. 5-1 shows the derived domestic monthly prices for Daqing from January 2005 to January 2012 and the corresponding Minas FOB prices (lag by one month). The figure shows that CNPC/PetroChina is the chief beneficiary of the international prices in recent years (FGE, 2011).

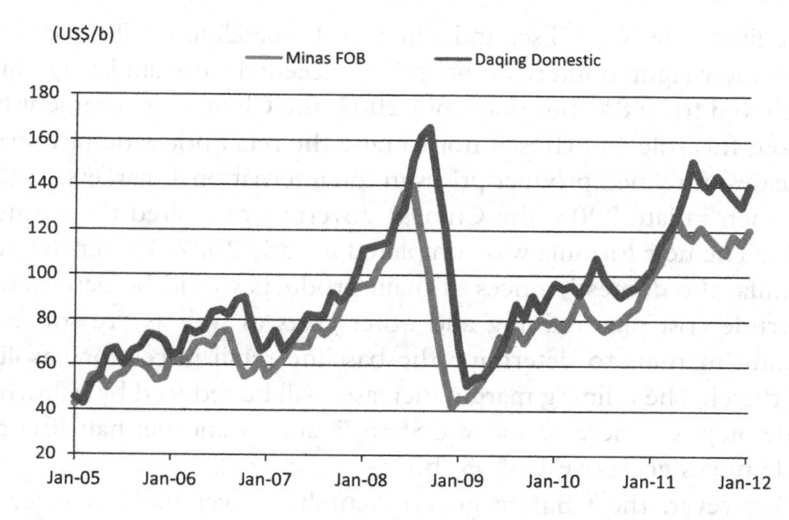

Fig. 5-1. Monthly Domestic Daqing Crude Prices Jan 2005–Jan 2012.
Note: Referring to derived domestic Daqing prices.

5.2.2. *Refined product pricing: Decade-long development*

As in the case of crude oil, China had a multi-tier pricing system for refined products prior to May 1994. The government moved in May 1994 to abolish the two-tier price system for refined products and to place the market of key refined products under the government's control. Following the May 1994 reform, prices for major refined products and petrochemicals, such as gasoline, kero/jet, diesel, part of domestic LPG, fuel oil, fertilizer, and agro-plastic membranes were subject to government regulations. For other products, such as asphalt, coke, paraffin wax, lube, imported LPG, and some petrochemicals, the prices were left to the market to decide.

For the regulated refined products, not only the retail prices but also ex-refinery prices were regulated by the NDRC (formerly SPDC) based on a formula. The formula was first introduced in June 1998 and then modified in October 2001. The October 2001 domestic gasoline and diesel prices were linked with the Singapore FOB (60%), Rotterdam FOB (30%), and NYMEX (New York Mercantile Exchange 10%) FOB prices. Prior to October 2001, only Singapore prices applied. Based on these links, the NDRC set and adjusted the baseline retail prices only when the weighted international prices exceeded a certain level, which is believed to be 8%. But since mid-2003, the Chinese government has broken this rule and chosen not to raise the retail prices despite sharp increases of refined product prices in the international markets.

Then in late 2006, the Chinese government altered the formula again. The new formula was completed in early 2007. Under the new formula, the domestic prices of main products would be determined by crude cost plus refining and other costs as well as "reasonable" refining margins to determine the baseline retail prices for gasoline and diesel. The refining margin increases will be reduced by half when crude oil prices increase above US$55/b and by another half after the crude prices go above US$65/b.

However, the Chinese government has never had a chance to implement the new formula as international oil prices soared again in mid-2007. As such, the practice of price fixing by the government continued until late 2008 and early 2009. The Chinese government has since reformed the price regime again. On May 9, 2009, the NDRC formally released the Preliminary Regulation on Petroleum Prices. The preliminary regulation has specific rules for setting prices on crude oil and refined products, such as gasoline, diesel, jet fuel, and aviation gasoline. The preliminary regulation was immediately put into effect with the following specifications. The preliminary regulation later became a formal regulation though the NDRC has retained the rights to follow the rules with its own discretion.

To summarize the discussion, for the past 13 years — since June 1998, when China officially announced the linkage of domestic and international prices on paper — China's price regimes employed by the National Development and Reform Commission (NDRC) for determining the domestic prices of these products have gone through 4 distinctive phases:

> June 1998 to September 2001: Domestic prices of main refined products (primarily gasoline, diesel, jet fuel, and kerosene) were linked to the Singapore market on a monthly basis. During the early years, the formula was not fully implemented.

October 2001 to January 2007: Domestic prices of main refined products were linked to three markets: Singapore, New York, and Europe on a monthly basis. From early 2004, the formulas were not fully implemented.

February 2007 to December 2008: The NDRC took full control of the prices and did not follow any particular role to set prices. As a result, before September 2008, domestic prices in China were sufficiently lower than that in Singapore. The Chinese domestic prices overtook that of Singapore since September 2008 even though there was no direct linkage of Chinese domestic prices with the international markets.

January 2009 to present: The NDRC has adopted a price regime, first introduced in early 2007 but never implemented, where Chinese domestic prices for gasoline, diesel, and jet fuel are based on crude cost, plus processing cost and a "reasonable" profit margin. As illustrated later, the actual regime is far more complemented. Furthermore, the NDRC has retained to rights not to follow the regime strictly, which is what they have been doing since mid- to late 2010.

At present, the price regime for main refined products subject to government regulation has the following key elements with the products divided in the two groups: prices under guidance and prices set directly by the government.

Prices under government guidance

These include gasoline and diesel retail and wholesale prices, as well as special wholesale prices of gasoline and diesel for railway, transportation, and other designated users. Under this category, there are several elements:

The NDRC set maximum retail prices for gasoline and diesel for each province. Maximum retail prices are set on the basis of the imported crude cost by adding the average processing cost, taxes, marketing markup, and reasonable profits.

Retailers may set their own retail prices as long as the prices do not exceed the maximum prices set by the government.

Wholesalers can set their own prices as long as they do not exceed the maximum wholesale prices set by the government. The wholesale–retail differentials shall not be lower than 300 yuan/t, which is US$5.16/b for gasoline and US$5.86/b for diesel.

For railway, transportation, and other designated users, maximum prices are set on the basis of maximum retail prices minus 400 yuan/t, which is US$6.89/b for gasoline and US$7.86/b for diesel. Actual prices to these users can be determined by buyers and sellers within the above limits.

Ethanol gasoline prices are set at the same level of pure gasoline with the same octane number.

Prices set directly by the government

This applies to gasoline, diesel, and jet fuel that are supplied to state reserves and the construction corps of the Xinjiang Autonomous Region. For these products, ex-refinery prices are set.
Frequency and Crude Price Range for Product Price Adjustments

Frequency: the regulation stipulates that for every 22 working days, if the average imported crude prices go up or down by more than 4%, price adjustments will be made by the NDRC.

Crude Price Range: the regulation further stipulates that as long as international oil prices are below US$80/b, the full formula will be used to determine the final prices of main refined products where a normal, reasonable refining margin will be assessed. If international crude prices exceed US$80/b, the refining margins will be reduced. If international oil prices are above US$130/b, the government will adopt appropriate fiscal policies to ensure price stability by not raising or, if necessary, raising retail prices by a very small amount.

Unconfirmed sources provide more information regarding how the "rational refining profit margins" are determined under the NDRC blueprint. It is as follows: if international oil prices are below US$80/b, the profit margins for refineries will be assessed at 5%. For prices above US$80/b, the profit margins will be reduced by 1% for every US$5/b of crude price increase. At a crude price of US$105/b, the profit margins will be reduced to 0%, but product prices will continue to be adjusted according to crude price changes until the crude prices hit US$130/b, after which the linkage of domestic prices for petroleum products at home with international crude prices will be severed. This nearly novel mechanism of price regime has not been officially confirmed by the NDRC. Fig. 5-2 shows the monthly wholesale and retail prices of gasoline and diesel for Beijing from January 2005 to April 2011.

Built into the chart is the appreciation of the Chinese currency renminbi (RMB). On July 21, 2005, China began relaxing control of the RMB exchange rate after pegging it on US dollar at US$1 = 8.28 yuan for more than a decade. Between July 2005 and July 2008, the RMB appreciated by 17.5% to reach US$1 = 6.83 yuan stayed there for the next two years. Under the mounting pressure from the West, particularly the US, the relaxation started since June 2010. On May

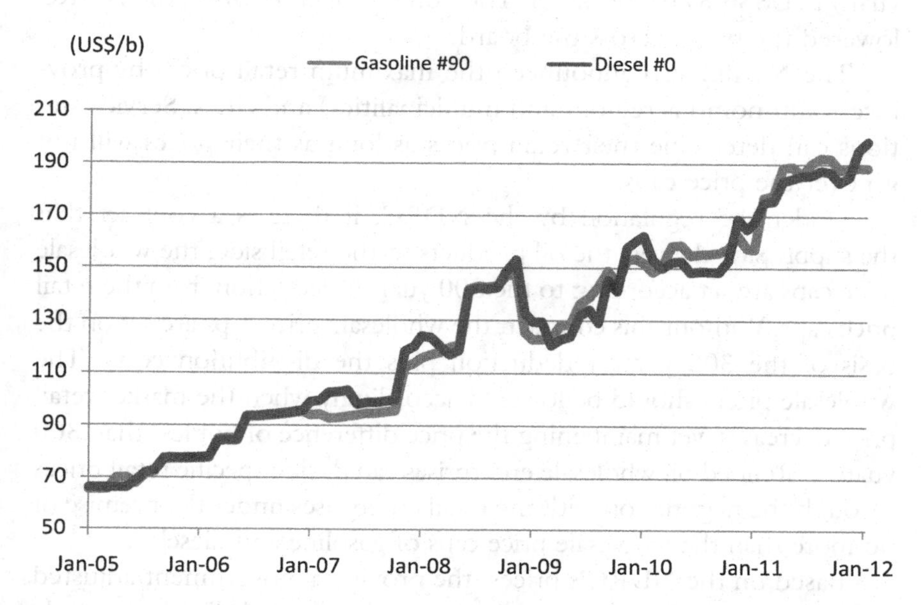

Fig. 5-2. Monthly Gasoline and Diesel Retail Prices in Beijing Jan 2005–Jan 2012.

27, 2011, the exchange rate was US$1 = 6.48 yuan, appreciated by 5.1% since June 2010 and by 21.7% from July 2005.

NDRC made price adjustments only three times in 2004, five times in 2005, and twice each in 2006, 2007, and 2008. The changes have become more frequent since early 2009. Even with number of adjustments fewer than they should be otherwise, the officially sanctioned retail prices for gasoline went up by 60% in Chinese yuan and 90% in US dollar between January 2004 and June 2008, with the difference between the factor of the exchange rate (appreciation of the Chinese currency against US dollar). Between January 2009 and December 2011, official gasoline prices in Beijing went up by 48% in terms of RMB and 59% in terms of US dollar.

The last price adjustment was in October 2011. On October 9, 2011, the NDRC decreased the prices of oil products, including prices supplied to the army and other sectors, as well as maximum retail prices by province. The prices for gasoline and diesel supplied to the army, Xinjiang Production and Construction Corps, and the state reserves decreased by 300 yuan/t (US$5.5/b) for gasoline and 300 yuan/t (US$6.3/b) for diesel. Then on October 9, 2011, the NDRC lowered the prices across the board.

The NDRC also announced the maximum retail prices by provinces (autonomous regions and municipalities) and cities. Service stations can determine their retail prices as long as their prices will not go over the price caps.

Under the regulation by the NDRC, if there is a contract that the supply side delivers the oil products to the retail side, the wholesale price caps are set according to the 300 yuan/t deduction from the retail price caps. Without this contract, the wholesale price caps are set on the basis of the 300 yuan/t deduction plus the distribution costs. The wholesale prices should be lowered accordingly when the market retail price decreases, yet maintaining the price difference of not less than 300 yuan/t. Refined oil wholesale enterprises can decide specific retail prices through the negotiation with the retail enterprises under the premise of no more than the wholesale price caps of gasoline and diesel.

Based on the NDRC's prices, the provincial government adjusted their retail prices in service stations for gasoline and diesel separately on the same day of October 9, 2011. The retail prices of gasoline and diesel were collected in main provinces as well as central cities.

NDRC also set the ex-refinery price cap for LPG; the price will be 0.92:1 based on the supply price of #90 gasoline for the army. Refineries can decide specific ex-refinery prices through the negotiation with buyers under the premise of no more than the ex-refinery price cap of LPG.

5.3. Petroleum Product Demand, Supply, and Trade: An Overview

China is currently the largest oil-consuming country as well as the largest crude oil importer in Asia. With a huge refining sector, China's need for petroleum products is supplied primarily by domestic refineries. In 2004, China's imports of refined products reached a peak of just under 1 mmb/d. It has since lingered between 850 kb/d and 950 kb/d. On the other hand, China's exports of petroleum products have increased, reaching a historic high of over 0.5 mmb/d in 2010 (FGE, 2011). In this section, we discuss the current situation and future prospects of China's petroleum product consumption, supply, imports, and exports.

It is very important to note that the total product demand and the demand for individual products are discussed here at the national level. When we later discuss the demand and supply for refined products for each province, the totals will differ slightly from the numbers presented in this chapter, mainly owing to the fact that some very small refineries are excluded from the provincial studies, plus the fact that provincial data do not necessarily add up to the national total.

Petroleum product demand in China is characterized by spectacular growth — especially since the beginning of this decade — and a radical transformation of the demand pattern where the share of lighter products has increased substantially. Fig. 5-3 illustrates the historical and projected product demand in China over a 50-year spectrum from 1980 to 2030. China is currently the largest oil consumer in Asia. For the past 30 years (1980–2010), the petroleum product demand growth averaged 5.8% per annum. The AAGR was

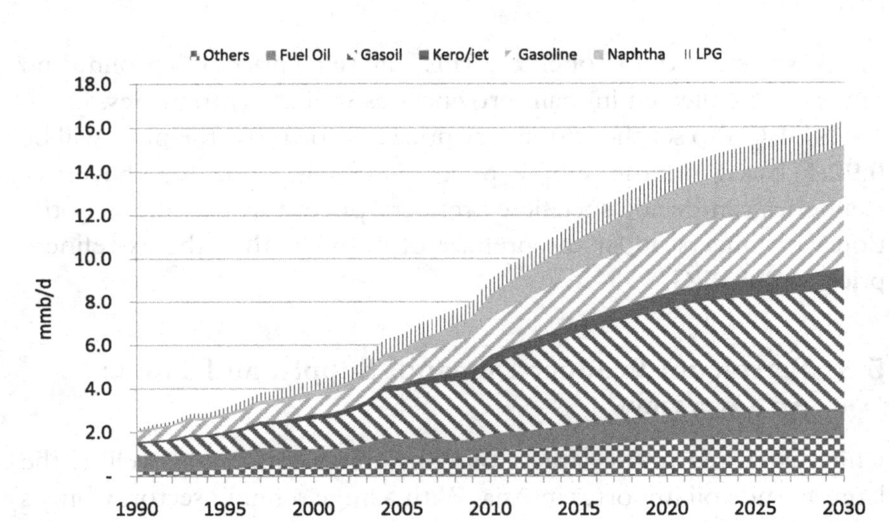

Fig. 5-3. China's Petroleum Product Demand, 1990–2030.

Note: 2011 data are preliminary and 2012–2030 data are projections.

slow at only 3.1% during the 1980s, accelerated to 7.2% in the 1990s, and went up even higher to 7.3% during the 2000s.

China's product demand pattern has undergone a major transformation in response to the country's past economic and energy policies. China's product demand slate in the early 1980s was heavily oriented toward bottom-of-the-barrel products, with fuel oil and crude oil for direct burning accounting for 47% of the total demand in 1980. This share has since fallen steadily, owing to the government's policy of minimization and eventual substitution of fuel oil use in power plants by coal. In 2010, fuel oil and direct burning of crudes and other specialized products constituted 10% of China's total product demand.

As the share of heavy distillates declines, the share of light to medium distillates was on the rise. The strong demand growth for transportation fuels, as well as for feedstock for China's growing petrochemical production capacity, has also contributed to lightening the country's product demand barrel.

The structure of China's domestic refinery output is closely related to the pattern of oil demand, indicating that the refining industry has made maximum efforts to meet the changing demand for oil products. In 1990, China produced 2.0 mmb/d of refined products. Fuel oil accounted for 27% of the barrel, followed by diesel at 27% and gasoline at 25%. In 2010, the total refinery output quadruped to 8.5 mmb/d, consisting of 38% of diesel, 22% of gasoline, and only a meager 5% of fuel oil.

China's product trade has been undergoing some dramatic changes during the 1990s and 2010s. Table 5-1 shows the imports and exports of individual products during the period 1990–2010 (FGE, 2011). On the import side, the notable changes between 1995 and 2010 were the following: (1) Rising imports of LPG till 2004 and then declined. (2) Emergence of naphtha as a large importing item since 2009; (3) Waning imports of diesel; (4) High imports of fuel oil, jet fuel, and other specialized products, particularly in recent years; (5) 2008 was an exceptional year because of the need to supply energy for the Beijing Summer Olympics.

For exports, the major characteristics during the 20-year period were: (1) gasoline exports were maintained at high levels (except for 2008); (2) the emergence of diesel and fuel oil as exporting items; (3) continuous exports of specialized products. At balance, China was a net exporter of petroleum products in 1990. After becoming a net importer, the next imports peaked in 2004 at 710 kb/d but have since come down. In 2010, the net imports were 489 kb/d.

Over the next 10 to 20 years, China's demand for petroleum products is expected to remain robust. Under the base-case scenario, China's overall petroleum product demand, including LPG, crude burning, and all other specialized products, is forecast to reach 11.5 mmb/d by 2015, and nearly 13.7 mmb/d by 2020 (see Fig. 5-3). However, beyond 2020, we believe major efforts are going to be made by the government to slow down the growth of fossil energy, and oil in particular. As such, the demand growth will be at slower rates. Under our base-case scenario, we forecast that China's total petroleum product demand will reach 14.8 mmb/d by 2025 and 16.0 mmb/d by 2030.

On the production side, overall refinery output will continue to increase as the Chinese refineries are set to process more crude oil. Our

Table 5-1. Petroleum Product Exports, Imports, Net Balances, 1990–2010 (kb/d).

	1990	1995	2000	2002	2004	2006	2007	2008	2009	2010
Imports										
LPG	—	73.9	152.7	199.0	203.2	170.2	128.8	82.2	129.7	101.4
Naphtha	0.3	10.3	2.8	5.6	1.2	14.9	24.9	17.9	61.7	67.7
Gasoline	3.9	3.7	—	—	—	1.4	5.3	46.1	1.0	0.0
Kero/jet	5.6	16.5	55.1	46.4	60.9	121.4	113.5	139.8	132.4	140.7
Diesel	45.9	125.0	5.3	9.7	56.0	14.4	33.1	127.1	37.5	36.7
Fuel Oil	12.0	121.0	270.9	304.7	560.0	513.8	443.7	400.2	441.9	422.0
Others	4.2	21.0	35.3	84.2	84.0	97.2	151.0	145.6	147.3	173.2
Total	72.1	371.3	522.2	649.7	965.2	933.4	900.2	958.9	951.5	941.8
Exports										
LPG	0.3	2.3	0.5	1.8	1.0	4.8	10.7	21.5	27.0	29.1
Naphtha	13.5	0.3	16.0	21.2	32.5	42.5	40.5	35.2	19.9	20.2
Gasoline	54.4	43.2	105.7	142.6	125.6	81.6	108.1	47.2	114.6	120.4
Kero/jet	6.0	3.6	15.8	13.5	16.2	24.7	29.9	34.2	45.1	42.8

(*Continued*)

Table 5-1. (*Continued*)

	1990	1995	2000	2002	2004	2006	2007	2008	2009	2010
Diesel	32.7	26.7	11.3	25.2	53.7	15.8	13.5	12.8	92.0	94.8
Fuel Oil	13.7	5.1	6.1	11.7	33.3	47.4	69.7	133.9	158.3	181.7
Others	33.8	28.7	61.3	54.0	78.8	103.7	91.2	91.5	37.2	46.2
Total	154.5	109.9	216.7	270.0	341.1	320.5	363.7	376.4	494.0	535.2
Balances (Net Exports)										
LPG	0.3	(71.7)	(152.2)	(197.2)	(202.1)	(165.4)	(118.1)	(60.6)	(102.7)	(72.3)
Naphtha	13.2	(10.0)	13.1	15.6	31.3	27.6	15.6	(17.3)	(41.8)	(47.5)
Gasoline	50.5	39.5	105.7	142.6	125.6	80.2	102.8	1.1	113.5	120.4
Kero/jet	0.4	(12.8)	(39.4)	(32.9)	(44.6)	(96.7)	(83.6)	(105.6)	(87.4)	(97.9)
Diesel	(13.3)	(98.3)	6.0	15.5	(2.3)	1.4	(19.6)	(114.3)	54.5	58.1
Fuel Oil	1.7	(115.9)	(264.8)	(292.9)	(526.8)	(466.5)	(374.0)	(266.2)	(283.6)	(240.4)
Others	29.5	7.8	26.0	(30.3)	(5.1)	6.5	(59.8)	(54.1)	(110.1)	(127.0)
Total	82.4	(261.4)	(305.5)	(379.7)	(624.1)	(612.9)	(536.6)	(582.5)	(457.5)	(406.6)

base-case assumption is that China will process 13.2 mmb/d in 2020 and 15.2 mmb/d by 2030. Petroleum product balance (excluding direct use of crude oil) in China by 2030. Under this base-case scenario, China's net petroleum product import requirements are forecast to decline continuously through 2025 and became a small net product exporter in 2025. However, China is likely to switch back to a net product importer again in 2030 as refining capacity additions slow down.

The vigorous refinery expansion and rising refining utilization rates have kept China's net product imports from going up during our forecast period to 2020. Beyond that, the net product imports may go up again.

5.3.1. *LPG demand, supply, and future growth*

The demand growth of LPG in the 1990s was unprecedented. For the entire decade, the average annual growth (AAGR) reached 18.4%, and consumption increased from 69 kb/d in 1990 to 697 kb/d in 2007. Accompanying this rapid growth was a rapidly expanding economy and increasing use of residential LPG primarily in South China. As a result, a sizable market was established and enormous investment opportunities were created for both foreign and domestic oil and gas companies in China.

However, the growth has been leveling off since 2007, when natural gas started penetrating the residential sector. As a result, LPG has become saturated or has been "crowded out" in many of these cities. In fact, between 2000 and 2010, the AAGR of LPG consumption in China became much lower at 5.7%, which was less than one-third of what was achieved in the 1990s. In 2008, LPG demand in China declined by 10%, the first and by far the deepest decline ever. LPG demand only grew by 3.3% in 2010. Still, from 1990 to 2010, total LPG consumption in China increased by a factor of eight. After overtaking South Korea in 1995 and Japan in 2003, China is now the largest LPG-consuming country in the Asia-Pacific region, with an LPG use of 692 kb/d in 2010.

The residential sector, coupled with a small amount of the commercial sector, dominates LPG use in China. In 2010, the residential and commercial sectors accounted for approximately 78% of the total LPG use or 544 kb/d. Back in 2000, the share of the residential/commercial sector was 85% or 338 kb/d. The industrial sector is the second largest user of LPG. In 2010, industry accounted for approximately 12% of China's LPG use, slightly up from 11% in 2000. As China moves away from using coal for industrial furnaces, the use of LPG and other petroleum products has increased. LPG is also used in the transport sector, with around 3% being used for automobiles. China uses little LPG in the petrochemical sector. China's domestic LPG is mainly produced from refineries, which contains propylene and butylenes. Thus, it is an excellent feedstock for the petrochemical industry. However, China is deficit in LPG and this has led to the minimum usage of LPG in the petrochemical sector.

At present, the share of LPG in the feedstock pool of ethylene production in China is low (less than 5%). Naphtha takes up around 65% of the share in the feedstock pool while light diesel, hydrocracked resid, and other refined products take up the rest. The remaining use of LPG is in the category of "others," which include power (electricity and heating), agriculture, and other sectors. The use of LPG for both electric power and public heating is limited in China.

China's domestic LPG production comes predominantly from refineries. Minor LPG production comes from gas processing plants. The refinery LPG production in China is closely related to the development of the refining sector. Expanding refining capacity, rising crude runs, and changing LPG yield, coupled with the changing markets, are the major factors determining LPG production in China. During the 1990s, China's LPG output grew rapidly at an AAGR of 13.8%. The AAGR has since declined to 9.2% between 2000 and 2010. Even though the crude throughput to the refineries grew rapidly in recent years, refinery LPG production has leveled off since 2007 as the LPG refinery yield has dropped from a peak of 8.8% in 2007 to 7.4% in 2010.

Non-refinery LPG from gas processing plants in the oil and gas fields accounts for a tiny of total domestic LPG supply. It is usually recovered from associated gas from the fields, but the recovery rate is very low in China due to limited technological capabilities and investments. Furthermore nonassociated gas output is higher than associated gas output in China at the present, and the trend is expected to continue in the future.

Accompanying this robust LPG demand growth in the 1990s and early 2000s was a widening gap between demand and domestic production, thus giving rise to rapidly rising requirements for LPG imports during that period. However, the imports reached the peak in 2004 and started declining thereafter.

Rising international LPG prices since 2004 have partly caused the drop in the requirement for imports. In 2008 alone, the imports were down by a whopping 36% in addition to the decline of 24% in 2007. The imports of LPG accounted for only 15% of total LPG consumption in 2010, down from the peak of 48% in 1998. In terms of the source of LPG imports, the Middle East accounted for two-thirds of the imports in 2010, where Iran, Qatar, UAE, and Saudi Arabia were the main players. Guangdong is the leading importer of LPG in China, accounting for 71% (72 kb/d) of the total in 2010, followed by Zhejiang at 1% (12 kb/d), and others.

China is an exporter of LPG as well, albeit at a small amount, since the regulation for LPG trade is more relaxed compared with other main refined products. The exports peaked in 1998 at 16.0 kb/d, but dropped to 2.4 kb/d in 1999 due to depressed international prices and robust domestic demand. The exports have increased again in recent years, jumping to 10.7 kb/d in 2007, 21.5 kb/d in 2008, 27 kb/d in 2009, and 29.1 kb/d in 2010 — the highest ever. Re-exports of LPG in some of the bonded terminal facilities in the coastal cities played a role in the rise in exports in the past three years. The major recipients of China's LPG are Vietnam and Hong Kong.

Under the base-case scenario, we project that China's LPG use will grow at an AAGR of 2.8% between 2010 and 2020 and 1.4% between 2020 and 2030, reaching 912 kb/d by 2020 and 1.05 mmb/d by 2030.

Under the base-case scenario, between 2010 and 2020, we see an AAGR of 6.3% for the industrial sector, 4.5% for the transportation sector, 2.1% for the residential/commercial sector, and 2.9% for others. Between 2020 and 2030, we see an AAGR of 2.2% for the industrial sector, 1.1% for the transportation sector, 1.4% for the residential/commercial sector, and –1.2% for others.

China's LPG production is set to grow in the future. Under the base-case scenario, we forecast that LPG production will increase from 624 kb/d in 2010 to 963 kb/d in 2020 and further up to 1.1 mmb/d in 2030 with an AAGR of 4.4% between 2010 and 2020 and 1.4% between 2020 and 2030. With the huge expansion of refining capacity and increase in crude runs, coupled with moderate growth in demand, we see constrained imports of LPG for the coming years.

Under our base-case scenario, we expect that China's LPG imports will be going down gradually to 2025, before rising up again slightly in 2030.

China exports LPG for several reasons: (1) geographical differences; (2) surpluses of individual refineries; (3) presence of excessive LPG storage; and (4) less restrictive government policies. The latter two are important as a freer market and the presence of surplus inventory gives LPG traders opportunities to export and import simultaneously. Over the coming years we see China's LPG exports to increase also because of the availability of large LPG storage facilities, or re-exports.

Under our base-case scenario, we expect that China's LPG exports will increase from 29.1 kb/d in 2010 to 35 kb/d in 2015, 59 kb/d by 2020 and 80 kb/d in 2030.

5.3.2. *Gasoline demand, supply, and future growth*

As discussed in Chapter 4, China has a huge capacity of fluid catalytic crackers (FCC) as well as resid catalytic crackers (RCC), which have been designed to deal with the heavy nature of the Chinese crudes as well as ensure sufficient production of gasoline. China's gasoline production has been going up steadily since 1990. However, the growth of gasoline production was below that of the overall crude runs, particularly since the early 1990s, leading to a lower share of gasoline in total crude runs.

The main reason of the declining gasoline-crude runs ratio is that China has a surplus of gasoline supply and for over a decade, the Chinese authorities have emphasized diesel supply security and frequently set targets for the Chinese refineries to raise the so-called diesel-gasoline production ratios. The share of gasoline in the country's total refining throughput was 16% in 1980; it increased to 23% in 1990 and an all-time-high of 28% in 1993, before declining to 24% in 2000, 22% in 2005 and slightly under 22% in 2010.

The gasoline produced in China mainly comes from FCC and RCC units. Others include reformate, straight-run naphtha, alkylates, MTBE, coker gasoline, polymerization gasoline, hydrocracking gasoline, and aromatics. In the recent years, the shares of reformate and MTBE have been increasing. In order to meet the gasoline specifications (specs) that have become increasingly stringent, China's reliance on hydrorefining to treat gasoline has been growing fast. To enhance octane numbers, China has built and used more reforming, MTBE, alkylation, and other units. Meanwhile, as the use of ethanol and methanol increases, they serve as natural enhancers of octane number for China's gasoline pool. More of these developments are discussed in this section.

China has come a long way to produce and use environmentally sensible automobile fuels. Until the mid to late 1990s, the pace toward setting stringent standards for auto fuels was slow. The country, however, has since acted rapidly to improve the overall quality of auto fuels (especially gasoline), and to introduce new specifications.

In 2000, China promulgated automobile gasoline specs, which is code-named GB17930–1999. This is below Euro II with a sulfur content of 1,000 ppm. By 2003, China had made available the new national specs for gasoline in which the sulfur content was set at 500 parts per million (ppm) and benzene content at 2%. It is called National Standards (NS) II which corresponds to Euro II specs. As of 2003, Beijing was the first city to use only Euro II spec gasoline, followed by Shanghai and Guangzhou. In July 2005, all cities in China adopted the standard of 500 ppm sulfur for gasoline.

In July 2005, Beijing was the first city to apply NS III emission standards and specs for gasoline.

In January 2008, Beijing led the country again by implementing NS IV emission standards and gasoline specs, where the sulfur content is down to 50 ppm. Main elements of this newest set of local specs of Beijing — China's first for NS IV gasoline.

A few large cities other than Beijing also have advanced programs to implement tougher specs. Guangzhou of Guangdong Province began introducing NS III emission standards and gasoline specs as early as September 2006. In Shanghai, most of the automobiles had met the NS III emission standards and gasoline sold met the NS III specs as well since 2007. Since early 2010, Guangzhou, Shanghai, and a few cities in Guangdong Province such as Shenzhen, Zhongshan, and Foshan have moved to adopt the NS IV specs for its automobile emissions, this was followed by Nanjing during the second half of 2010. Nationwide, NS III for all automobile emissions has been adopted since January 1, 2010.

Currently, all gasoline in China is unleaded. In terms of octane number, the trend is that the share of higher-octane gasoline is increasing every year. From 2006 to 2010, the share of 90 RON (research octane number) gasoline went down from 40% to 16%, while the share of 93 RON gasoline went up from 48% to 67%.

Altogether, the share of gasoline with an octane number of 92 and above accounted for 82% of the total gasoline pool in 2010, up from 60% in 2006. For the premium grades of RON 97 and 98, their combined share was 11%, up from 8% in 2006. Overall, China's gasoline consumption growth has closely followed the growth of gasoline production. During the past two decades, the expansion and modernization of the automotive industries and the switch to trucks instead of trains for short-distance hauls in the 1980s and 1990s have increased the demand growth for gasoline. In China, gasoline is mainly used for passenger cars, trucks, motorcycles, and other light vehicles. Between 1990 and 2010, the consumption of gasoline grew at an average annual rate of 6.9%, while the annual growth for gasoline production averaged at 6.6%. In 2010, gasoline use reached 1.68 mmb/d, up from 442 kb/d in 1990 and 817 kb/d in 2000.

China has long been a net exporter of gasoline. The exports, however, have declined since 2003 when they reached the peak of

176 kb/d. In 2008, China exported 47 kb/d of gasoline, the lowest since the late 1990s, affected mainly by the need to supply the Chinese market in preparation for the 2008 Summer Olympics in Beijing. In 2009, the exports rose to 115 kb/d and went up further to 120 kb/d in 2010. On the import front, the years that China imported any meaningful volumes of gasoline were 1993 (51 kb/d), 1994 (25 kb/d), and then 2008 (46 kb/d). In 2009 and 2010, China imported virtually no gasoline.

Singapore was the largest recipient of China's gasoline exports in 2010, accounting for 42% (51 kb/d) of the total, followed by Indonesia at 40% (48 kb/d), and Vietnam at 9% (11 kb/d). Liaoning is the largest gasoline exporting province in China — it accounted for 63% (76 kb/d) of gasoline exported from China in 2010, followed by Guangdong at 11% (13 kb/d), and other provinces.

For future gasoline demand, the driving force is the rapid growth of China's automobile fleet. The auto industry has developed at a spectacular rate. In 1990, the civilian auto population or vehicle stock was 5.5 million. The auto stock reached 16.1 million by the end of 2000 and some 78 million by the end of 2010.

In 1990, China produced 514,000 cars and trucks. The output increased to 2.1 million in 2000, 5.7 million in 2005, and then tripled to 18.3 million in 2010 (Fig. 5-4), though the production showed no growth in 2011. In terms of car sales, China sold 13.6 million cars in 2009 and overtook US, whose car sales plunged by some 40%, to be the world's largest car market. With a sale of 18.1 million in 2010 and 18.5 million in 2011, China continued to be the No. 1 car market.

Over the next 10 to 20 years, China's automobile population (which is also called on-road stock) is forecast to reach 209 million in 2020, and 310 million by 2030 under the base-case scenario.

Accompanying the auto population growth, an improvement in the efficiency of the autos used in China is expected, which, coupled with a drastic increase in congestion, will lower the gasoline and diesel consumption per vehicle. The assumption for use of gasoline and diesel per car is very important for projecting the future demand for the auto fuels. In addition to automobiles, there are other vehicles such as motorcycles that are powered by gasoline. Based on the future

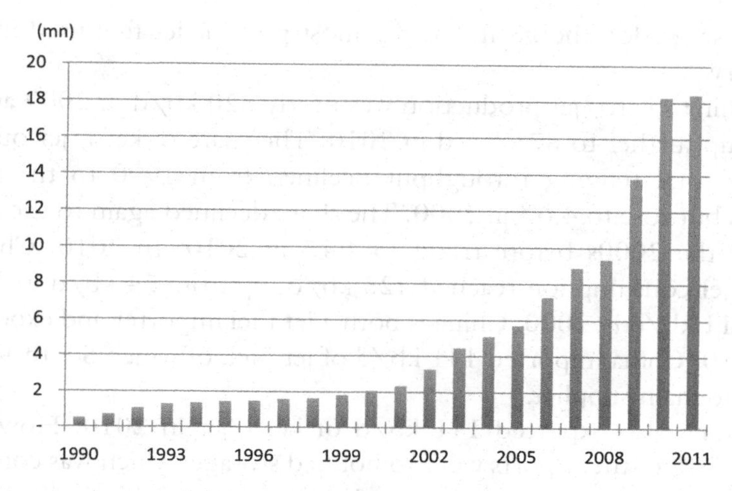

Fig. 5-4. China's Automobile Production, 1990–2011.

growth of the automobile industry and the growth of other gasoline-powered vehicles, our base-case forecast indicates that the gasoline consumption will increase steadily by 2030.

On the production side, the gasoline output is expected to go up, and the net-export status for gasoline is forecast to continue throughout the forecast period. More use of imported crudes that are nonwaxy and lighter is part of the reason why gasoline output is projected to continue staying relatively high during the forecast period.

5.3.3. *Kero/jet demand, supply, future growth*

In China, kero/jet includes jet fuel, lamp kerosene, and other types of kerosene. Lamp kerosene is mainly used in rural areas for lighting, where electricity is either not available or inadequate in supply. Lamp kerosene is also used for other lighting equipment. As in the case of late 2010, kerosene is also used for power generation in certain quarters of the country where power shortage is present.

Jet fuel is used for various kinds of aircraft turbines. Based on the weather conditions, jet fuel has four grades: #1, #2, #3, and #4 fuels.

Of these grades, the #3 fuel is the most popular jet fuel used in the country.

China's kero/jet production was nearly 320 kb/d in 2009 and it went up further to 371 kb/d in 2010. The share of kero/jet output in the total refining throughput declined from 1990 to the mid-1990s but rose to 4.6% in 2000. The share declined again to the middle of the 2000s before rising to 4.4% in 2010. In 2010, China's kero/jet consumption reached 425 kb/d, up from 74 kb/d in 1990 and 211 kb/d in 2000. China is both a jet fuel importer and exporter. In 2010, China imported 141 kb/d of jet fuel, of which South Korea was the main supplier.

China also exported 141 kb/d of kero/jet in 2010. However, nearly 70% of the exports went to bonded storage, which was counted as domestic consumption in our balance analysis. Typically Hong Kong is the largest recipient of China's actual jet fuel exports. Shanghai was the largest recipient of imported jet fuel in 2010, accounting for 53% (56 kb/d) of the total, followed by Beijing at 27% (29 kb/d), Guangdong 16% (17 kb/d), and others.

Over the next 20 years, lamp and other kerosene consumption will continue to grow slowly, and the demand for jet fuel will grow fast. On the supply side, domestic production of kero/jet is expected to grow as well, but we expect China's jet fuel imports to soar over the coming years.

5.3.4. *Diesel demand, supply, and future growth*

Rapid industrialization and motorization of the agricultural sector, coupled with growing interest in diesel autos, have been the major driving forces behind the accelerated diesel oil consumption since the 1990s. In this section, we will discuss just diesel and leave diesel-range products that are used as petrochemical feedstock to a later section. The latter includes not only light gasoil but also heavy gasoil, vacuum gasoil (VGO) streams, and hydrocracking resids (which currently accounts for only a small share of ethylene production).

Although diesel can be used for transportation, agriculture, power generation, and other areas, the specifications are established for three types of diesel, namely, light diesel, heavy diesel, and marine diesel, which are based on the distillation cuts and modes of production. Light diesel currently accounts for more than 80% of the diesel production in China. Light diesel is used by high-speed diesel engines. Based on condensation points, or the weather conditions under which the fuels can be used, China has the following brands of popular light diesel: #10 (used in engines equipped with a preheating device), #0 (used in areas with temperatures of 4°C and above), #–10 (used in areas with temperatures of –5°C and above), #–20 (used in areas with temperatures between –5°C and –14°C), #–35 (used in areas with temperatures between –14°C and –29°C), and #–50 (used in areas with temperatures between –29°C and –44°C).

Prior to 2000, light diesel had three grades for each brand: premium grade, first grade, and regular grade. New specs, codenamed GB252–2000, were adopted in 2000, when the three grades were consolidated into one. The maximum allowable sulfur content is now 0.2% (or 2,000 ppm) for all light diesels. For cetane number, the minimum requirement is 45, a rather low standard. For refineries that use intermediate-based crudes (as opposed to paraffinic-based or naphthenic-based crudes), or use middle distillates from cat crackers as diesel components, the cetane requirement is even lower at 40.

For large cities, more stringent auto diesel specs have been adopted since 2003, wherein the maximum sulfur content is limited to 500 ppm and the minimum cetane number is 49. These new specs are considered recommendations by the Chinese government and they are being gradually applied to the country as a whole. In other words, in China today, not all provinces and cities use Euro spec diesel yet. For many, 2,000 ppm diesel specs are still acceptable, though the actual sulfur content in diesel is lower. This is an indication of how the adoption and implementation of diesel specs lags behind that of gasoline.

Once again, Beijing leads the country in applying more stringent specs for automobile diesel, partially because of the need for the Summer Olympics in 2008. In July 2005, Beijing moved to NS III specs on automobile diesel, which lowered the sulfur content to

350 ppm. Finally, starting January 2008, Beijing moved to NS IV emission standards for automobiles and specs for automobile diesel, where the sulfur content has been lowered to 50 ppm.

Nationwide, the country was scheduled to start applying NS III emission standards for diesel cars and specs for automobile diesel on July 1, 2008. However, that had been postponed to January 1, 2010. The country has since been on NS III specs for automobile diesel. Like gasoline, Guangzhou and Shanghai adopted NS III for emissions and automobile diesel specs in 2008 already. As mentioned earlier, since early 2010, Guangzhou, Shanghai, as well as Guangdong cities of Shenzhen, Zhongshan, and Foshan have moved to adopt the NS IV specs for its automobile emissions, this was followed by Nanjing during the second half of 2010. This applies to both gasoline and diesel.

Diesel is now the largest component of the production pool of China's refined products. In 2009, China produced 2.9 mmb/d of diesel, up from 533 kb/d in 1990 and 1.4 mmb/d in 2000. The share of diesel in total refining throughput increased rapidly from 24% in 1990, 36% in 2000, and 39% in 2009. In 2010, China's diesel output went up further to 3.2 mmb/d, but its share in total crude runs went down slightly to 38%.

China's total diesel consumption amounted to 2.8 mmb/d in 2009, up from 547 kb/d in 1990 and 1.4 mmb/d in 2000. In 2010, China's diesel demand went up to nearly 3.2 mmb/d. The average annual growth rate of diesel consumption was 8.7% between 1990 and 2010.

In 1997, China imported some 150 kb/d of diesel, the highest since early 1993, with a net import of some 100 kb/d. The imports declined in subsequent years and then went up again to 56 kb/d in 2004 (booming demand) and 127 kb/d in 2008 (need for Olympics). In the meantime, China's diesel exports fluctuated widely. In fact, China was a net exporter of diesel in 7 out of 11 years between 2000 and 2010. In 2009, China's net diesel exports increased to 92 kb/d and they went up further to 94 kb/d in 2010.

Of China's 37 kb/d of diesel imports in 2010, 32% (12 kb/d) came from South Korea, 24% (9 kb/d) from Japan, 19% (7 kb/d) from Russia, 10% (4 kb/d) Singapore, and the rest from other countries. Guangdong was the largest recipient of imported diesel in 2010, accounting for 54% (20 kb/d) of the total, followed by Shanghai 26% (9 kb/d).

Over the next 10 to 20 years, diesel consumption is forecast to grow at a rate that will be higher than the average overall growth rate for petroleum products. Transportation sector will continue to drive the demand growth of diesel. Under our base-case scenario, diesel demand is expected to increase to 4.0 mmb/d in 2015, 4.8 mmb/d in 2020, and 5.6 mmb/d by 2030. On the supply side, diesel production is expected to increase even faster during the same forecast period, making China a diesel exporter during the forecast period.

5.3.5. *Fuel oil demand, supply, and future growth*

Fuel oil accounted for a large share of petroleum product output in China in the past, but the Chinese refiners for many years have tried hard to crack more fuel oil and to raise the light-to-medium product yields. The efforts since the mid-2000s resulted in a dramatic decrease in fuel oil production, in both relative and absolute terms. On the demand side, the Chinese government is continuing its policy of restricting the use of fuel oil for power generation, although the fuel is favored by some local governments and joint-venture power plants. Finally, locally owned small refineries have continued to survive and have increasingly relied on using fuel oil as feedstock.

For end use, there are three types of fuel oil in China: resid fuel oil, bunker fuel oil, and marine bunker fuel oil. Resid fuel oil is used in industrial boilers, power generation, and the metallurgical industry.

Overall, specifications for fuel oil as a whole are not well developed in China. Traditionally, fuel oil produced from Chinese refineries using domestic crudes contains low sulfur. This has been changing since the late 1990s as more imported sour crudes are used and more high sulfur fuel oil is imported. Generally, there is no limit on sulfur content for fuel oil used as bunker fuels in China. Fuel oil for power generation and industrial use can have 1%–2% sulfur, and the specifications for power and industrial use are expected to be tightened slightly in the future. For some coastal cities, China may adopt 0.5% fuel oil for power generation and industrial use after 2012.

As far as specs are concerned, for industrial boilers with different sizes, fuel oil has four grades: #20, #60, #100, and #200.

Bunker fuel oil is used to power engines for ocean carriers and tankers. Marine bunker fuel oil is used for warships. China has been known to import high sulfur fuel oil in Asia. However, some local governments, particularly those in the South and the Lower Yangtze Region, have increasingly tightened the sulfur specs for fuel oil use.

The fuel oil supply and demand data includes bunker fuel oil.

China consumed 617 kb/d of fuel oil in 2009, down from the peak level of 811 kb/d in 2004 and 742 kb/d in 2006 and about the same level as in the mid 1990s. In 2010, fuel oil demand was 553 kb/d. The drop in fuel oil consumption since 2004 is mainly due to the decreased fuel oil usage for power generation and, to a less extent, in the industrial sector. Since 2005, some small power plants and ceramics plants have started to use coal instead of fuel oil. In addition, under pressure to protect the environment, an increasing number of power plants and industrial consumers have started using gas or LNG in place of fuel oil in the coastal cities, especially in South China. Fuel oil demand in the power sector dropped from about 236 kb/d in 1990 to 202 kb/d in 2000, 200 kb/d in 2006, and sharply to only 94 kb/d in 2010.

In China, small refineries have very limited access to crude oil supply, so they have to rely on fuel oil as their raw materials. Fuel oil consumption for refining increased notably from the early 2000s to 2008 as the fuel oil throughput into the local refineries increased. However, the consumption of the refining sector decreased since early 2009, due to the rise in the consumption tax on fuel oil from 0.1 yuan/liter (US$2.4/bbl) to 0.8 yuan/liter (US$19/bbl) in January 2009. In addition, the Chinese government hiked the fuel oil import tariff from 1% to 3% in January 2010, and this policy added further pressure to the survival of the local refineries.

Among the sectors, only bunker fuel oil demand showed continuous rapid growth from 25 kb/d in 1990 to 175 kb/d in 2010. The share of fuel oil in the refining throughput has declined continuously since the 1990s and leveled off at around 5% in recent years. Therefore, even though the crude throughput to the refineries grew rapidly in the past two decades, fuel oil production was down from 600 kb/d in 1990 to 376 kb/d in 2000 and further down to 338 kb/d in 2009. In 2010, however, the production rose to 388 kb/d.

As domestic fuel oil production decreased while its demand was stagnant, China remains as one of Asia's largest fuel oil importers. The levels of imports vary from year to year. In 2009, China's imports of fuel oil were 441 kb/d, down from 513 kb/d in 2006 but up from 395 kb/d in 2008. In 2010, fuel oil imports were 422 kb/d.

In 2010, Singapore and Venezuela were the two biggest sources of fuel oil imports by China, both accounting for 19% of fuel oil #5–7 imports, followed by Malaysia at 18% (76 kb/d), Russia at 15% (64 kb/d), and South Korea at 9.9% (41 kb/d).

Fuel oil imports entering China via the Qingdao port in Shandong Province reached 183 kb/d in 2010, accounting for 43% of the total fuel oil imports and making it the top destination for fuel oil import destination to the Chinese market. In Shandong Province, 90% of the imported fuel oil was consumed by local refineries. Imports into Huangpu port in Guangdong Province have dropped drastically in recent years. Huangpu port used to be the top fuel oil import destination until it was overtaken by the Qingdao port.

In recent years, China's fuel oil exports also increased substantially from less than 40 kb/d before 2004 to 133 kb/d in 2008 and further up to 158 kb/d in 2009. In 2010, exports were 182 kb/d. China's fuel oil exports are mainly to Panama and Hong Kong.

In 2010, Singapore was the biggest source of fuel oil imports by China, accounting for 19% (79 kb/d) of fuel oil #5–7 imports, followed by Venezuela at 18% (77 kb/d), Malaysia at 18% (76 kb/d), Russia at 15% (64 kb/d), and South Korea at 10% (41 kb/d).

Shandong was a major fuel oil importing province in 2010 at a whopping 51% (215 kb/d), followed by Guangdong at 19% (79 kb/d), and Zhejiang at 12% (50 kb/d). The leading role played by Shandong is mainly due to the hungry need of locally owned refineries there using fuel oil as feedstock.

Over the next two decades, despite the efforts of Chinese refiners to further crack crude oil, the increase in crude runs will raise the fuel oil output moderately. It is worth noting that a larger amount of the fuel oil will be used as refinery fuel that is not reported in the national total. On the demand side, fuel oil consumption will continue to grow at a moderate rate before leveling off after 2020. As a result, the net fuel oil import requirements are forecast to decrease in the coming years.

5.3.6. *Petrochemical feedstock demand, supply, future growth*

Petrochemical feedstock, or chemfeed, in a broad sense, includes any petroleum feedstock used in the production of olefins, aromatics, fertilizers, synthetic fibers, and other petrochemicals. The feedstock ranges from C2/C3/C4 from oil and gas to light diesel, hydrocracking resid, fuel oil and others. In this sense, condensate as a feedstock is also included.

In China, a special category has been created for chemfeed, which is called "light distillates for petrochemicals." The Chinese statistics for "light distillates for petrochemicals" refers to the amount of chemical feedstock that is explicitly supplied from the refineries to the petrochemical plants. The refineries, however, often do not report those chemical feeds that are transferred within the integrated petrochemical complex. As such, the data of the light distillates for petrochemicals reported in China is only part, albeit a substantial part, of all chemfeed used in the petrochemical sector. Moreover, the abovementioned chemfeed includes naphtha; not all naphtha is included in the data. Keeping this in mind, the production of light distillates for petrochemicals in China amounted to 878 kb/d in 2009, up from 192 kb/d in 1990 and 438 kb/d in 2000. The share of light distillates for petrochemicals in China's total refining throughout sharply increased from 9% in 1990 and 12% in 2009. In 2010, the production increased sharply by 30% to reach 1.14 mmb/d with the yield increased to 13.5%. This is due to the maximization of production for light distillates for petrochemicals to meet the rapidly rising demand as China added about 4 million tonnes/year of new ethylene capacity in last quarter of 2009 and early 2010.

Since chemfeed is not listed separately for petroleum product balance for China or for any country in the Asia-Pacific region, we divide it into two parts: naphtha and others. Others include C2/C3/C4, light diesel, hydrocracking resid, and other distillates. For the national product balances discussed in this, naphtha is separately listed and we group all the rest to "other products." For provincial product balances discussed later in the book, we cannot separate naphtha either. So the entire chemfeed is included in "others."

While light diesel was the most important feedstock for ethylene production in China in the past, its share in total ethylene feedstock has been declining. Over the next 10 to 20 years, the use of other diesel-range feedstock such as VGO and hydrocracking resid is expected to increase. A very important reason why the amount of projected diesel-range chemfeed is so large is that many new ethylene projects plan to make maximum use of the feedstock source from the existing refineries. Although demand for naphtha will be very strong as discussed later, use of other chemfeed such as the diesel-range distillates will also increase.

Naphtha is an increasingly important part of chemfeed in China, particularly for the olefin industry. However, the official statistics for naphtha are misleading. China has reported production, consumption, and trade of naphtha for years, but the data refer only to the portion that is commercially available for exports. In recent years, China has had an internal reporting system that lists naphtha separately, and it appears to be large enough to match the needs for ethylene production. However, even this number does not include all naphtha used by individual petrochemical companies for the production of aromatics and the small amount that is burned. To complicate things further, the internal reporting of naphtha and the numbers recorded as "light distillates for petrochemicals" overlap each other. In other words, not all naphtha reported (which is itself not complete) is included in the reported data of "petrochemical feedstock," and the portion of naphtha that is included in the latter is not all included in the reported naphtha.

China, surprisingly, was a net exporter of naphtha from 2000 to 2008. In 2009, it switched to a net importer of naphtha and we expect the net import volume will rise in the future. Over the next 10 to 20 years, naphtha consumption in China is forecast to grow at a rapid pace as China aggressively expands its capacities of ethylene and aromatics plants. As discussed in detail in Chapter 4, between the end of 2010 and end of 2015, China will add 5.6 mmtpa of new ethylene capacity, increasing the total ethylene capacity to 21.6 mmtpa. From end 2015 to end 2020, another 6 mmtpa new capacity will be added. China is also expanding its BTX (benzene, toluene, and xylene) capacity. China is expected to add 9.4 mmtpa of BTX capacity by 2020 under the firm and likely category. Of which, about 6 mmtpa of para-xylene capacity will be added. Our forecasts take into account the fact that China intends to maximize the use of chemfeed from within the existing refineries, which will give a chance for more middle distillates to be used as petrochemical feedstock.

On the supply side, domestic production of naphtha will also increase but is expected to lag behind the demand. Therefore, China's net naphtha imports will exceed 100 kb/d by 2020 and reach 313 kb/d by 2030 under our base-case scenario.

5.4. The Outlook for Oil Demand, Supply, and Trade in China

5.4.1. *Crude oil demand, supply, and trade*

Since the 1970s, China's crude oil trade has had two important turning points. One is in 1985, when China's crude oil exports peaked at 601 kb/d while imports were zero. The other one is 1996, when China became a net crude oil importer for the first time since the early 1970s. By 2011, China's crude imports reached an all-time high of 5.1 mmb/d, while the exports fell to 50 kb/d.

Crude exports

China began to export crude as early as the 1970s after production from Daqing and other fields accelerated. During the mid-1980s, China was the largest crude oil exporter in Asia. The exports peaked in 1985 before entering a long-term decline. While exporting 601 kb/d of crude in 1985, China did not import a single barrel of crude during that particular year. The exports have since declined to 480 kb/d in 1990 and 208 kb/d in 2000. China's exports declined further to merely 62 kb/d in 2010 and 50 kb/d in 2011 (Fig. 5-5).

China's exported crude has been destined to only a handful of countries in recent years. Japan is the largest importer of the Chinese crude. Ever since Japan started the importation of Chinese crudes, the two countries had an intergovernment agreement for a long-term Chinese oil supply to Japan. In recent years, negotiation on the sales of Daqing crudes to Japan had become increasingly difficult because of disagreements over quantity and prices of the crudes delivered. The intergovernment agreement came to a final halt in early 2004. This has affected the Japanese imports of Chinese crudes significantly, though the volumes have been declining for many years.

In 2010, China exported a meager 12 kb/d of crudes to Japan, accounting for 20% of the total, down from 159 kb/d (51% share) in 1998. China is now exporting more to South Korea, the US, and Singapore, but overall the volumes are small.

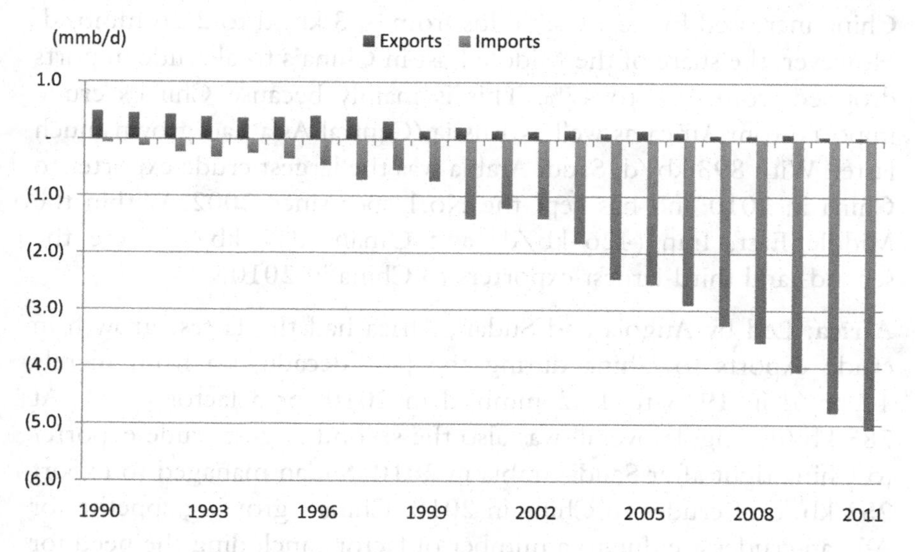

Fig. 5-5. Crude Exports and Imports, 1990–2011.

Crude imports

Until the late 1980s, China had never been a large crude importer. During the 1950s and early 1960s, although China had a large deficit in oil trade, most of the imports were in the form of refined products. China's refining capacity began to increase rapidly only after the Daqing oil field was discovered and put into production. As a result, the highest imports of crude oil were 13 kb/d before the 1970s and 35 kb/d before the late 1980s. Since 1988, however, crude imports have increased dramatically. Even so, China was a net crude oil exporter for every single year from 1971 to 1995. It became a net crude oil importer again in 1996.

In 2010, China imported 4.8 mmb/d of crude oil, up from 58 kb/d in 1990 and 1.3 mmb/d in 2000. In 2011, the imports went up further to 5.1 mmb/d. In 2010, Guangdong was the largest crude oil importing province, followed by Zhejiang, Shandong, Liaoning, Shanghai, Jiangsu, and other provinces.

In terms of sources of crude imports, some unique features are worth observing:

Middle East: Between 1998 and 2010, Middle East crude exports to China increased by nearly six folds from 333 kb/d to 2.26 mmb/d. However, the share of the Middle East in China's total crude imports dropped from 61% to 47%. This is mainly because China's crude imports from Africa as well as Russia/Central Asia had grown much faster. With 893 kb/d, Saudi Arabia was the largest crude exporter to China in 2010 and has kept the No.1 spot since 2002. Within the Middle East, Iran (426 kb/d) and Oman (317 kb/d) were the second- and third-largest exporters to China in 2010.

Africa: Led by Angola and Sudan, Africa had the fastest growth in crude exports to China during the past decade, up from merely 44 kb/d in 1998 to 1.42 mmb/d in 2010, or a factor of 31. At 788 kb/d, Angola overall was also the second-largest crude exporter to China right after Saudi Arabia in 2010. Sudan managed to export 252 kb/d of crudes to China in 2010. China's growing appetite for African crudes are due to a number of factors, including the need for heavy sweet crudes, CNPC's increasing investment in Sudan and other African countries, and growing arbitrage opportunities because of the changing sour-sweet crude price differentials.

Russia/Central Asia/Europe/Latin America/Others: This group is now dominated by Russia and Kazakhstan, though Latin American countries of Venezuela and Brazil have become notable players. Between 1998 and 2010, crude exports to China from this group increased by a factor of over 14, with the highest growth coming from Russia, which grew from under 3 kb/d in 1998 to 284 kb/d, around half of which was transported by rail. However, the exports by rail have stopped since the end of 2010 when the crude pipeline began operations. Russia is now China's 5th largest crude exporter. Kazakhstan's crude exports also increased from 8 kb/d to 184 kb/d during the same period, while Venezuela's exports went up from nothing to 126 kb/d.

Asia-Pacific Region: One of the most dramatic changes is the shrinking share of the crude exports to China from the Asia-Pacific region itself. After peaking at 282 kb/d in 2004 (12% of China's total imports), crude exports to China from this region declined to 176 kb/d (5% of the total) in 2010.

Future growth

By 2015 and 2020, China's crude import requirements are forecasted to be 7.5 and 9.7 mmb/d, or about 64% and 69%, respectively, of the country's crude oil use. By 2030, China crude import requirements will be 11.9 mmb/d, or 76% of the country's total oil consumption.

Where will all these future imports come from? Obviously, China will seek to import crudes from all possible sources. On an overall basis, the crude export availability from the Asia-Pacific region will decline. China, having anticipated this decline, has already started diversifying its sources and is likely to import more Atlantic Basin crudes to meet its needs for sweet crudes. Beyond the sweet crudes, the only viable alternative for satisfying China's growing appetite for imported crudes will be those from the Middle East. The Middle East is an important crude exporter to China but its share in China's total crude imports plunged to 45% in 2007 from the peak of 62% in 1998. However, the share of the Middle East rebounded to 51% in 2011. As China's needs are massive, it is inevitable that the Middle East will grow further in importance as an exporter.

Other important sources of crudes are those from Central Asia and Russia, as well as the Latin American countries. CNPC will expand its 200 kb/d Kazakhstan crude pipeline to 400 kb/d by 2013 and it has already started the 300 kb/d Russian East Siberia–China crude pipeline. CNPC is also firming up plans to build a huge refinery (possibly 400 kb/d) in Jieyang, Guangdong, with Venezuelan PDVSA to specially target Venezuelan heavy sour crudes. Our base-case forecasts shows that the share of Middle East crude exports to China are expected to go up to 60% (5.8 mmb/d) in 2020 and 61% (7.3 million b/d) by 2030.

5.4.2. *Overall oil demand, supply, and trade*

If we put crude oil and petroleum products together, China's net oil imports reached an all-time high of 5.1 mmb/d in 2010 and

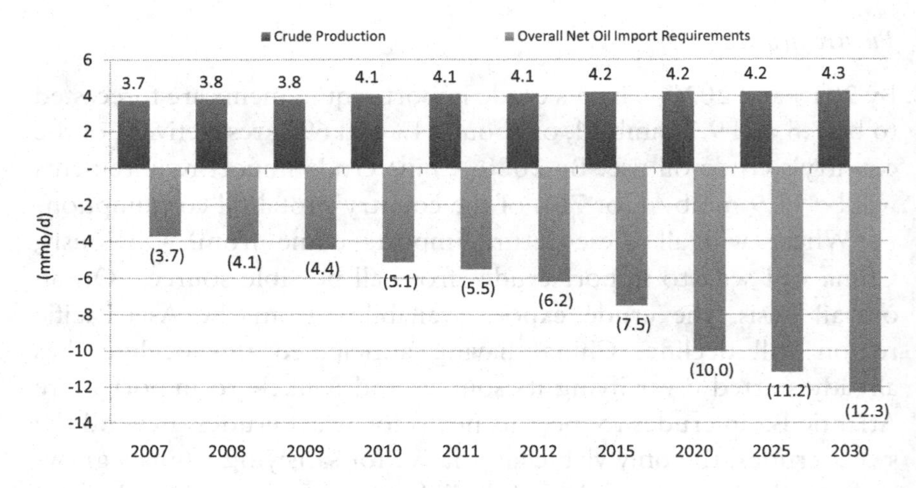

Fig. 5-6. China's Crude Oil Production and Overall Oil Imports Requirements, 2007–2030

Note: Data for 2012–2030 data are forecasts.

5.5 mmb/d in 2011. Back in 1985, China had a net oil export of over 700 kb/d. With flat oil production and rising demand, China's net oil imports are expected to rise to 7.5 mmb/d in 2015, 10.0 mmb/d by 2020, and 12.3 mmb/d by 2030, consisting of significantly higher amounts of crude imports.

As for the product trade, the situation is more complicated. The net product import requirements are projected to be lower during most of the forecasting period, thanks to the rapid buildup of the refining capacity. Toward 2030, China may develop surpluses for all products as a whole. Of course, beyond 2020, there is a high degree of uncertainty. The final balances will also depend on the speed of refining capacity expansions beyond 2015.

chapter 6

Natural Gas Use, Pricing, and Future Growth

China did not engage in international gas trade until the mid-1990s, and the country lacked long-distance gas pipelines, except for those built in Sichuan Province in Southwest China. As a result, the country consumed only what it produced for decades. For industrial and residential consumers alike, consumption was primarily in or near the regions where the natural gas was produced. No gas-fired power plants were built during that period. The structure of natural gas consumption in China prior to the mid-1990s had therefore followed a unique pattern that is different from the consumption patterns in many other countries.

China then entered a transitional period that lasted a decade, when it began exporting natural gas to Hong Kong in 1996 and building long-distance pipelines from Ordos to Beijing, Xinjiang to Shanghai, and Sichuan to Wuhan between 1997 and 2006. The year 2006 marked a new era for China as the country became an importer of natural gas for the first time as the first cargo of liquefied natural gas (LNG) arrived in the Guangdong Dapeng receiving terminal at the end of May 2006. Three and a half years after China imported its first LNG cargo, the country started to import pipeline gas from Turkmenistan and the volume is ramping up at the moment.

Looking toward the future of China's natural gas use, there are many uncertainties. It is a new experience for both China and potential foreign investors to develop a market for natural gas that will be much bigger than it is today. Fortunately, the transitional period from the mid-1990s to end-2000s provide some guidance for China's future direction. During this transitional period, China had experimented in all features concerning the establishment of a nationwide natural gas market — the development of nonassociated gas fields, construction of long-distance gas pipelines, imports of LNG and pipeline gas, establishment of competitive pricing regimes, the development of natural gas for power generation, local distribution of natural gas in cities, and wholesaling and retailing. China has gradually gained experience in these areas, though more still needs to be done.

In this chapter, we review the past and current situations of natural gas consumption in China with a focus on the period from the mid-1990s, including overall consumption, consumption patterns, and the past and current price regimes. We will then review the evolution of the natural gas price regimes, followed by an outlook for future natural gas consumption in China under different scenarios, with discussions of the future sectoral uses of natural gas. Finally, a discussion of the likely future imports of natural gas into China is presented at the end of the chapter.

6.1. Natural Gas Consumption: Historical Perspectives and Sectoral Split

Until the mid-1990s, China's natural gas consumption followed production closely. Since 1996, gas production from the offshore Yacheng gas field has been exported to Hong Kong. Then China became a natural gas importer in 2006 for the first time in history after the first cargo of LNG arrived in Guangdong's Dapeng terminal near Shenzhen. End of 2009 marked another milestone for the China gas market as Turkmen gas started to flow to China through the Central Asia–China gas pipeline.

In 2009, China's natural gas use was up by 13%, reaching 8.6 bscf/d, up from 1.5 bscf/d in 1990, 2.3 bscf/d in 2000, and 4.5 bscf/d in 2005 (Table 6-1). In 2010, gas consumption increased further to 10.5 bscf/d. The average annual growth rate (AAGR) of China's total natural gas consumption was 4.8% between 1990 and

Table 6-1. Natural Gas Output, Trade, and Consumption, 1990–2011./[a] (mmscf/d)

Year	Output	Consumption	Imports	Exports	AAGR-C/[b]
1990	1,480	1,453	—	—	—
1991	1,555	1,519	—	—	4.5%
1992	1,528	1,514	—	—	(0.3%)
1993	1,622	1,589	—	—	4.9%
1994	1,699	1,663	—	—	4.6%
1995	1,736	1,690	—	3	1.6%
1996	1,946	1,699	—	180	0.5%
1997	2,197	1,863	—	285	9.7%
1998	2,252	1,906	—	266	2.3%
1999	2,438	2,035	—	293	6.7%
2000	2,625	2,315	—	261	13.8%
2001	2,934	2,608	—	291	12.7%
2002	3,160	2,776	—	276	6.4%
2003	3,388	3,229	—	178	16.3%
2004	4,000	3,771	—	256	16.8%
2005	4,772	4,521	—	297	19.9%
2006	5,665	5,402	90	290	19.5%
2007	6,699	6,760	381	260	25.2%
2008	7,748	7,806	435	324	15.5%
2009	8,250	8,569	723	321	10.0%
2010	9,280	10,528	1,654	390	21.7%
2011	9,971	12,639	3,028	309	20.1%

[a]Data for 2011 are preliminary.
[b]AAGR-C = average annual growth rate for consumption.

2000, and it accelerated to 16.7% between 2000 and 2011 as more gas distribution infrastructures were built and came onstream. Gas consumption grew faster than that of primary energy consumption as a whole. As a result, natural gas' share of the primary commercial energy (including noncommercial biomass) mix rose from 1.6% in 1990 to 3.5% in 2009. China's share of natural gas in total primary energy consumption, however, is still far below the regional average in the Asia Pacific. Regional distribution of natural gas use in China is uneven, making long-distance pipelines necessary for developing the natural gas market in China.

Natural gas plays an important role in China's chemical industry (fertilizer) and in regions that are close to gas-producing fields. In

2010, the share of industrial natural gas use was estimated at 34%. The residential and commercial sectors ranked second in natural gas use at 33% of the total. Electric power and heat accounted for around 20% of total natural gas use in 2010.

6.1.1. *Industrial and chemical sectors*

The industrial sector is still the leading user of natural gas in China. In 2010, industrial use of natural gas, which includes the chemical sector, accounted for approximately 34% of the total gas use, or 3.6 bscf/d, which was down from the peak level of about 60% in the mid-1980s and about 50% in the mid-1990s.

The chemical sector accounted for approximately 30% of all industrial use of natural gas in 2009, or around 1 bscf/d, where natural gas is used as a feedstock. Back in the 1980s and early 1990s, the share of natural gas use in the chemical sector was around 60% of total industrial consumption of gas.

China is the world's largest fertilizer producer. In 2009, fertilizer production — including nitrogen, phosphate, and potassium fertilizer — amounted to 63 mmt, up 19 mmt in 1990 and 32 mmt in 2000. Despite the large production volume, China imports fertilizer each year while exporting at the same time.

Nitrogen fertilizer (or urea) accounts for about 70%–75% of total fertilizer production in China. Of the nitrogenous fertilizers production companies in China, 62% use coal as feedstock and 26% use natural gas as feedstock. Of the total urea output, coal-based urea accounts for about 80% while natural gas-based urea makes up almost all the other share.

In addition to synthetic ammonia, one other major use of natural gas for other purposes is feedstock for the production of methanol. This is one of the unique characteristics of current natural gas consumption in China.

Aside from the gas used in the chemical sector, we expect that industrial natural gas consumption in the other areas, which accounts for 70% of the total industrial gas use at the moment, will grow rapidly, possibly in the range of 15%–18% annually in the next 10 years.

Overall, we expect that the industrial use of gas will continue to drive the demand of natural gas in the future.

6.1.2. *Residential and commercial use*

The residential and commercial use of natural gas has been growing fast since the mid-1990s, thanks to the rapid expansion of long-distance pipelines.

In 2010, the residential and commercial use of natural gas reached 3.5 bscf/d, accounting for 33% of the national total, up from 12.0% in 1995 and 14.6% in 2000. The AAGR of the residential/commercial use of natural gas was 15.7% during the 1990–2010 period, higher than 10.4% for natural gas use as a whole. The AAGR for residential and commercial use was even higher at 20.9% between 1995 and 2010, compared to 13.0% for natural gas as a whole. Natural gas is only one of the many "gases" used in China's urban cities. LPG and coal gas are the other two key gases competing with natural gas. LPG consumption in the coastal city has slowed down significantly since the early 2000s onwards compared to that in 1996–2000, mainly because of the competition from natural gas in the cities that gas pipelines are built.

6.1.3. *Power generation*

Until the mid-1990s, the utilities in China did not use natural gas for power generation and heating. Less than 100 mmscf/d of natural gas was consumed before 1997. Power plants and heating using natural gas have since been built but the rapid expansion did not start until after 2003, when the West–East pipeline was being built and the LNG contract for the Guangdong LNG terminal was signed.

In 2010, the gas-fired power generation and heating consumed 2.1 bscf/d of natural gas, accounting for 20% of total natural gas use, up from only 5% in 1995. At the start of 2011, China had over 30 GW of gas-fired power capacity installed, accounting for only about 3% of the total installed electricity generation capacity.

The current gas-fired power plants are mainly located in the South, the Lower Yangtze, and the North regions, which account for nearly

95% of the total gas-fired plant capacity in China. Many of those gas power plants are not base-load power generators, but they only ramp up their utilization rates substantially in the peak power demand seasons.

6.2. Natural Gas Pricing

The current natural gas pricing regime of China has four components:

(A) Ex-plan prices = wellhead prices + purification fee
(B) Transportation tariff
(C) Prices at the city gate = A + B
(D) End user prices = C + City distribution tariff

After extraction and before being channeled into pipelines for transportation, natural gas has to be purified to remove or reduce to satisfactory levels various contaminants such as sulfur, water, and carbon dioxide. The degree of purification depends on the quality of the natural gases. The purification has to be carried out before the gas is transported in order to protect and prolong the pipeline's life A tariff has to be imposed for the use of pipelines for gas transportation.

For end users, gas purification and pipeline user fees are added to the wellhead price to form the final price. Like wellhead prices, natural gas transportation and purification charges have also been regulated by the government, but changes have been made, too. Large industrial users pay ex-plant prices plus a transportation tariff.

To summarize, the chain of natural gas supply in China has the following features:

- Gas sales companies receive gas from producing companies and sell gas to gas-distribution companies. Normally, the gas sales company and the producing company are the same. As such, prices charged by sales companies are ex-plant prices.
- Gas distribution companies receive gas via pipelines. As such, they pay two prices: ex-plant prices and pipeline tariffs.
- Gas distribution companies then send gas to end users.

During the above process, the central government regulates ex-plant prices and pipeline tariffs while local companies determine additional tariffs that are part of the end user prices.

6.2.1. *Ex-plant prices*

Prior to 2002, China separated the wellhead prices and the purification fee, and both were set by the government. The wellhead prices and purification fee have since been combined and are now called ex-plant prices. The government regulated ex-plant prices for natural gas (Wu and Wang, 2009).

The mechanism of setting energy prices in China has undergone some major changes during the past two decades. Before 1980, all energy prices were set by the central government, usually at very low levels. Natural gas is no exception and was perhaps one of the lowest-priced sources of energy in the past. For quite a long time, the price of natural gas in China has been kept low, and this has been one of the major impediments to greater production of natural gas.

In the early 1980s, while economic reforms in China were spreading rapidly, energy price reforms also started. In the gas sector, however, real price reforms started only in 1987. Between 1985 and 1987, the national average wellhead natural gas price per 1000 m^3 increased from 59 yuan to 68 yuan, while the actual production cost went up from 74 yuan to 99 yuan per 1000 m^3. Because of the sharply increased losses of gas-producing enterprises, the government began in 1987 to seriously assess the price situation for natural gas production. In 1987, the State Planning Commission (now the NDRC) divided natural gas output by producing enterprises into two parts (in-plan and out-of-plan production) and applied two different prices. The out-of-plan prices were two or three times higher than the in-plan prices but covered only 10% of total production. Both prices were higher than the prices in the past.

In general, the reforms were slow in the late 1980s and early 1990s, but their implementation has since been modestly sped up, as natural gas prices have been raised several times.

In 1992, Sichuan ended the dual-price system, raised the average prices, and started applying different prices to different users. Provinces outside Sichuan continued to use the dual-price system, but the overall prices were higher. In May 1994, China once again drastically raised the in-plan wellhead natural gas prices, and out-of-plan prices became applicable again in both Sichuan and other provinces. The out-of-plan price was set at 900 yuan per 1000 m^3 but with a band of 10% so that the price could be set in the range of 810 to 990 yuan per 1000 m^3.

In March 1997, the Chinese government raised the state-regulated wellhead natural gas prices. The highest rate was assessed on commercial use of natural gas in Sichuan Province, which was 925 yuan per 1000 m^3, or US$3.12 per mmBtu. Gas producers can continue to sell gases outside the government plan, at prices that are determined by the markets. The 1997 price system lasted until 2002.

Before the post-2002 price regime is discussed, the issue of gas purification needs to be mentioned here.

Purification of natural gas is important not only because it is part of the final prices to end users but also because it affects the life of natural gas pipelines and therefore the pipeline economics. In China, the natural gas purification process includes desulfurization, dehydration, sulfur recovery, and residue gas cleaning. The purpose of the purification is to produce clean gas that meets the specifications set by the government. China's current natural gas specifications were set in 2001 and are divided into three categories: I, II, and III.

Type I is the cleanest, while type III has the lowest standards. Under the planned economy in the past, all types of natural gas were set at the same price, and purification efforts were not given high priority. Even during the 1980s and 1990s, the issue of gas quality was not properly addressed, and the purification fee set by the government is extremely low and insufficient for covering the cost. For instance, the state-regulated gas-purification fee, on the basis of 1000 m^3 (1 km^3) is 40 yuan (US$0.13/mmBtu) for fertilizer and 50 yuan (US$0.16/mmBtu) for other users, yet the cost of purifying gas ranges from 70 to 80 yuan (US23–26¢/mmBtu). Losses have therefore accumulated for producing companies that have purification plants. China has since raised the fee and decided in 2002 to merge the purification fee to wellhead prices to form the ex-plant prices, which were raised at the time and again later, discussed as follows.

After merging the purification fee with wellhead prices to form the ex-plant prices, the Chinese government raised the ex-plant prices in January 2002. The government has also divided the natural gas pricing into two categories: first-tier prices and second-tier prices. The majority of the sales were subject to the first-tier pricing, formerly called "in-plan" pricing. In the meantime, in 2002, the government stipulated that prices for self-sales could be set at 10% above or below the baseline prices, which was 980 yuan/km^3 (US$3.32/mmBtu).

On December 26, 2005, China's NDRC announced the decision to raise ex-plant natural gas prices nationwide and indexed natural gas prices with other fossil fuels. As a result of the move, ex-plant prices for industrial and commercial use were raised by 50 to 150 yuan per 1000 m^3 (US$0.17 to $0.50 per mmBtu), and that for fertilizer production were by 50 to 100 yuan per 1000 m^3 (US$0.17 to $0.33 per mmBtu). Starting in 2006, gas subject to the first-tier pricing covers pretty much all natural gas fields that were previously distributed according to state plans. These include gas from the Chuan-Yu, Changqing, Qinghai, and Xinjiang fields, and a portion of the gas from Dagang, Liaohe, and Zhongyuan. For gas from all other fields, second-tier pricing will apply. Based on this division, 85% of China's domestically produced gas is subject to first-tier pricing and 15% is subject to the second-tier pricing regime.

Under the 2005 pricing regime, all first- and second-tier natural gas prices are guidance prices. That means the user and producer can set their final prices within 10% of the government-set baseline prices. The government would adjust the baseline prices based on oil prices, but for any two consecutive years the increase shall not be more than 8%.

In November 2007, the NDRC drastically increased the ex-plant prices for the various sectors. For instance, the average price for the industrial sector was up by 50% from around 800 yuan/km^3 (US$3.13/mmBtu) to 1,200 yuan/km^3 (US$4.69/mmBtu). The move reflected the government's resolve to hike natural gas prices. It is, however, also an indication that the government does not necessarily follow transparent rules to deal with the energy pricing issues.

After a period of 2.5 years, on May 31, 2010, the NDRC announced that the ex-plant baseline price of the domestic on-shore natural gas is increased by 230 yuan/km^3 (US$0.94/mmBtu) across the board (Table 6-2). The NDRC has also merged the two-tiered gas pricing for Dagang, Liaohe, and Zhongyuan gas fields and allowed the buyers and sellers to negotiate gas prices within an upper limit of 10% above the benchmark price, same as before, but there will be no lower limit versus just 10% below the benchmark price before.
For CNG used in transportation, its price will be set at least at the ratio of 0.75 versus the maximum gasoline retail price. The NDRC also estimates that the monthly gas bill for a household will just go up by 4.6 yuan (US$0.67), based on a 0.23 yuan/cbm (US$0.91/mmBtu) hike in the city gas selling price, which implies a full pass-through for gas distributors. Subsidies may be also provided to low income groups and taxi drivers.

6.2.2. *Transportation tariff*

Some of the pipelines built in China have more than 20 years of history, and their technologies are outdated. There are several problems associated with the old natural gas pipelines in China. First, the utilization rate is generally low. Because over one-fourth of the pipelines, especially those in Sichuan Basin, were built in the 1970s or before, their utilization rates are very low, often at 50%. Second, the maintenance cost is high for Chinese natural gas pipelines because of the low utilization and inefficient operations. Gas transportation losses in China amount to over 1% of the total natural gas transported for old pipelines. Finally, the high pipeline utilization cost has not been fully compensated because of the low regulated transportation tariffs.

Table 6-2. Baseline/[a] Ex-Plant Natural Gas by Field Before and After June 1 2010

Gas Fields	Users	Price before June 1 2010 (yuan/km^3)	Price after June 1 2010 (yuan/km^3)	Price before June 1 2010 (US$/mmBtu/[b])	Price after June 1 2010 (US$/mmBtu/[b])
Chuanyu Gas Field	Fertilizer	690	920	2.83	3.77
	Industrial (Direct Supply)	1,275	1,505	5.22	6.16
	City Gas (Industrial)	1,320	1,550	5.40	6.35
	City Gas (Non-industrial)	920	1,150	3.77	4.71
Changqing Gas Field	Fertilizer	710	940	2.91	3.85
	Industrial (Direct Supply)	1,125	1,355	4.61	5.55
	City Gas (Industrial)	1,170	1,400	4.79	5.73
	City Gas (Non-industrial)	770	1,000	3.15	4.09
Qinghai Gas Field	Fertilizer	660	890	2.70	3.64
	Industrial (Direct Supply)	1,060	1,290	4.34	5.28
	City Gas (Industrial)	1,060	1,290	4.34	5.28
	City Gas (Non-industrial)	660	890	2.70	3.64
Xinjiang Gas Fields	Fertilizer	560	790	2.29	3.23
	Industrial (Direct Supply)	985	1,215	4.03	4.97
	City Gas (Industrial)	960	1,190	3.93	4.87
	City Gas (Non-industrial)	560	790	2.29	3.23
Dagang/Liaohe/ Zhongyuan Gas Fields	Fertilizer	1st tier/2nd tier/avg	940	2.70/4.01/2.91	3.85
	Industrial (Direct Supply)	660/980/710	1,570	5.40/5.65/5.49	6.43
	City Gas (Industrial)	1,320/1,380/1,340	1,570	5.04/5.65/5.49	6.43
	City Gas (Non-industrial)	1,230/1,380/1,340	1,170	3.4/4.01/3.85	4.79
		830/980/940			

(*Continued*)

Table 6-2. (*Continued*)

Gas Fields	Users	Price before June 1 2010 (yuan/km^3)	Price after June 1 2010 (yuan/km^3)	Price before June 1 2010 (US$/mmBtu/[b])	Price after June 1 2010 (US$/mmBtu/[b])
Other Gas Fields	Fertilizer	980	1,210	4.01	4.95
	Industrial (Direct Supply)	1,380	1,610	5.65	6.59
	City Gas (Industrial)	1,380	1,610	5.65	6.59
	City Gas (Non-industrial)	980	1,210	4.01	4.95
WE#1 Pipeline	Fertilizer	560	790	2.29	3.23
	Industrial (Direct Supply)	960	1,190	3.93	4.87
	City Gas (Industrial)	960	1,190	3.93	4.87
	City Gas (Non-industrial)	560	790	2.29	3.23
Zhongwu Pipeline	Fertilizer	911	1,141	3.73	4.67
	Industrial (Direct Supply)	1,311	1,541	5.37	6.31
	City Gas (Industrial)	1,311	1,541	5.37	6.31
	City Gas (Non-industrial)	911	1,141	3.73	4.67
Shaanjing Pipelines	Fertilizer	860	1,060	3.52	4.34
	Industrial (Direct Supply)	1,230	1,460	5.04	5.98
	City Gas (Industrial)	1,230	1,460	5.04	5.98
	City Gas (Non-industrial)	830	1,060	3.40	4.34
Sichuan-to-east Pipeline Average		1,280	1,510	5.24	6.18

[a]Final prices can be negotiated within a floating range with an upper limit of 10% but no lower limit.
[b]Exchange rate for June 2010: US$1 = 6.83 yuan

Table 6-3. Transportation Tariffs for Gas Pipelines with Different Lengths.

Distance of Transportation (km)	1976–1991 (yuan per 'km^3)	1991–1997 (yuan per 'km^3)	1997–April 2010 (yuan per 'km^3)	April 2010–Present (yuan per 'km^3)
<50	30	33	36	116
50–100	35	38	41	121
101–200	40	43	47	127
201–250	50	53	58	138
251–300	55	58	63	143
301–350	60	63	68	148
351–400	65	68	74	154
401–450	70	73	79	159
451–500	75	78	85	165
Distance of Transportation (km)	**1976–1991 (US$/ mmBtu)[a]**	**1991–1997 (US$/ mmBtu)[b]**	**1997-Present (US$/ mmBtu)[c]**	**April 2010-Present (US$/ mmBtu)[c]**
<50	0.16	0.10	0.15	0.48
50–100	0.18	0.12	0.17	0.50
101–200	0.21	0.14	0.19	0.52
201–250	0.26	0.17	0.24	0.57
251–300	0.29	0.18	0.26	0.59
301–350	0.32	0.20	0.28	0.61
351–400	0.34	0.22	0.30	0.63
401–450	0.37	0.23	0.32	0.65
451–500	0.39	0.25	0.35	0.68

[a]Exchange rate used US$1.00 = 5.32 yuan for 1991.
[b]Exchange rate used US$1.00 = 8.29 yuan for 1997.
[c]Exchange rate used US$1.00 = 6.83 yuan for H1 2010.

The gas transportation tariff in China is set by the government and has been low historically. After several increases, the fees are reasonable after the hike in April 2010 (Table 6-3).

However, both ex-plant prices and transportation tariffs are set differently for the cross-regional gas pipelines and gas fields associated with them. For transportation tariffs in particular, the rates are much higher than what a standard chart for pipeline tariff may suggest, mainly because of the long distances and new policies. On April 25, 2010, the NDRC issued a document called "*The Notice of Adjusting the Pipeline Transportation Tariffs for Natural Gas*," which raised the price by 80 yuan/km^3 (US$0.32/mmBtu). The price adjustment is applicable in 11 provinces including Tianjin, Hebei, Liaoning, Jilin, Heilongjiang, Shandong, Henan, Chongqing, Sichuan, Yunnan, and Qinghai.

The following is a summary of the situation for these long distance pipelines.

First and Second Ordos–Beijing Pipelines: The first Ordos–Beijing pipeline became operational in 1997. In 2005, the second Ordos–Beijing pipeline came online. The ex-plant price was 830 yuan per km^3 (US$3.05/mmBtu), while the transportation tariffs vary from 310 yuan/km^3 (US$1.14/mmBtu) for Shanxi Province and 480 yuan/km^3 (US$1.77/mmBtu) for Tianjin.

West–East First Pipeline: From the latest price change in June 1, 2010, the ex-plant price for city gas is 790 yuan per km^3 (US$3.24/mmBtu), while the transportation tariffs vary from 660 yuan/km^3 (US$2.70/mmBtu) for Henan Province to 840 yuan/km^3 (US$3.44/mmBtu) for Shanghai.

Zhong–Wu Pipeline: The Zhong–Wu pipeline project has been operational since the end of 2004. It starts from Zhong Xian county of Chongqing to Wuhan, the capital city of Hubei. The situation is more complicated because it divides users into different categories.

Puguang–Shanghai Gas Pipeline: The Puguang gas has the highest ex-plant price in China, at 1,510 yuan/km^3 (US$6.3/mmBtu). The high ex-plant price and pipeline tariffs are to compensate and incentivize Sinopec to develop the challenging Puguang gas field, purify the high sulfur gas, and transport the gas to the end consumers through the challenging territories. It is reported that the gas allocation for different provinces are: Sichuan, 194 mmscf/d;

Chongqing, 194 mmscf/d; Hubei, 77 mmscf/d; Jiangxi, 29 mmscf/d; Anhui, 77 mmscf/d; Zhejiang, 179 mmscf/d; Jiangsu, 227 mmscf/d; and the rest to Shanghai. However, because of the high Puguang gas price, many end-users have reportedly not taken up the volume.

West–East Second Pipeline: It is reported that the pipeline tariff from Horgos to Shanghai is 1,080 yuan/km^3 (US$4.5/mmBtu).

6.2.3. *Final prices to end users*

For many individual urban users — including industrial, commercial, and residential users — the final prices could vary widely, depending on the location of the cities and how the natural gas is obtained. There are no linkages among different cities on retail gas prices, because the sources of supply are different.

We expect that a full pass-through of the ex-plant price hike and the pipeline tariff increase as well as the new expensive gas streams will eventually show in the end-user prices across the country by mid-2011. This is because many local governments have stakes as partners in the joint-ventures with the gas distributors in city gas distribution projects, thus it is in their interest to facilitate the pass-through. In fact, in many cities, the end-user prices have been increased by more than the amount of ex-plant price hike. The end-user price generally increased the most in the industrial sectors (excluding fertilizer producers), followed by commercial sectors, CNG cars, and then the residential sector. In China, price for nonresidential use is higher than that for the residential use; cities that are further away from the gas supply sources have a higher price.

Retail natural gas prices across different cities in China ranged from the low level 1.25 yuan/m^3 (US$4.96/mmBtu) in the city of Xining, Qinghai Province, to the mid-level 2.5 yuan/m^3 (US$9.92/mmBtu) in Shanghai, and to the highest level 5.93 yuan/m^3 (US$23.53/mmBtu) at Liuzhou in Guangxi Autonomous Region in July 2010. This wide range is the best indication of how natural gas prices differ from one city to another. The retail prices for most of the cities in July 2010 are still the same as those in August 2009, which indicates that the 230 yuan/km^3 (US$0.94/mmBtu) ex-plant price hike in May 30, 2010, is still not reflected in the end-user prices up to July 2010. Change in the city gas retail prices requires public hearing and the approval of the local government, which delay end-user price changes. Nonetheless, starting in August, city gas retail prices started to increase across the country, up by more than the 230 yuan/km^3 (US$0.94/mmBtu) in most of the cities, especially for those that will take in the expensive Puguang gas from Sichuan. For example, the city gas price is up by 250 yuan/km^3 (US$1/mmBtu) in most of the cities in the Shaanxi province, 330 yuan/km^3 (US$1.35/mmBtu) in Zhejiang, 320 yuan/km^3 (US$1.31/mmBtu) in Chongqing, and 460 yuan/km^3 (US$1.88/mmBtu) in Chengdu (the highest hike among the cities).

However, China's consumer price index in October 2010 rose to a 25-month high of 4.4% year-on-year (y-o-y), well above the government's full year target of 3%. In order to curb inflation, China's State Council issued a "16-point" directive, which entails 16 new policy measures to stabilize consumer goods prices. One of these new measures — the slowing-down of price reforms — went into full swing in mid-November. Thus, several provinces have suspended hiking retail natural gas prices for the residential sector. For example, Henan Province in Central China has frozen a city gas price increase plan that was approved in mid-November. Other provinces like Anhui, Jiangsu, Guangdong, and Hebei have also said that they will put their city gas price hike on hold.

Although inflationary pressures have put China's natural gas pricing reforms on hold, we believe that the Chinese state oil companies will continue to lobby and press the government to resume gas price reforms in 2011.

If natural gas is used, the power sector is the most sensitive to prices. For those cities that intend to promote the use of natural gas for power generation, the price is generally set at levels that are lower than those for most other sectors. However, in many cities, the prices for power generation are the same as the prices for the industrial sectors.

6.3. Outlook for Natural Gas Demand, Supply, and Imports

Natural gas consumption in China has been growing rapidly since the mid-1990s. Over the next 10 years and beyond, the consumption is forecast to grow continuously at robust rates.

6.3.1. *Future growth under the base-case scenario*

Our forecast of China's gas consumption over the next 10 years is bullish, which is based on the following macro-observations.

First, China has huge potential natural gas resources. Although the proven volumes are very low, the growth rate of natural gas production can nonetheless be very high.

Second, China is facing serious environmental problems because of its heavy reliance on coal. On an overall basis, approximately 70% of smoke pollutants, 90% of sulfur dioxide (SO_2), and 60% of nitrogen oxides (NOX) are attributed to coal-burning, which has led to widespread air pollution in urban areas where economic and industrial developments are at advanced stages in China. Acid rain caused by coal-burning has spread from areas south of the Yangtze River to the rest of the country, and about 40% of China's land area is now affected by acid rain. In Guangdong, the most developed province in China, 70% of the area has acid rain, costing the province close to US$1 billion a year. China has 7 of the 10 worst polluted cities in the world. There has been a rising cry from the public to prevent the environment from worsening and, better yet, to improve the environment over the long term. Natural gas is the best alternative for replacing coal, although cleaner oil products and renewable energy will also play important roles in these environmental efforts.

Third, natural gas has a variety of uses in different sectors of the economy. In theory, natural gas could serve as a substitute for coal and oil for about 70% of total energy consumption. The actual level of substitution will be determined by supply availability and overall economics.

The rapid growth of demand in the industry, power and residential sectors will continue to drive consumption of natural gas in China.

Finally, the rapid economic growth in China, especially in the coastal areas and south China has provided a solid foundation for the country to switch to or use more clean energy such as natural gas. Because of the supply potential, import options, substitutability, and low starting point, natural gas consumption in China can grow at a rate that is much faster than any other form of energy and faster than the overall economic growth during the next 20 years. This forms the basis of our optimistic projections for future natural gas production in China during the forecast period.

However, China still faces challenges and impediments to effectively develop the natural gas sector and markets. These challenges include but are not limited to the following:

Regulatory issues: The Chinese gas market is still fragmented. Regulations of individual fields, pipelines, city gas markets, and foreign investment vary widely from one to another. Lack of transparency has created huge uncertainties for investment in various segments of the gas sector developments.

Infrastructure: Despite the rapid build-up of trunklines in the past 10 years, the total length is far less than that in the US and Europe. China still has a long way to go to build sufficient pipelines to move gas around. The fact that the Chinese government regulates transportation tariffs does not help the growth of pipeline business over the long run. Also, it is not sustainable in the long run for the state oil companies to have monopolies over major long-distance pipeline projects in China. For CBM development, lack of sufficient pipelines and the absence of third-party access regime is a serious constraint.

Price regimes: China regulates natural gas prices. The NDRC needs to approve all prices for new projects, imported LNG, and future imported pipeline natural gas. The government may be slow in approving projects and assessing market prices. This has often delayed the negotiations of LNG imports and prolonged the talk on cross-border pipeline projects. Since China's natural gas consumption is partially supply driven, lack of supply leads to the use of natural gas that is below the desirable levels.

Restrictions on foreign investment: China has, in theory, opened up various segments for foreign investment. In reality, because most upstream and pipeline businesses are in the hands of the three state oil companies, foreign investment in these areas is constrained. As for gas distribution networks and marketing, city governments are not uniform in their policies, leading to confusion and difficulties for foreign investment.

Taking consideration of all the factors, China's natural gas consumption is forecasted to reach 27.7 bscf/d by 2020 and 40.8 bscf/d in 2030 under our base-case scenario, up from 8.6 bscf/d in 2009. (Table 6-4).

It is very important to note that the forecast is for natural gas consumption, which takes into consideration not only the desire of the consumers to use natural gas but also the supply availability, import options, and infrastructure constraints. The consumption forecast is therefore different from the demand forecast, which

Table 6-4. Projected Natural Gas Balance, Base-Case, 2008–2030 (mmscf/d).

Year	Output	Consumption	Imports	Exports
Current				
2008	7.7	7.8	0.4	0.3
2009	8.3	8.6	0.7	0.3
2010	9.3	10.5	1.7	0.4
2011	10.0	12.6	3.0	0.3
Forecasts				
2015	13.6	19.3	6.1	0.4
2020	17.7	29.1	11.9	0.5
2025	21.8	35.6	14.4	0.5
2030	25.7	43.2	18.0	0.6

measures only the volumes that consumers may wish to use at the prevailing prices. Although China can import any amount of gas in theory, actual consumption is constrained by the availability of domestically produced gas, since building import facilities will take a long time and has political and economic implications. In other words, Chinese consumers may demand more natural gas but end up consuming less, because of the many constraints that still remain.

6.3.2. *Sectoral use in the future*

As long distance pipelines are built both within China and from Central Asia and Myanmar — and possibly from Russia — and as China begins to import LNG, regional distribution of natural gas consumption in the future promises to be drastically different from the distribution at present and in the past. The three major sectors will play an important role in determining the future consumption growth of natural gas in China: industrial, residential/commercial and power.

Industrial sectors

We expect that industrial sectors will continue to lead the growth of natural gas consumption in the next 10 years with an AAGR of 13.1% for 2010–2020. While natural gas use in the chemical sector will continue to increase, its growth rate in this sector is expected to be lower than the rates in other major sectors. The other key industrial uses of natural gas, including the glass and ceramics, metals, and building materials sectors, will grow at a robust rate as they switch from heavy oil or coal to gas as their source of fuels. Given increasing concerns about large emissions of sulfur dioxide and other environmental issues caused by the heavy use of coal, the government is expected to encourage more use of natural gas — a cleaner energy source — in those sectors. From 2020–2030, we expect that the AAGR of gas use in the industry will slow to 4.1%.

Residential/Commercial

The residential sector is another leader in future natural gas consumption. Under the base-case scenario, the residential and commercial sector use of natural gas — with residential use being the more dominant of the two — is expected to have an AAGR of 7.5% between 2010 and 2020, and 3.3% between 2020 and 2030.

Power generation

Although China is hungry for power, the limitation of price and resource availability will keep gas consumption in the power sector lower than that in the industrial and residential and commercial sectors. In terms of growth rate, the use of natural gas for power generation is expected to grow at 11.2% between 2010 and 2020 and then 4.4% between 2020 and 2030. The use of natural gas for power generation could grow faster but the costs of gas-fired plants are rising, which limit the rapid construction of new power plants. Gas-fired power has to compete with coal-fired plants. Apparently, appropriate government policies, including taxes on heavy polluters, will have to be in place in order to improve the cost structure of the power industry using different fuels — in a transparent way — so as to make investment in gas-fired power plants more attractive.

Other sectors

Use of natural gas in other sectors is more or less residual of the above-mentioned three major sectors. The gas use in the oil and gas field is still large but its share is shrinking. The use of compressed natural gas (CNG) in automobiles is an exception and is expected to grow very fast. Currently, the country has about 40,000 CNG cars and 1,400 CNG stations. Several major gas-producing provinces, including Sichuan, Qinghai, Xinjiang, and Hainan, as well as medium-sized and large cities such as Beijing, Tianjin, Shanghai, Chongqing, and Shenzhen (Guangdong Province), all are expanding natural gas use to the transportation sector.

6.3.3. *Prospects for China's natural gas imports*

China's needs to import natural gas are a result of the expected strong demand in the country (Wu and Fesharaki, 2005b). These imports — including their timing, sites, and volumes — will in turn be one of the determining factors of projected natural gas consumption in China. As such, the volumes of imports will directly affect the volumes consumed during the forecast period. Here, we briefly discuss imports under the base-case Scenario.

Since 2006, the Guangdong LNG terminal has been operational, which sources LNG from Australian's NWS.

For 2010, in addition to the Guangdong LNG terminal, China imported LNG from BP's Tangguh in Indonesia for its Fujian LNG terminal, from MLNG of Petronas for the Shanghai LNG terminal, spot cargos during summer and winter. Pipeline gas imports from Turkmenistan have also started since end 2009.

For 2015, China will import full contract volumes from Australia's Northwest Shelf, BP's Tangguh, MLNG's Tiga, Qatargas-II for CNOOC, and Qatargas-IV for PetroChina and supply from Total's portfolio as well as partial contractual volumes from Gorgon/Shell, Exxonmobil's PNG LNG, Gorgon/ExxonMobil, and Curtis LNG/BG. Additional volumes of LNG will be imported too. Meanwhile, we assume pipeline gas from Turkmenistan will ramp up and that from Myanmar will come onstream in 2015. By 2015, 2.64 bscf/d of gas will be supplied from Central Asia and Myanmar.

For 2020, more LNG imports are expected. For pipeline gas, we assume the Russian pipeline from West Siberia will be onstream by 2017. By 2020, a total of 6.65 bscf/d of pipeline gas will be supplied from Central Asia, Russia, and Myanmar.

For 2025, we expect that China will import more LNG. A Russian pipeline from East Siberia will also start supply to China and a total of 8.3 bscf/d of pipeline gas is expected.

For 2030, more LNG will go to China, and China will import a total of 11.4 bscf/d of piped gas.

Altogether, China is projected to import 12 bscf/d of natural gas by 2020 18 bscf/d by 2030.

6.3.5. *Unconventional gas use: An overview*

Current situation

Compared to CBM production, the actual utilization of CBM is even lower. While two-thirds of CBM production from surface wells — out of a low production level — is used, less than one-third of the extracted CBM is actually consumed. Altogether, the overall utilization of CBM is around 38% of total CBM production in China at present.

Before the first commercial CBM pipeline linking up with the West–East gas pipeline was completed in late 2009, CBM was mainly used in the residential sector of the areas around coal mines. Currently, China has 10 coal mines where the extraction of CBM exceeded approximately 10 mmcf/d individually, while the number of households that use CBM reached approximately 1 million. The use of CBM for power generation has just started. At the start of 2010, China had approximately 920 MW of CBM-fired power plants. The capacity has since increased to some 1,500 MW by the start of 2011, utilizing some 290 mmcf/d of CBM. With the connection of the CBM pipeline with conventional gas pipelines, CBM use is expanding to the faraway consuming centers in coastal areas.

While the long-distance pipelines are being developed rather slowly, China has increasingly used CBM in the liquefied form. At the start of 2010, China had three liquefied CBM projects (LCBM) in operation, two under construction, and one proposed. From these projects, the production capacity in operation is around 48 mmcf/d, the production capacity under construction is 76 mmcf/d, and the proposed capacity is 28 mmcf/d.

All factors considered, we project that CBM use in China will reach 2.9 bcf/d in 2020 and 4.1 bcf/d in 2030. It will also account for 8% of total gas consumption by 2020 but down slightly to 70% by 2030 (Fig. 6-1).

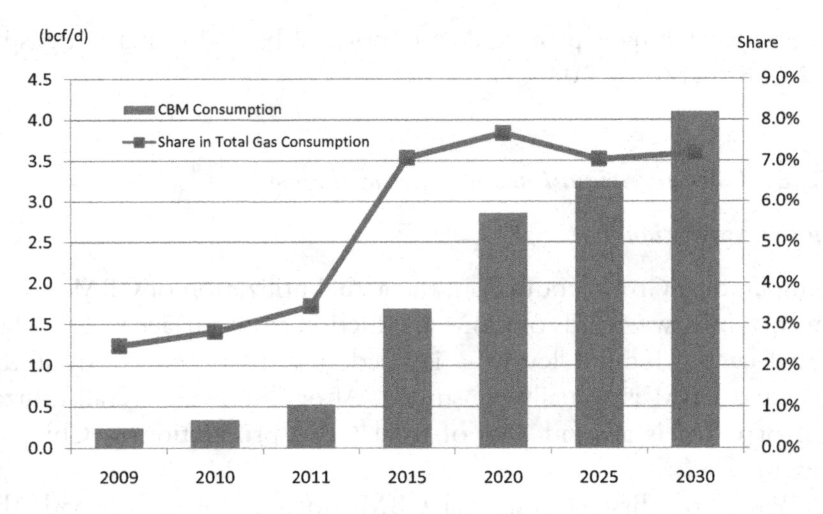

Fig. 6-1. Outlook for CBM Consumption in China.

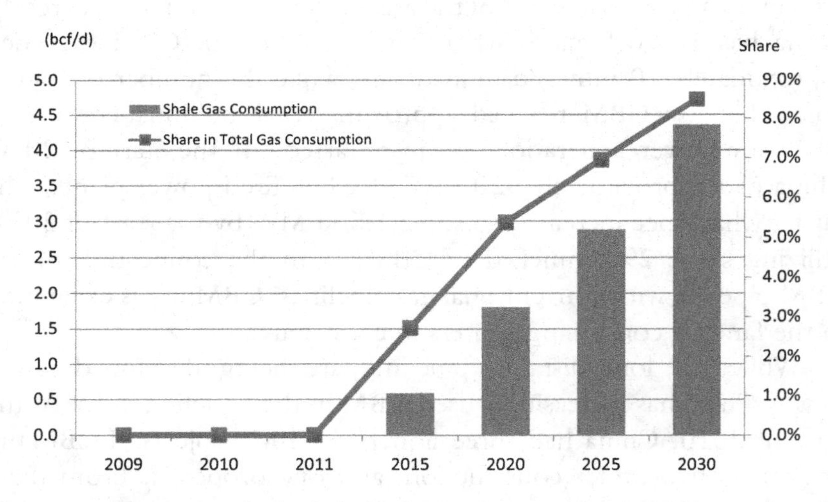

Fig. 6-2. Outlook for Shale Gas Consumption in China.

In a similar fashion, we project that China's shale gas use will reach 1.8 bcf/d in 2020 and 4.4 bcf/d by 2030. It will also account for 5% of total gas consumption 2020 and 9% by 2030 (Fig. 6-2).

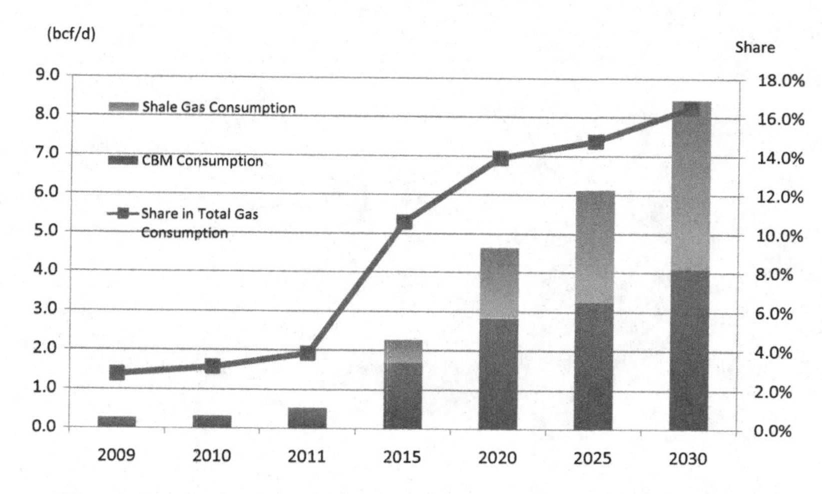

Fig. 6-3. Outlook for Unconventional Gas Consumption in China.

On a comparable basis, and if we add up CBM and conventional natural gas, unconventional gas production is forecast to reach 4.6 bcf/d by 2020 and 8.4 bcf/d by 2030 (Fig. 6-3). It will thus account for 14% of total gas consumption by 2020 and 17% in 2030.

chapter 7

Outlook for China's Liquefied Natural Gas and Pipeline Gas Imports

China became Asia's fifth importer of liquefied natural gas (LNG) in 2006, joining Japan, Korea, Taiwan, and India. It has shown impressive LNG demand growth over the course of its relatively short import history. In 2010, it imported a total of 9.4 mmt, up from a mere 0.7 mmt in 2006. For 2011, China's LNG imports reached 12.2 mmt. In 2010, imported LNG accounted for 12% of China's total natural gas use. The share went up further to 13% in 2011 (with another 3% from imported pipeline gas) and is poised to grow more. While China's economic growth prospects and vast population imply almost unlimited LNG import potential, we expect the nation's LNG import outlook to be heavily affected by price as well as the development of domestic gas — both conventional and unconventional.

7.1. LNG Imports and Supply Contracts

Overall, China is not yet "addicted" to gas, especially comparatively expensive LNG imports. Although Beijing is keen to encourage gas use to achieve environmental objectives, the nation has a range of other, relatively cheap energy options. Before 2006, China relied on domestic production for 100% of its natural gas supply. In 2011,

China imported 12.2 mmt, the fourth largest in Asia after Japan, Korea, and India.

The three NOCs — CNOOC, PetroChina, and Sinopec — are the only authorized importers of LNG at present. CNOOC is currently the leader, but PetroChina is catching up fast. Currently, China has 10 long-term LNG supply contracts, all are sales and purchase agreements (SPAs). Based on these full contractual volumes of 33.03 mmtpa, CNOOC accounts for 49% of the total, PetroChina 22%, and Sinopec 29%. Under these mostly long-term contracts, current and future LNG supplies to China are Australia, Indonesia, Malaysia, Qatar, Pupua New Guinea (PNG), and others. LNG projects under these contracts supplying to China now and in the future include Northwest Shelf (NWS) LNG, Tangguh LNG, MLNG Tiga, Qatargas III, Qatargas IV, PNG LNG, Gorgon LNG, Australia-Pacific LNG, and Queensland Curtis LNG etc.

Chinese companies have actively sought other supply opportunities as well, but their status is slightly more nebulous than the deals listed earlier. But if even a handful of these deals actually materialize, the existing modest gap between forecast Chinese demand and contracted supply would be rapidly eroded. The onus is therefore on existing LNG exporters to tie up what short-term sales opportunities they can, if they have the desire and means, to capture a small and potentially instant-vanishing window of opportunity.

7.2. Receiving Terminals

Table 7-1 illustrates the build-up capacity of individual Chinese LNG terminals from 2009 to 2015 (FGE, 2011). The terminal capacity is not a good indicator for LNG demand in China as it is believed that many of those will run far less than 100% capacity. By the end of 2011, China has five terminals that are operational with a combined receiving capacity of some 19 million tonnes per annum (mmtpa). This is likely to go up to a whopping 62 mmtpa by the end of 2015.

Table 7-1. China LNG Terminals' Capacities (Operational, Under Construction and Approved) (mmtpa).

Owner	Terminal Name	Start-Up Date	2009	2010	2011	2015
CNOOC, BP and others	Guangdong LNG	2006	5.5	6.7	6.7	13.5
CNOOC and FDIC	Fujian LNG	2009	2.6	2.6	2.6	5.2
CNOOC and Shenergy	Shanghai LNG	2009	3.0	3.0	3.0	6.0
Kunlun Energy* and Dalian government	Dalian LNG	2011	—	—	3.0	6.0
Kunlun Energy*, Pacific Oil and Gas and others	Rudong LNG	2011	—	—	3.5	6.5
CNOOC and others	Zhejiang LNG	2012	—	—	—	3.0
PetroChina	Shenzhen	2013	—	—	—	2.0
CNOOC	Zhuhai	2013	—	—	—	3.5
Sinopec and Huaneng	Qingdao LNG	2014	—	—	—	3.0
PetroChina, Beijing and Hebei Governments	Tangshan LNG	2013	—	—	—	3.5
CNOOC and Hainan Development Holding	Hainan LNG	2015	—	—	—	2.0
CNOOC and others	Tianjin	2013	—	—	—	5.2
Sinopec and others	Guangxi	2015	—	—	—	3.0
Total			**11.1**	**12.3**	**18.8**	**62.4**

7.3. Outlook for Future Growth of LNG Imports

Future Chinese LNG imports are assessed in the overall context of natural gas use in the country as well as on the basis of LNG demand, supply, and trade in Asia and the world at large.
The key drivers of overall LNG demand growth are:

Strong economic growth.

Rapid growth of demand in the industrial, power, and residential sectors.

Use of natural gas as a cleaner fuel.

Growing list of long-term LNG contracts.

Rapidly growing but still insufficient domestic natural gas production.

Slow progress of pipeline gas imports.

Fig. 7-1 illustrates our LNG demand forecast under different cases.

LNG demand forecasts under our base-case scenario have the following assumptions:

They are in line with China's natural gas consumption forecasts under the base-case scenario presented earlier in the book.

Contractual LNG import prices (DES) are in the range of US$12–18/mmBtu throughout the forecast period 2012–2030.

LNG terminals will be built as long as supply contracts are secured.

Under our base-case scenario, China is expected to import 26 mmt in 2015, 41 mmt in 2020, and 51 mmt in 2030.

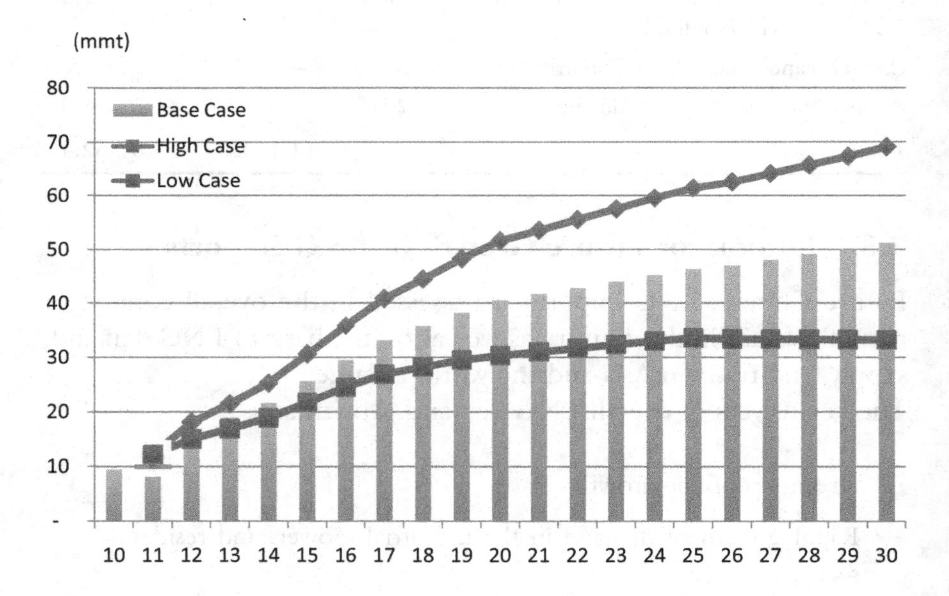

Fig. 7-1. High, Low, and Base-Case LNG Imports of China.

Note: Data for 2012–2030 are forecasts.

The possible constraints for China to reach its full forecast market potential, particularly the LNG import potential under the base case, lie in five areas: (1) The ability of individual Chinese importers, namely CNOOC, PetroChina, and Sinopec, to accomplish "resource pooling" and "price pooling;" (2) competition of natural gas from domestic fields and via pipeline imports; (3) competition of unconventional gas; (4) competition of other fuels such as coal, hydroelectricity, nuclear power, LPG, and other oil and energy fuels; and (5) future LNG import prices.

Resource Pooling and Price Pooling: PetroChina has the greatest domestic resources to carry out the "pooling" strategies, helps explain why PetroChina has been — and could afford to be — more aggressive in signing LNG contracts with slopes near or close to crude oil parity. It produced 6.6 bscf/d of natural gas in 2009 and is expected to increase its production quickly in the future. Also, as the driver behind the West–East pipelines, PetroChina is in a position to offset higher LNG acquisition prices by pooling LNG with its lower-priced domestic production. For its part, CNOOC had the advantage of contracting for relatively low-priced LNG from Australia and Indonesia in 2002, so it too has some pooling options, which can help blunt the effects of importing higher-priced LNG in today's less-forgiving environment. Other than the relatively "low-priced" deals CNOOC landed earlier this decade, the firm has hitherto focused its LNG importing efforts in South China and the Lower Yangtze region, which are far-away gas producing areas and have to pay high gas price (Fig. 6). With the highest paying capability in those areas, CNOOC appears to be successful in managing its LNG supply contracts and terminal projects. By contrast, Sinopec is the least advantaged as it does not have significant cheap domestic gas production (only about 10% of domestic production) for "pooling" nor existing cheap LNG contracts. This is why Sinopec lags far behind the other two players in securing LNG supply contracts and moving forward with its LNG terminal project.

Competition from indigenous gas and pipeline imports: In terms of prices and with the exceptions of LNG imported into Guangdong and

Fujian terminals, LNG going to China cannot compete with most of the gas produced domestically, despite pricier gas from newer fields in the Southwest, the Northwest, the West, and offshore China. However, since it is almost certain that China's domestic gas production will be insufficient to meet growing demand, the impact of "domgas" on LNG demand is less severe than what it may appear to be.

Another source of competition to LNG is imported pipeline gas. Part of the Turkmenistan–China gas pipeline just began operating, and volumes will increase to 3 bscf/d. With a border price of $7.90/ mmBtu (at Brent price = US$80/bbl), the Turkmenistan gas is not cheap. Similar prospects exist for imports from Myanmar and Russia. In other words, Chinese LNG import prices could be on par or competitive compared with the existing and potential future pipelined gas imports.

Competition of unconventional gas: Of the three major types of unconventional gas, China is already a large producer of tight gas. Tight gas data have been lumped together with conventional gas and it is already in the pool of China's natural gas production and demand. China has developed another type of unconventional gas — coal-bed methane (CBM) for over 15 years. However, the results are disappointing by far. Finally, China has barely started the exploration of shale gas since 2009.

Despite all these obstacles, China has the huge potential to developing CBM and shale gas in the coming decade. Various factors, such as price regime, government support, infrastructure, and structure of investment companies that hindered the past development of CBM have improved. China now has a greater need for gas. If the prices are right, investment of CBM and shale gas will be spurred. There is still a huge uncertainty regarding the size of unconventional gas development in China. If the production of unconventional gas is large enough, future LNG imports may be affected.

Competition of other fuels: Imports and use of LNG in China in the future face competition from a number of fuels such as coal, hydroelectricity, nuclear power, LPG, and other oil and energy sources. While natural gas can largely edge out LPG in the residential area, the use of natural gas for power generation is a major area of concern. The power sector will find it tough to compete with coal unless the Chinese governments — central or local — intervene with more restrictive coal-use policies. The same holds true for the industrial sector. In the residential sector, natural gas can compete well with LPG but for home heating, the situation is complex as coal is still being used. Overall, China is sensitive to natural gas prices and if they are high enough, additional demand can be killed.

LNG import prices: As far as LNG is concerned and in light of the four areas discussed earlier, the level of import prices will ultimately affect the volume of imports. Our view is that China is still sensitive to the LNG import prices. If the regional LNG prices are too high, China's ability of importing LNG will be severely affected. Alternatively, if the LNG prices are low enough and LNG can compete well in the three areas mentioned above, imports can be significantly higher.

In end 2009, China became the first Asian country to import both LNG and pipeline gas with the start-up of the Central Asia–China international pipeline. Pipeline gas imports are set to become one important part of Chinese gas supply in the future. The country has started construction on the Myanmar–China pipeline since June 2010 and has also been negotiating with Russia for pipeline gas imports for over a decade. In this chapter, we review the status of China's pipeline gas imports from Central Asia, Myanmar and Russia, and then present our projections of the gas imports to China to 2030. These are part of the assumptions concerning China's regional and provincial natural gas demand, supply, and balances elsewhere in this study.

7.4. Central Asia–China Pipeline Gas

The Central Asian countries used to be republics within the former Soviet Union. Currently, three Central Asian countries share common borders with China: Tajikistan, Kirghizstan, and Kazakhstan.

Four Central Asian countries have rich gas resources, which are Turkmenistan, Kazakhstan, Uzbekistan, and Azerbaijan. With huge amounts of gas reserves and relatively small domestic gas demand,

Central Asian countries have the potential to export large amounts of gas. Besides supplying gas to Russia, they are also keen to export gas directly to other countries (such as China, Iran, India, and European countries) because more outlets can allow them to diversify away from exposure to Russia. China started to import Turkmen gas in December 2009 after the completion of the Central Asia–China pipeline. The pipeline runs from Gedaim in Turkmenistan and passes through Uzbekistan and Kazakhstan to reach Horgos in Xinjiang, where it connects to the domestic second West–East pipeline to transport the gas to Shanghai, Guangdong, and Hong Kong. The investment of the project is all financed by CNPC.

The international section of the Central Asia–China pipeline is 1,833 km (1,139 miles) and has two parallel lines — A and B. The pipeline runs 188 km (117 miles) through Turkmenistan, 490 km (304 miles) in Uzbekistan, and 1,404 km (872 miles) in Kazakhstan.

In 2010, China imported about 430 mmscf/d, mostly from the Bagtyyarlyk block on the right bank of Amu Darya River, of which PetroChina has a production sharing contract with Turkmengaz. China's imports rose 1.4 bscf/d in 2011. In the long-run, we expect China will import 2.9 bscf/d of natural gas from Central Asia and 5.8 bscf/d by 2030.

7.5. China's Gas Imports from Myanmar

CNPC and Myanmar's Ministry of Energy have signed a MOU to construct, operate, and manage the parallel Sino–Myanmar oil and gas pipelines in mid-June. Investment in the oil pipeline is estimated to be US$1.5 billion and on the gas pipeline, with a 1.16 bscf/d (12 bcm/y) of capacity, is US$1 billion (some reports state that it is more than US$2 billion). CNPC will own 50.9% of the project and Myanmar Oil and Gas Enterprise (MOGE) will own the remaining 49.1%. They have started construction in June 2010 and it is possible that it could be completed by 2013/2014.

Gas will be transported via a 32-inch offshore pipeline and via a 36-inch onshore pipeline to China. Daewoo and its partners own and operate the offshore pipeline while PetroChina will own and operate the onshore pipeline although Daewoo, its partners, and the Myanmar government will have an option to participate. But in any case, PetroChina will maintain a majority stake. In early 2010, India's ONGC paid out nearly US$168 million on an 8.35% share in the China–Myanmar pipeline and Gail spent US$84 million for a 4.17% stake in the gas pipeline.

The source of the gas will be from key blocks in the Shwe gas fields and other gas fields. The blocks in the Shwe gas fields are owned by a consortium that consists of Daewoo International (51%, operator), ONGC (17%), GAIL (8.5%), KOGAS (8.5%), and Myanmar Oil and Gas Enterprise (15%). In their preliminary development plan released in October 2009, Daewoo International intends to spend US$1.7 billion commercializing the gas finds in the three gas fields, Shwe and Shwe Phyu in Block A-1 and Mya in Block A-3, in the next three years. Gas production is not expected until 2013 and the field life is put at 28 years. In 2009, CNPC signed an MoU with the Daewoo led consortium to import 500 mmscf/d from 2013 for 20–30 years from Block A-1 and A-3.

Given the short distance of 900 km (559 miles) to reach Kunming, China, the expected lower pipeline tariff will help ensure its competitiveness in the Chinese market. However, the challenge is that prices for domestically produced natural gas prices have traditionally been set low in Southwest China where Kunming and the Yunnan Province are located, though lately wellhead prices for newer fields in Sichuan have been raised substantially. Under our base case, we expect that China will start to import Myanmar gas from 2015 and the amount could reach 841 mmscf/d by 2020, 1 bscf/d by 2025 and 1.2 bscf/d by 2030.

7.6. China's Gas Imports from Russia: Will It Ever Happen?

Russia is the richest country in the world in terms of proven natural gas reserves. Despite huge reserves, production capacity, and exporting capability, Russia has transported only limited Volumes of LNG into the Asia-Pacific region through the Sakhalin II LNG project but zero pipeline gas to the region. However, the potential for establishing links with Asia is huge, because Russia's untapped natural gas resources in East Siberia and the Russian Far East are very large. Even West Siberia, despite its distance from Asia and the competing European market, also offers a potential for links with China. In the "Energy Strategy of Russia 2030" document released by the Russian government in 2009, Russia has a plan to export 6–7 bscf/d of pipeline gas to Asia by 2030.

On September 27, 2010, CNPC and Gazprom signed a framework agreement on natural gas imports from Russia, under the witness of the Chinese President Hu Jintao and his Russian counterpart Dmitry Medvedev. Both sides have agreed on commercial parameters of the potential gas supply to China, including pipeline transmission capacity, total supply volume, supply duration, and payment conditions. However, they are yet to agree on the gas delivery price, which is the key stumbling block since negotiations started in 2004. Under the framework agreement, Gazprom will provide 2.9 bscf/d (30 bcm/y) of gas to China from the West Siberian fields in the first phase of supply, and another 3.7 bscf/d (38 bcm/y) from East Siberia gas fields will be supplied in the second phase. The 2.9 bscf/d gas will be from the West Siberian fields and Rosneft's untapped Kharampur fields in northwest Siberia as well as private producer Novatek's neighboring gas and condensate fields. The 3.7 bscf/d gas could be from Sakha-Yakutia and Sakhalin gas fields. According to their plan, a final contract, including the volumes, routes and prices, will be signed in mid-2011. If everything proceeds smoothly, gas from Russia could start flowing to China from the West Siberian fields by 2015. Under our base case, we believe that Russia will only start to supply gas to China in 2017 because some delays are expected.

There are four projects in Russia that involve China one way or another and at various points in time during the past many years. These four are the Irkutsk gas pipeline project; the Sakha oil, gas, and pipeline project; the Sakhalin oil, gas, and pipeline project; and the West Siberia gas pipeline project (Table 7-2). Among these project proposals and ideas, the West Siberia project was once considered the least possible. However, since 2006, Russia has been championing this project and it thus has come to the forefront. Likewise, the

Table 7-2. Current Natural Gas Pipeline Projects from Russia.

Project Name	Pipeline Route	Length		Capacity	Status
		km	miles	(bscf/d)	
West Siberia	West Siberia–Altai Republic–Xinjiang–Shanghai and Guangdong	7,000	4,350	2.9	Likely
Sakhalin	Sakhalin–Harbin–Shenyang–Beijing	1,950	1,212	0.8–3.9	Likely
Irkutsk	Kovykta–Irkutsk–Manzhouli (Heilongjiang)–Shenyang (Liaoning) then (1) Dalian–Yellow Sea–South Korea; (2) Beijing	4,800	2,983	2.9	Inactive
Sakha (Yakutsk)	Yakutsk (Sakha)–Changchun (Jilin)–Beijing–Qingdao (Shandong)–Seoul (Korea)–Kitakyushu (Japan)	4,800	2,983	2.9	Inactive

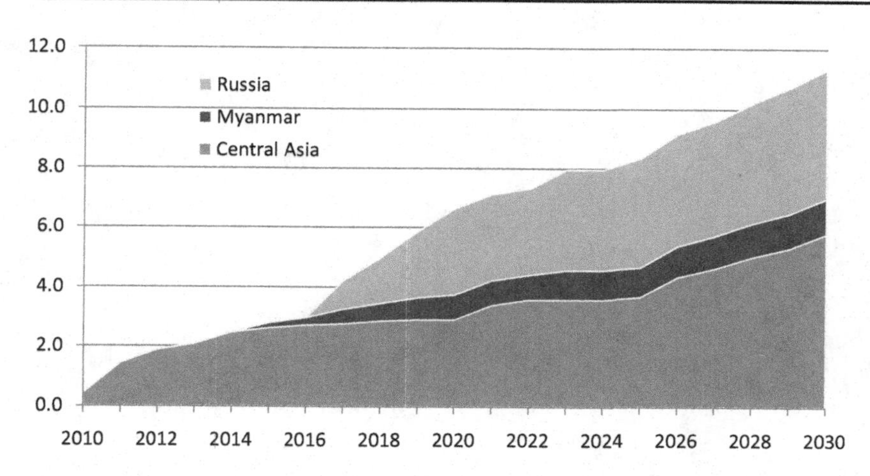

Fig. 7-2. International Pipeline Gas Imports, 2010–2030.

Note: Data for 2012–2030 are forecasts.

Irkutsk–China–South Korea pipeline project was high on the list of likely projects and has been put on the back burner because of the continued disputes over pricing issues and Gazprom's plan for using Kovykta's gas in local markets. The Sakhalin–China pipeline project was promoted by ExxonMobil strongly for a while but is facing new challenges at present.

7.7. Outlook for China's Pipeline Gas Imports: A Review of All Options

Under our base case, we expect that Myanmar and Russian gas will start to flow to China in 2015 and 2017, respectively (Fig. 7-2).

Altogether, we expect that the total capacity of pipeline gas imports to China will reach 6.6 bscf/d (68.7 bcm/y) by 2020 and 11.4 bscf/d (117 bcm/y) in 2030 under our base-case scenario. International pipeline gas import's share of total gas demand in China will increase from 11% in 2011 to 23% in 2020 and 26% in 2030.

chapter 8

Energy Security in China: Regional and Global Implications

This chapter touches upon the issue of energy security in China. Until the early 1990s, China had long been a net energy exporter. The country became a net oil importer in 1993, the first time since the 1960s. For China, energy security first and foremost means oil supply security (Chen, Cheng, and Wu, 2008; Leung 2011). It also means natural gas and coal supply security. For decades, China managed in the past to produce nearly all the energy it needed. However, the country's energy imports, primarily oil, have increased significantly since the 1990s, while exports have been declining. Currently China is a net importer of all three types of fossil energy — oil, natural gas, and coal.

As discussed elsewhere in the book, China's energy dependence can therefore be characterized primarily by its heavy dependence on coal and growing dependence on imported oil and natural gas and, to a lesser extent, coal itself. As an economy striving to become modernized and industrialized, China's reliance on coal for meeting over two-thirds of its commercial energy use is not healthy. Chief among the disadvantages of coal use are the huge environmental problems it causes as well as the enormous waste and inefficiency for burning coal directly. While the dominant role of coal in China's future energy requirements will not change fundamentally over the next 10 to 15 years, efforts have been made by the Chinese government to ensure that the share of coal in total energy consumption declines. This means cleaner energy products should be used, including oil, gas, nuclear power, and hydroelectricity. For oil and gas in particular, China's domestic resources are unfortunately limited, and production is insufficient to meet the growing demand. The inevitable result is a larger dependence on imported oil and gas.

The objectives of this chapter are to examine the major elements of China's emerging energy security strategies This chapter is divided into several sections. Section 8.1 identifies China's energy vulnerabilities. Section 8.2 discusses China's major components of energy security strategies. Section 8.3 examines one component of China's energy security: strategic petroleum reserves (SPRs) while Section 8.4 reviews another component, China's overseas oil and gas investment. Finally, the role of China in the Asia-Pacific region as well as the world as whole are assessed in Section 8.5, while the role of China in Asia's oil and gas industries and markets is also discussed.

8.1. China's Energy Vulnerabilities

China's energy system is vulnerable in many areas (Seligsohn, 2011). Six major vulner-abilities can be identified.

Structural mismatch between energy consumption and production

First and foremost, the rising energy use and the structural mismatch between energy consumption and production represent one of most serious vulnerabilities in China's energy system. Despite all the skepticism over the accuracy of the official growth data, the Chinese economy has been growing at a spectacular rate for over three decades. China is expected to enjoy high growth rates over the next 15 to 20 years. Even with a low energy–economic linkage, it means enormous amounts of energy requirements for China over the long term. By 2030, it is expected that China's primary energy consumption will be double the actual consumption of 2010.

While the increasing energy requirement is challenging enough in itself, the greater challenge is in determining the right energy mix. The structural mismatch between China's energy resource availability and energy consumption is one of the most serious problems facing China today. China lacks high-quality premium fuel to meet its energy needs despite the relative abundance of coal and other energy resources.

China needs clean, high-quality energy to support its economic growth for the coming decades. Yet the current availability of China's energy resources cannot meet this challenge. For instance, the share of natural gas, hydroelectricity, and nuclear power are still very low in China. Structural problems also exist within the individual energy sectors. Within China's coal sector, upstream mining is well developed, but the investment is lacking for coal washing, shaping, transportation, distribution, and coal-water slurry. For the power sector, power generation, transmission, and distribution are not well coordinated, leading to bottlenecks in many markets.

The Chinese government has long realized these structural problems. The steps being taken by the government include the following: (1) Promote hydroelectric power generation; (2) Promote nuclear power; (3) Promote natural gas developments and utilization; (4) Speed up structural reforms within the energy sectors; (5) Promote renewable energy development.

Rising energy imports and energy security

China's growing oil and gas demand and the lack of domestic supply is the biggest structural mismatch the country is facing today, and the gap is growing rapidly. For China, therefore, in terms of energy security, oil supply security is the most important issue. While natural gas imports may add to the security problem, they may also be viewed as a way to manage the growing dependence on oil through energy diversification. As such, China's planned natural gas imports in the form of liquefied natural gas (LNG) and by pipelines add a new dimension to the energy security issue.

Energy use and environmental protection

The third energy vulnerability is the conflict between energy use and environmental protection (Jiang, 2011; Ladislaw *et al.*, 2009;

Zhang, 2010). China is currently the world's largest sulfur dioxide polluter and the second largest carbon dioxide emitter. According to the World Bank, of the 20 most heavily polluted cities in the world in the mid 2000s, 16 were in of China. At the beginning of this decade, about two-fifths of China's land territory were affected by acid rain, with the Lower Yangtze region the most heavily affected.

Despite the government's efforts to promote the use of clean and premium fuels, it is inevitable that China continues to rely on coal to meet the bulk of its energy demand in the foreseeable future. The massive use of coal has caused substantial damage to the environment and serious public health problems. At present, half of coal use in China is the direct burning of raw coal, either as a fuel or for power generation. Obviously, the Chinese government has made great efforts to manage coal consumption and control the damage made to the environment. However, China has a very long way to go before it is able to reduce coal consumption to under 50% of the total energy consumption and to apply basic clean coal technologies to the majority of its coal use.

Low per-capita energy consumption and energy efficiency coupled with increasing difficulties for energy conservation and efficiency improvement

Despite the fact that China is the largest primary energy consumer, its per-capita energy consumption is the same as world average and far below the levels of developed countries. The low per-capita energy consumption has presented a huge challenge for China. The reason is that as the Chinese economy develops, an increase in per-capita energy consumption is inevitable, which means increasing energy requirements for the country in the coming decades.

In the meantime, China's energy efficiency is still low (Levine, Zhou, and Price, 2009; Song, 2005; Xuan, 2004), yet the promotion of energy conservation and efficiency is becoming increasingly difficult (Prince *et al.*, 2011). For the past 20 years, China has applied various energy conservation technologies and achieved impressive results. The task, however, has become increasingly difficult as the country continues to open up and move toward a market economy despite a large gap between China and the more advanced countries in energy efficiency. China now needs to establish a market-oriented policy framework and invest substantially in new energy technologies to further promote energy conservation (Bambawale and Sovacool, 2011). If China fails to further promote energy conservation, in order to maintain its high economic growth, energy demand in China may rise to unprecedented levels that are impossible to sustain.

To deal with the challenge, the Chinese government continues to explore ways to establish new mechanisms that can promote energy conservation and comprehensive utilization of resources under the condition of the market economy. During the 11th Five-Year Program (FYP), which covered the period from 2006 to 2010, the Chinese government had given energy conservation and efficiency improvement a top priority in China's future energy development. Finally, ensuring energy supply security continues to be featured in the 12th FYP, which covers the 2011–2015 period. However, China is still far from reaching their targets.

Management and regulatory reform of the energy sector

In almost all areas of the energy sector, ranging from coal to power, many problems exist in the management and regulatory system. For coal, low efficiency, heavy pollution, and lack of competition continue to plague the sector. For oil and gas, functioning free markets are far from fully established. For power, it takes time to end the long-term monopoly and establish competitive markets. For all energy sectors, a well-functioning regulatory framework either does not exist or is incomplete.

The Chinese government has tried for decades to reform the management and regulatory system of the energy sector. Reform of the oil and gas industries started as early as the mid-1980s. Reform of the coal sector has been going on for nearly two decades. Power sector reform is relatively new. On an overall basis, the process is slow and has been proceeding on a trial and error basis. As of today, there is still a lot to do to demonopolize the energy markets as well as establish a functional regulatory framework.

Weak energy supply system in rural areas

Energy supply in China's vast rural area is very inefficient. Currently, China's consumption of noncommercial biomass — used exclusively in rural areas — accounts for about 8% of China's total primary energy consumption (primary commercial energy consumption plus noncommercial biomass) in 2010. China currently has approximately 25 million people in rural areas who have no access to electricity. The massive use of biomass, often in primitive ways, is ecologically destructive and economically inefficient.

Rural energy development has long been one of the focuses of China's energy policy. The government has tried for decades to promote the commercialization of biomass use in rural areas and extend the electric power grid to remote areas. With slightly less than half of China's total population, or over 650 million people, living outside of urban cities and towns, it is an enormous challenge to further promote the commercialization of energy use in rural areas.

Among these vulnerabilities, the structural mismatch between energy production and consumption, as well as rising oil imports and the consequences for energy security, are considered the most threatening. Many Chinese scholars believe that although China needs more total energy during the coming decades, China's lack of clean, premium, and high-quality fuels is a bigger problem. Adequate supply of clean and high-quality energy will support the government's goal of rapid economic growth to improve the environmental and ecological conditions of the country and lift China out of the group of lower-income countries and become an advanced developing country. However, to obtain sufficient energy products of clean, premium, and high-quality nature, China has to not only substantially increase its investment in oil, gas, hydroelectricity, nuclear power, and clean coal technologies but also import more oil and gas, leading to the important issue of energy security.

As for energy security, its importance is growing and will soon become the biggest energy vulnerability facing PRC. If China feels that its energy security is jeopardized, many of the other energy policy goals such as the use of clean and high-quality fuels, economic efficiency improvement, environmental protection, and energy sector reform will be negatively affected. As such, a good energy security policy is very important for the country as well as for the rest of the world.

8.2. Elements of China's Energy Security

Despite the fact that China became a net oil importer in 1993, the net imports were no more than 750,000 b/d (kb/d) and share of total oil consumption was under 20% between 1993 and 1998. Both volume of imports and the share have since increased rapidly. The share of net oil imports on total oil consumption increased from 18% in 1998 to 45% in 2005, 56% in 2010 and 57% in 2011.

Added to the rising import dependence are price volatility in the global oil markets and instability in the Middle East, energy security has already become a policy item and is visible in China's overall energy planning (Wu and Lim, 2008). As such, energy supply security in general and oil supply security in particular has become one of the top concerns for the Chinese government since the beginning of the new millennium (Zhao, 2010, Downs, 2006, Wu and Storey, 2008).

For China's 10th Five-Year Plan, two energy security items were incorporated for the first time. At the strategy level, the government set the following as one of four energy strategies for energy developments through 2005 — to optimize energy mix while ensuring the overall energy security. Specifically for oil and gas, the establishment of SPSs was written into the 10th Five-Year Plan for the first time. The plan called for the establishment of a petroleum storage system to ensure petroleum supply security and enhance the government's capability for stabilizing the market. During the 11th FYP (2006–2010), Phase I of the SPR system was actually completed. Diversification of petroleum imports is emphasized at the same time to reduce the overall risk of supply interruptions.

To formulate national energy security strategies, elements suggested by scholars and experts and considered by the government include the following (Xu and Yang, 2004; Zhang, 2002; Qin, 2004; Kennedy, 2010; Wu, 2007; Lewis, 2008):

- Adjust energy consumption and production structures and reduce dependence on oil through coal gasification, liquefaction, and development of nuclear power, etc.
- Establish strategic upstream oil and gas reserves in certain parts of the country, as well as, enhance domestic oil and gas exploration and production (E&P) activities.
- Actively participate in the formation of a regional community and establish a regional energy security system.
- Establish an oil futures market.
- Diversify the sources of oil and gas imports, increasing the share of oil and gas imports from Russia and Central Asia (Liao, 2006).
- Strengthen overseas investment by state oil companies, particularly in the Middle East, Asia Pacific, Russia, and Central Asia.
- Undertake different ways of trade to avoid transaction risks.
- Increase the investment in an oil and gas infrastructure and open more channels to imports.
- Establish government-controlled SPRs.
- Increase mandatory oil reserves for large oil companies.

In addition to the above, the following measures were also recommended to the Chinese government to deal with China's energy security issues (Xu, 2007; Chen, 2003; Gao, 2003):

- Form a centralized government agency for energy management.
- Draft, discuss, and implement a coherent national energy policy.
- Enhance energy information gathering and research capabilities.
- Establish efficient energy markets and get rid of elements in the energy managing system that hinders energy security formulation and implementation.
- Establish an energy security response system.
- Strengthen efforts on improving energy efficiency and conservation.
- Step up efforts on clean coal technologies and coal efficiency.
- Divide up domestic and global energy supply to different zones and define China's energy needs accordingly.

- Participate in or initiate more bilateral and multi-lateral cooperation on energy (Garrison, 2008; Wu *et al.*, 2008).
- Regard ocean transportation as an important element of China's energy security.
- Provide government and financial support to Chinese energy shipping companies.
- Encourage strategic cooperation between state oil and shipping companies.
- Use of more nuclear power.
- Promotion of renewable energy development.

In general, there are three dimensions for analyzing energy security: foreign policy and geopolitical dimension, economic dimension, and environmental dimension, although some (Clarke, 2010) may add military as the fourth dimension. For China, all three dimensions are intermingled with each other and drive the issue of energy security in the country. As such, key factors driving China's energy security strategy can be summarized as follows.

Economic factor: Ensuring China's long-term economic growth

The Chinese Communist Party (CCP) continues to rule the country under a one-party system. Political legitimacy of the government has been a question for CCP, particularly under today's global environment where democracy is the mainstream form of governance for most major countries in the world. CCP believes that one way to gain legitimacy, is to keep the economy growing continuously and vigorously over the long term. For the past three decades, they have been very successful in doing that. However, the challenge is mounting over the next 20 years and beyond. One of the biggest challenges is energy supply, where not only huge amounts of total energy but also high-quality fuels and security of energy supply are also needed. The Chinese government feels increasingly less certain if the current energy supply system is sufficient in meeting the challenge. The uncertainty has continued to drive the energy security issue to higher levels.

Geopolitical factor: Reducing China's energy vulnerabilities

With current rising imports of oil and future growth in oil and gas imports, China believes that it has become increasingly vulnerable to future energy supply interruption. Since the early 21st century, China has begun to look to Russia and possibly Central Asia as alternative routes for its future oil and gas imports. The change is gradual and it is not at all easy to develop an energy trade relationship with Russia and Central Asia, but China has since made a big progress in this area. Geopolitical concerns will continue to drive China's energy security policy.

Environmental factor: Protecting the environment and avoiding ecological degradation and disasters

China's energy security policy is also driven in part by the desire to protect the environment and avoid ecological degradation and disasters. Although there are advocates within the country calling for more use of coal as a way to address rising security issues, the mainstream view is still to continue China's current transformation to cleaner energy products with higher quality. For coal, China intends to adopt a more positive position by promoting advanced coal technologies and clean technologies. As such, the environmental factor has become an element in China's quest for energy security. In fact, the reason that China is so concerned about oil and gas security is to find a reliable way to use more oil and gas for the benefit of improving the energy consumption structure and protecting the worsening environmental conditions of the country.

8.3. SPRs: An Important Element of Energy Security Strategies

The goal of China's SPRs program is mainly to reduce the impact of a crude oil supply disruption. China first officially formalized the SPR program in the 10th Five-Year Program in 2001 and construction started on the 5.8 million m^3 Zhenhai base three years later in June 2004 (Wu and Zhang, 2009). By the end of 2008, construction of Phase I was completed, with a total capacity of 16.4 million m^3 (103 million barrels (mmb)). China is currently building the Phase II sites and aims to have them completed by 2012/2013, with a total planned storage capacity of 26.8 million m^3 (169 mmb). By 2015/2016, China aims to complete Phase III and bring the total SPR (Phases I, II, and III) to about 80 million m^3 (500 mmb).

The National Petroleum Reserve Center (NPRC), established in December 2007, is in charge of China's SPRs. The NPRC is supervised by the National Energy Administration (NEA), which is under the National Development and Reform Commission (NDRC). The NDRC is in charge of policy and planning of SPRs. The Administrator of the NEA, Mr. Liu Tienan, is also one of the ten NDRC vice chairmen. The NPRC organizes reserve base construction, procures oil, and makes utilization and turnover decisions. During Phase I, CNPC/PetroChina, Sinopec, and Sinochem were responsible for facilities construction, maintenance, and reserve site filling, all implemented on behalf of the NPRC.

The sites for China's SPR Phase I are Zhenhai, Zhoushan, Huangdao, and Dalian as shown in Construction began in 2004 and was completed at the end of 2008. All four sites are above ground, located in the coastal cities, and near refining centers. They were filled in March/April 2009 and Mr. Zhang Guobao, the former NEA Administrator, told the media in June 2009 that the average crude procured price for SPR Phase I was US$58/b. This implies that the government has approached crude purchases strategically and bought crudes when prices were perceived to be low. We believe that about 40 mmb of crudes were purchased from August 2006 to June 2007 and about 60 mmb of crudes were purchased from October 2008 to April 2009.

Under Phase II, eight strategic stockpiling bases with a total capacity of 26.8 million m^3 (169 mmb) are being built. Half of these projects have already been completed and the rest will be in place by late 2012 or early 2013. Furthermore, it is possible that the NDRC may decide to expand existing Phase I sites. While the four Phase I sites are all located at important coastal ports and above ground, the NDRC has shifted focus in selecting the Phase II sites. It has chosen sites in inland provinces, with access to various crude pipelines connecting to the international Kazakhstan–China, Russia–China, and maybe Myanmar–China crude. The NDRC is also testing underground facilities, with feasibility studies under way for several underground sites.

It is likely that some flexibility for operating the SPR sites is allowed and the government may be experimenting with different methods to run the SPR program. In fact, there are signs that China has actually allowed crudes from the initial four Phase I sites to be drawn and refilled. Overall, the NDRC could divide China's SPRs into three categories: a truly national SPRs, commercial storage by state oil companies, and commercial storage by local government or private companies.

Similar to the crude filling for Phase I, we expect that the government will continue to approach the crude fillings for Phase II strategically and only import crudes to fill their tanks when the market is weak. It is unlikely that China will import crudes for the SPR Phase II sites during a bullish crude market because of:

- High crude prices.
- Chinese government's sensitivity for being blamed as the one that pushes up the crude price.

Therefore, the impact of Chinese SPRs filling will be more to support a weak crude market rather than further pushing up a bullish market.

8.4. China's Overseas Oil and Gas Investments

China began investing in overseas upstream oil and gas areas in the 1990s and intensified its efforts in the latter part of the decade. Since 2000, Chinese state oil companies have made a bigger push to expand overseas, which is favored and encouraged by the Chinese government. The Chinese state oil companies have thus been taking advantage of the central government's growing concern over potential disruptions to their energy supplies to realize their desires of having larger business operations around the world. "Going out" has become part of the overall investment strategy for every state oil company in China. In recent years, China has increased its overseas investment for oil and gas assets in both numbers and size. China's total overseas investment since the 1990s is estimated to have amounted to over $90 billion by the end of 2011.

CNPC leads the charge in overseas upstream petroleum investment. CNOOC, through its publicly listed subsidiary CNOOC Limited, has followed CNPC's lead in the pursuit of overseas ventures. Sinopec, together with Sinopec Corp, comes in third in its overseas energy investment activities. In addition to these three, state oil trading company Sinochem Corporation, two non-oil state companies, China International Trust & Investment Company (CITIC) and ZhenHua Oil Company, and two Chinese sovereign wealth funds (SWEs) have also engaged or begun investing in oil and gas overseas.

All major Chinese oil and gas companies have become very aggressive in making direct acquisitions after the global financial crisis in 2008. China has since stepped-up direct acquisitions significantly, with the past three or four years accounting for about three quarters of the total amount of money spent since the early 1990s.

After slightly more than 10 years of overseas investment, Chinese overseas equity production reached about 1.3 mmb/d in 2010 (Fig. 8-1), which was more than the Japanese or Korean overseas equity crude production. The 2010 level has increased by 13% from the 2009. Of the total equity production in 2010, CNPC/PetroChina accounted for 58%, followed by Sinopec for 28% and CNOOC at 8%.

Across the regions, African and Former Soviet Union (FSU) countries (mainly Kazakhstan) made up the bulk of overseas equity crude production in 2010, with 45% and 32%, respectively. We believe that currently about half of equity production is brought back to China. Most of the Sudanese equity crude production and Kazakh production are brought back to China at the moment.

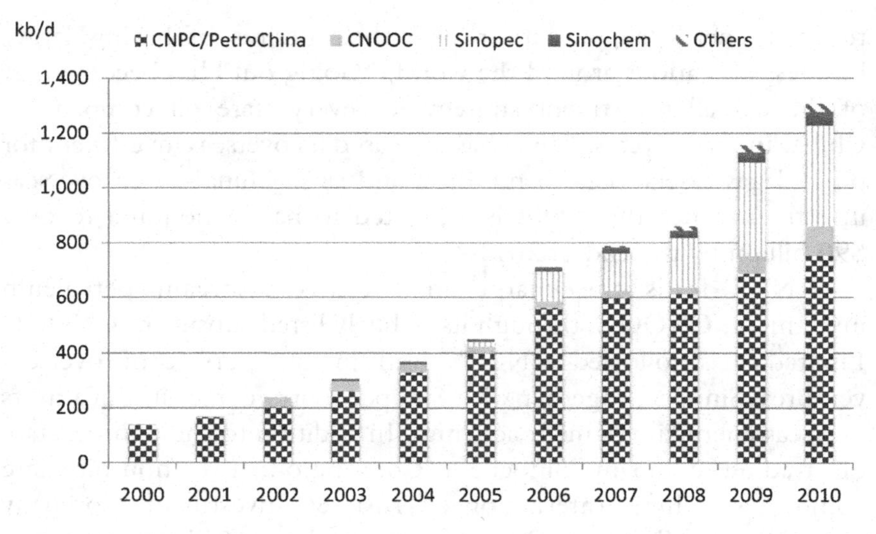

Fig. 8-1. China Overseas Equity Crude Production, 2000–2010.

CNPC/PetroChina

CNPC/PetroChina is currently engaged in some 100 overseas cooperative projects. The company owns oil and gas assets and interests in 27 countries and provides oil field services, engineering, and construction in 49 countries worldwide.

CNPC/PetroChina holds the dominant position in both upstream production and midstream distribution in China. CNPC/PetroChina has ambitions towards becoming an international oil and gas company, both in the upstream and downstream oil and gas business. The company has stated that the aim is to build a global downstream trading business. CNPC/PetroChina is also building infrastructure to import gas from Turkmenistan (operational), Myanmar (under construction), and possibly Russia.

CNPC/PetroChina is also the first Chinese state oil company to invest in the overseas petroleum sector. Oil production from fields that CNPC/PetroChina was involved in reached 1.5 mmb/d in 2009. CNPC/PetroChina's equity oil amounted to 752 kb/d in 2009, up from 137 kb/d in 2000 and 400 kb/d in 2005. Overall, CNPC/PetroChina's overseas petroleum investment activities are concentrated in Africa, South America, Central Asia, and the Middle East. More detailed investment projects in individual countries are reviewed as follows.

About 60% of the current overseas production of CNPC/PetroChina is from Sudan (about 230 kb/d) and Kazakhstan (about 200 kb/d). It is believed that most of the Sudanese and Kazakh crudes are exported back to China.

Sinopec

Sinopec began investing overseas later than CNPC/PetroChina and CNOOC. In 2010, Sinopec's equity oil production surged to 368 kb/d, up sharply from 90 kb/d in 2006.

Sinopec's upstream global upstream expansion is necessary and makes sense because the company needs oil to feed its domestic refineries. Additionally, there is the incentive to diversify its business away from China's downstream business, where prices are still under the control of the Chinese government. Sinopec has over 5 mmb/d in refinery assets mainly in the Yangtze River Delta, Pearl River Delta, and along the Bohai Bay areas, but Sinopec domestic crude output in China is about 850 kb/d, the required crude runs by its vast refineries. Therefore, Sinopec has said that it will make upstream oil assets acquisition the firm's priority for its globalization strategy. But it does not rule out the possibility of acquiring downstream assets if those assets prove attractive.

Currently, Sinopec is involved in over 30 overseas oil and gas projects in Angola, Iran, Algeria, Oman, and others. At the same time, Sinopec has managed to secure engineering and construction contracts to build or upgrade refineries in other countries like Iran.

CNOOC

CNOOC's overseas operations began in the mid-1990s. The company has around 35 overseas projects in 10 countries. CNOOC's overseas upstream assets are more focused on gas production. In 2010, overseas net oil production was 109 kb/d.

For overseas investment, CNOOC has repeatedly stated that it is value focused and will not buy overseas assets at an excessive price. There is recent evidence to support the company's statement. CNOOC has invested in Indonesia, Nigeria, Australia, Myanmar, and other countries.

Other Chinese oil and gas companies

Before the early 1990s, Sinochem held China's oil import and exports monopoly. Said monopoly has since eroded in the face of the expansion of Sinopec and CNPC/PetroChina. With a shrinking business scope in oil trading, Sinochem has begun expanding into upstream exploration and production along with refining and oil marketing, particularly after China's entry into the World Trade Organization (WTO). In 2001, the State Council granted Sinochem the rights to conduct overseas upstream oil and gas exploration and production activity. In March 2002, Sinochem setup the Sinochem Petroleum Exploration and Production Company Ltd for oversea investment. Compared with the other three Chinese state oil companies, Sinochem's overseas activities are less extensive. Sinochem is currently seeking opportunities in the Middle East, Africa, and Latin America.

Other Chinese companies that are interested in overseas oil and gas investment include Sinochem, CITIC, ZhenHua Oil Company, China Aviation Oil, as well as the Chinese SWEs.

Sinochem

Sinochem equity oil production from overseas projects is 49 kb/d in 2010.

CITIC

As far as energy is concerned, CITIC, through its Hong Kong–listed company CITIC Resources Holdings, has been investing in power plants and other power generation efforts. For the most part, their investments have been in China and Hong Kong, though they have, for example, been involved in building power generators for Uzbekistan as part of a political effort to strengthen ties with that country. CITIC's first move overseas is in Kazakhstan.

ZhenHua oil company

ZhenHua Oil is a small state-owned company established in 2003. Its business includes overseas petroleum investment, oil trade, and petrochemical investment in China. The parent company of ZhenHua Oil is China North Industries Group Corporation, who has links to the military. ZhenHua Oil's overseas operations include blocks in Syria, Kazakhstan, and Pakistan.

Yanchang petroleum

In April 2008, Yanchang Petroleum signed an agreement with Hong Kong–listed oil and petrochemicals company Sino Union and Towngas to develop an onshore block in Madagascar. Each company will contribute about US$150 million (estimated) to develop Block 3113 and will also jointly manage the block's exploration, production and operation. The block covers an area of 8,320 sq km (3,212 sq miles).

China's two Sovereign Wealth Funds (SWFs)

China's two SWFs for overseas energy investment refers to the State Administration of Foreign Exchange and China Investment Corp. (CIC). The former has investment Total, BP, and other companies while the latter also invests in energy and resources related companies. CIC has a partnership with Penn West Energy Trust, an Alberta Oil Sands Calgary-based company, to develop oil sands properties in the Peace River area of northern Alberta.

China cross-border crude pipelines

In addition to aggressively investing in overseas upstream assets, CNPC has also made substantial investment to build crude and gas pipelines to import oil and gas from overseas. Some of the crude pipelines have come online recently. CNPC is expanding the Kazakhstan-China pipeline from 200 kb/d to 400 kb/d, which could be operational by 2013/2014. PetroChina has started its 300 kb/d Russian-China pipeline in early 2011 for importing the ESPO crudes. Furthermore, CNPC started construction of a 440 kb/d crude oil pipeline from Myanmar to China.

Loan for oil deals

In addition to gaining overseas assets via corporate acquisition and bid rounds, China has taken advantage of the financial crisis' limited and expensive commercial credit by offering a total of US$90 billion in loans to several oil and gas producing countries. The concept of loans for oil was first introduced by China with the Angola oil-backed loan in 2004. China provided Angola with a US$4 billion oil-backed loan for energy, health, education, water, and infrastructure. China then extended the loan by anther US$500 million before signing a US$2 billion oil-backed loan in 2007. In early 2009, China provided another US$1 billion loan to Angola. As a result of these oil backed loans, China has forged a close relationship with Angola and about 40% of Angola's crude output (more than 700 kb/d) is currently exported to China. At the Shanghai Cooperation Organization meeting in February 2005, China agreed to a US$6 billion loan to Russia in exchange for Rosneft guaranteeing to supply 380 million barrels (averaging about 200 kb/d) up to 2010. In February 2009, China agreed to provide another US$15 billion loan to Russia's Rosneft and a US$10 billion loan to Transneft over the next 20 years. In return, Rosneft will export 300 kb/d of oil to China for 20 years, starting from 2011. China also signed loan deals with Venezuela, Kazakhstan, Brazil, Turkmenistan, Bolivia, Ecuador, and Ghana in exchange of long-term oil or gas supply. Those countries could repay the loan through revenues from oil sales, by selling upstream assets to Chinese oil and gas companies, or through supplying crudes to China. Given the limited credit and high interest rates available in the secondary market during the financial crisis time, it is very likely that Chinese lenders will be able to negotiate a good return on their investment in future loans for oil and gas deals. Furthermore, China wants to build goodwill with oil- and gas-producing countries by providing them with much needed capital.

Motives of China NOCs for overseas investments

Although high-profile oil diplomacy has helped Chinese NOCs to clinch deals, the Chinese NOCs usually recognize the opportunities first, initiate the negotiations over prospective investment, and move and seek the support of the government for financial and diplomatic support if needed (Zhang, Zhou and Ebbers, 2011; Wu, 2008).

The three Chinese NOCs are — their net profits are comparable to the international majors. The Chinese government allows the NOCs to keep their profits as long as they invest properly. More importantly, if the NOCs do not spend their profits quickly enough, it is possible that the government may get back those earnings. Hence, given the huge amount of cash they earned every year and the urgency to spend it, the NOCs aggressively expand to the overseas markets and they also demand a lower rate of return (than the IOCs) for their investment. Furthermore, compared to the domestic energy business, there is no prescribed limit to the kinds of business operations the NOCs or the Chinese private oil company like Yanchang Oil or Brightoil can invest in overseas. Thus, with both the freedom to maneuver and opportunity to grow bigger, oil and gas overseas investment are appealing to many Chinese companies. It is also usually easier to get the central government to approve overseas investment plans than it is for new domestic proposals.

The internal competition among the Chinese NOCs also shapes their overseas investment. The three NOCs (CNPC/PetroChina, Sinopec, and CNOOC) and other players (Sinochem, and a few others) justify their existence in many ways, including maintaining size through continuous expansion. Simply put, the larger the company, the more easily it can justify its importance and argue "what is good for it is good for the country." In the quest to outdo the others, the Chinese NOCs may not make their investment entirely based on commercial reasons. Also, some of their overseas investments are partly to help them to facilitate their domestic expansion or dominance. The Chinese companies also have many other motives similar to other foreign companies for overseas investments, such as seeking international profits, diversifying and fully capitalizing their technol-ogies and labor forces.

In short, with tighter global oil supply and the Chinese government's growing concern over energy security, the Chinese NOCs will continue their aggressive push in overseas oil and gas investments. We expect that the Chinese NOCs, but not the Chinese government, will take the lead in overseas investments as they did in the past. Because they have their individual strategies and motives, their overseas investments are poorly coordinated and they could still compete with each other for the same overseas projects, though this type of competition has increasingly been subject to the Chinese government scrutiny.

In a global context, the impact of China's overseas investments is growing fast. The Chinese NOCs have become huge competitors and key participants in global energy merger and acquisitions deals. Furthermore, they have committed to spend billions of dollars with its partners in exploring and developing giant oil and gas fields in the Middle East to increase global supply. On the one hand, the growing Chinese investment in the overseas oil and gas market may crowd out some private investment as well as investment from the state oil companies in the other countries such as those from India, Korea, Brazil, Malaysia, Russia, and others. On the other hand, the Chinese investment has also contributed to global oil supply positively. It remains to be seen if the Chinese NOCs will become more efficient and act as true global players through these overseas activities and competition.

8.5. Regional and Global Implications

8.5.1. *China's oil industry in the regional and global context*

At present, China is Asia's largest oil- and gas-consuming country, refiner, crude oil importer, as well as oil and gas producer as well (Wu and Fesharaki, 2007; Wu *et al.*, 2008). During the 2000–2010 period, China accounted for nearly 70% of incremental oil demand growth in the Asia-Pacific region. Over the next 10 to 20 years, the role of China in Asia's oil and gas markets will continue to grow.

8.5.2. *Outlook for regional oil production and product demand: Role of China*

The Asia-Pacific region has been the most important contributor to the global oil demand growth (Wu and O'Kray, 2007). Between 1990 and 2011, the total increase in oil demand for the world as a whole was approximately 23 mmb/d, of which nearly 15 mmb/d, or 66%, came from Asia (Table 8-1). The region has been largest oil consumer in the world after surpassing North America in 2007 (IEA, 2010; IEA, 2012).

Overall, Asia's demand growth is significantly higher than the oil demand growth for the world as a whole. As a result, the share of the Asia-Pacific region in world total oil demand is expected to rise from 31% in 2011 to 35% in 2020 and 36% in 2030. Back in 1990, the Asia-Pacific region accounted for 20% of the world oil demand. Since the beginning of millennium, the Asia-Pacific region's demand growth has been driven primarily by China as well as India. China's role can be assessed from various angles.

- Between 2000 and 2011, the incremental demand of the Asia-Pacific region was 7.5 mmb/d, of which 71% or 5.4 mmb/d was in China.
- In 2011, China accounted for 35% of the Asia Pacific's petroleum product demand. The share was 15% in 1990 and 21% in 2000 (Fig. 8-2). China's share in the world oil demand also increased from 3.0% in 1990 to 10.9% in 2011.
- In 2004, China surpassed Japan to be region's largest oil-consuming country. In 2010, China registered a demand increase of some 1 mmb/d, over 70% of the growth seen in the Asia-Pacific region as a whole.

Table 8-1. Global and Asian Incremental Oil Demand, 1990–2011 (kb/d).

Year	World	Asia-Pacific Region	Share of AP (%)
1990	390	639	163.9
1991	520	661	127.1
1992	530	773	145.9
1993	120	812	676.3
1994	920	766	83.2
1995	1,218	1,101	90.4
1996	2,003	827	41.3
1997	1,783	821	46.0
1998	751	(286)	—
1999	1,623	970	59.8
2000	671	307	45.8
2001	711	194	27.3
2002	650	585	89.9
2003	1,597	737	46.2
2004	2,967	1,109	37.4
2005	1,672	606	36.3
2006	1,049	761	72.5
2007	1,300	737	56.7
2008	(270)	47	—
2009	(1,060)	473	—
2010	2,820	1,422	51.5
2011	780	838	107.5
TOTAL	**22,685**	**14,901**	**65.7**

Notes:
[1]World is from IEA April 2012 OMR.
[2]AP is from DBS12.

- Between 2011 and 2030, the region's demand will increase by 10.6 mmb/d under our base-case scenario, of which the 6.6 mmb/d is expected to be in China, which is over 60%.
- As result, the share of China in Asia's total oil demand is expected to increase to 43% by 2030 (Fig. 8-3) (FGE, 2011; EIA, 2011a, 2011b, 2011c, and 2012; BP 2011).
- However, unless US experiences a huge decline, China is unlikely to surpass the latter to be the world's largest oil-consuming country until after the middle of the next decade.

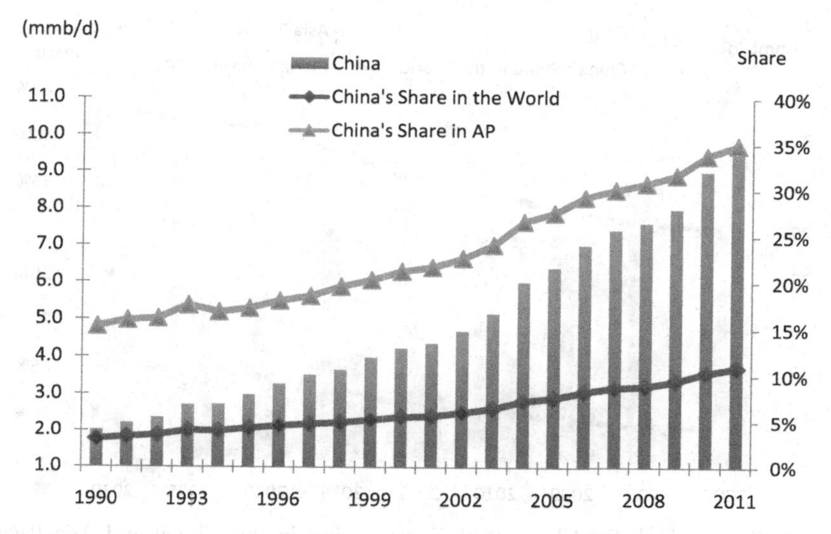

Fig. 8-2. China's Oil Consumption in the Global and Asia Pacific Regional Contexts, 1990–2011.

Note: 2011 data are preliminary.

8.5.3. *Outlook for regional oil production and role of China*

While the Asia-Pacific region's demand for oil is surging, its own production can satisfy only half of its needs. Adding the Russian Far East, whose crudes are exported to Asia, the major oil producers in Asia and the Pacific are China, Indonesia, Malaysia, India, Australia, Vietnam, Brunei, and Thailand. These eight countries plus the Russian Far East accounted for 97% of the total regional crude production in 2010. In 2010, the Asia-Pacific region's crude oil production was 8.09 million b/d, up from 7.77 million b/d in 2009.

Toward 2020, an increase in oil production is expected to be seen in China, India, Malaysia, and the Russian Far East, and to a lesser extent Thailand, the Philippines, and Brunei. However, production is forecast to decline in Indonesia, Australia, and a few other countries. Overall regional production, under the base-case scenario, is forecast to grow gradually by 2015, reaching 8.55 mmb/d but decline to 8.33 mmb/d in 2020 (see Table 7-1).

Since Asian crude production is unable to satisfy existing regional oil demand, the gap between supply and demand continues to widen.

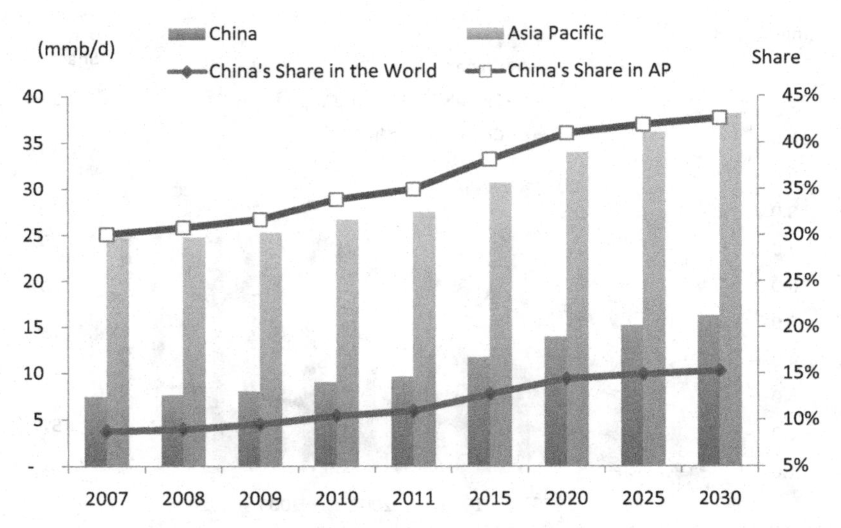

Fig. 8-3. Outlook for China's Oil Consumption in the Global and Asia-Pacific Regional Context.

Note: 2015–2030 data are forecasts.

The result will be a major increase in oil import dependence. In 2010, the net oil import requirements of the Asia-Pacific region amounted to 18.6 million b/d, about 69% of regional product consumption. Based on our base-case projections, the region's overall oil import dependence is expected to rise to 70% by 2015 and 74% by 2020. As such, the net oil import requirements, including both crude and refined products, are forecast to reach 24.7 million b/d by 2020.

The Asia-Pacific region is a net importer of both crude oil and refined products. While the situation for refined products will be discussed later, the deficit for crude oil is much larger, simply because of the huge refining capacity built in the region. Asia's crude imports come in part from within the region, but more is from outside the region. As for extra-regional imports to Asia, the Middle East plays a dominant role both at present (Fig. 8-4) and by 2020.

China's impact on the regional oil market has been reflected in its evolving and changing role, as both an oil importer and an exporter during the past two plus decades, and this will continue for many years to come. As such, China's influence on Asia's oil supply and trade can be summarized as follows:

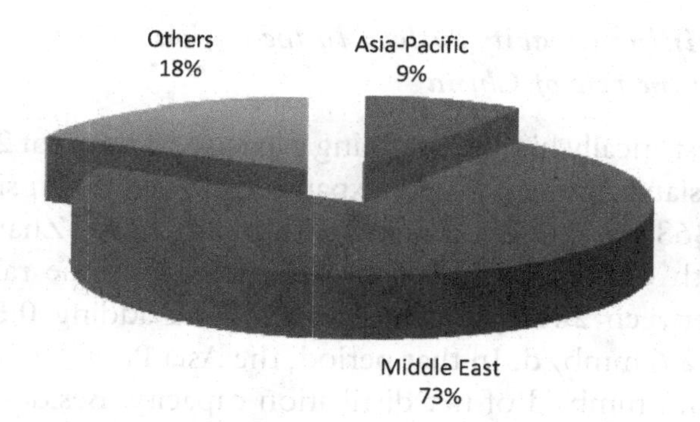

Fig. 8-4. Crude Oil Imports of the Asia-Pacific Region: 2010.

Note: Total crude imports: 18.3 million b/d.

- Despite its huge and growing oil imports, China is still Asia's largest oil producer. In 2010, China produced 4.06 mmb/d of crude oil, accounting for 50% of the regional total. This share was higher than 43% for both 1990 and 2000. In fact, due to the unprecedented growth from offshore oil fields, China's increment oil production in 2010 accounted for 85% of the net growth of oil output for the region.
- In 2010, China imported 4.8 mmb/d of crude oil, accounting for 26% of the region's total imports. China is the region's largest crude oil importer.
- By 2020, China will still be the region's largest crude oil producer and its share in the region is expected to increase slightly to 51%.
- By 2020, we expect China to import 9.7 mmb/d of crude oil, accounting for around 40% of the region's projected crude imports.
- As a crude oil exporter, China's role is shrinking. In 2010 China's crude exports were only 21 kb/d. Back in 1985, China was the region's largest crude exporter. Toward 2020, China's crude exports are expected to go below 10 kb/d.
- China's gross oil imports — including both crude oil and refined products — are expected to increase rapidly. The gross imports are expected to amount to 7.3 million b/d in 2015 and 9.5 million b/d by 2020, playing a leading role in the region's total imports.

8.5.4. *Refining capacity outlook in the region and the role of China*

After the historically high net refining capacity addition of 2.2 mmb/d in 2009, Asian refining capacity expansion slowed down significantly, with only 368 kb/d of net refining addition in 2010 (Zhang and Wu, 2011). Both China and India have plans to continue raising CDU capacity between 2011 and 2015, with India adding 0.52 mmb/d and China 2.6 mmb/d. In that period, the Asia Pacific will add a total of almost 3.3 mmb/d of net distillation capacity. Besides China and India, Pakistan and Vietnam are likely to expand their refining capacity by 140 kb/d and 200 kb/d, respectively, by end 2015.

Asian primary distillation capacity at the start of 2011 was 29.4 mmb/d. Between the start of 2011 and the end of 2015, Asian refining capacity is set to increase by 3.1 mmb/d on a net basis, raising the net regional CDU capacity to around 32.5 mmb/d. Between the beginning of 2016 and end of 2020, it is likely that the Asia-Pacific region will add another 2.9 mmb/d of capacity, raising the total to 35.4 mmb/d.

More specifically, China's role in Asia's refining sector and future buildup can be seen as follows.

- Overall, China plays an important role in the Asia Pacific regional refining capacity expansion. China's refining capacity at the start of 2011 accounted for about 39% of the region's total (Fig. 8-5).
- By 2015, China's CDU is expected to increase to 13.9 million b/d, or 43% of the regional total.
- Toward the end of 2020, China's CDU capacity is likely to increase further to 16.1 mmb/d, accounting for 46% of the regional total.
- In other words, between the start of 2011 and the end of 2020, the region is likely to add 5.9 mmb/d of total CDU capacity on a net basis, of which nearly 80% is expected to be in China.
- Indeed, China will continue to be the largest refiner of the region for the rest of the decade, racing to the top to surpass the US to be the world's largest refinery beyond 2020.

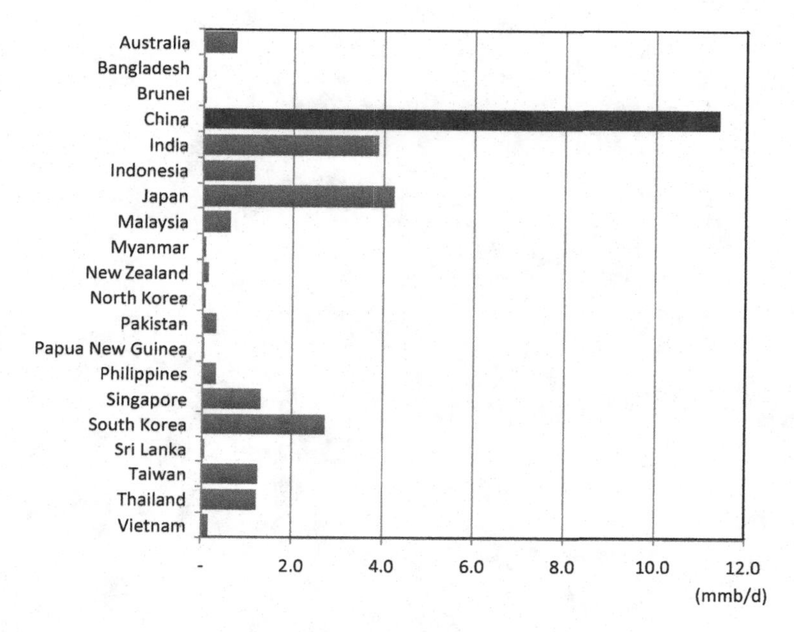

Fig. 8-5. Asia Pacific Distillation Capacity, Start of 2011.

8.5.5. *China's gas industry in the regional and global context*

In the Asia-Pacific region:

- Until 2009, China was the smallest LNG importer in the region.
- It overtook India in 2010 to be the fourth largest LNG importer. In 2011, China remained the fourth largest importer after passing Taiwan but India's imports were slightly ahead of China's again.
- It is likely to surpass Taiwan to be the third largest LNG importer in Asia in 2011.
- By 2020, its LNG imports are likely to be on par with that of Korea.
- In terms of total natural gas consumption, China surpassed Japan to be the largest in 2009.
- China is the only country in Asia that imports LNG and pipeline gas simultaneously.

[illegible] Sources: [illegible] 2011.

8.5.5 [illegible] in the Asia Pacific region

- [illegible] LNG [illegible] region. [illegible] 2010 [illegible] Taiwan [illegible] LNG [illegible] Japan [illegible] Taiwan [illegible] the third largest LNG importer in Asia in 2011.
- [illegible] in 2006.
- China [illegible] LNG [illegible]

chapter 9

Regional Developments and Future Growth

This chapter presents an analysis of the provincial and regional demand, supply, and net balances for oil (by products) and natural gas in 1995, 2000, and 2005–2010, with projections to 2015, 2020, 2025, and 2030. The chapter organized as follows: Section 9.1 describes how the country is divided into eight regions for this book, instead of the traditional six. Section 9.2 discusses social and economic developments and differences among the regions. Regional production and consumption of natural gas are reviewed in Section 9.3, while distribution of other primary energy production is provided in Section 9.4. The future growth is presented in Section 9.5 for oil and Section 9.6 for natural gas.

9.1. Division of Regions

Ever since the People's Republic of China was founded in 1949, the country has been divided into six regions, which were originally where regional bureaus of the Chinese Communist Party (CCP) were seated in the 1950s and part of the 1960s. After the CCP abolished those regional bureaus, the way of dividing the country into six regions remained. The regions shown in Fig. 9-1 are Northeast China, North China, East China, Central South China, Southwest China, and Northwest China.

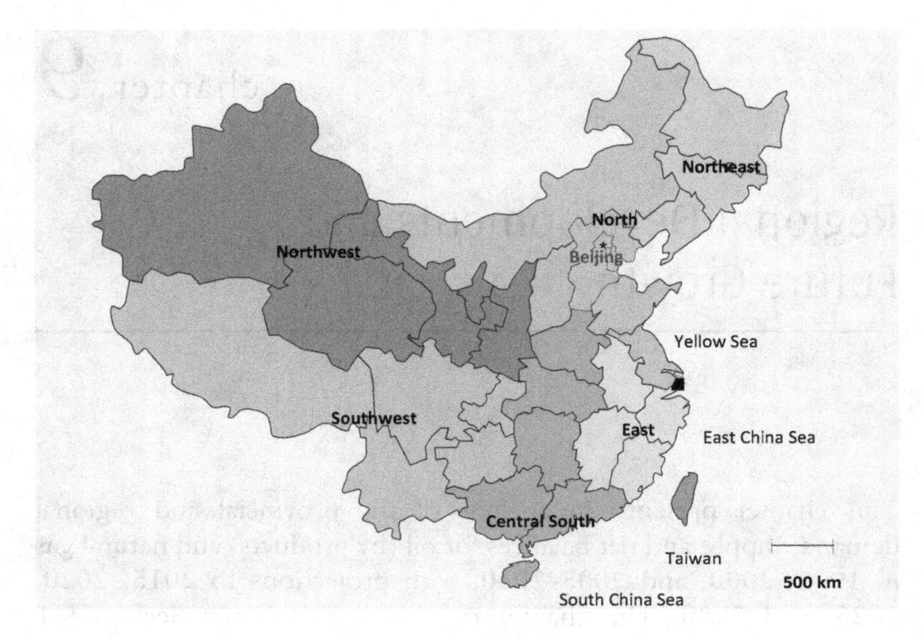

Fig. 9-1. Traditional Division of Regions.

Note: This is an illustrative nonofficial map of China.

The grouping of provinces in this way is not necessarily suitable for our study in which downstream oil sector developments and petroleum products demand, supply, and net balances are analyzed. To better understand China's oil sector developments, refining business, and petroleum products demand and supply today, in this book, we divide the country into eight regions that reflect current differences in regional developments, particularly the rapid growth and role of the coastal provinces in China's economic development and energy consumption.

These eight regions are the Northeast, the North, the Middle Yangtze, the Lower Yangtze, the South, the Southwest, the Northwest, and the West (shown in Fig. 9-2). Under this new division, the fast-growing Guangdong Province in South China is in the same group as the adjacent coastal province of Fujian, and the northern province of Shandong is in the same group as Shanxi, Tianjin, and Beijing.

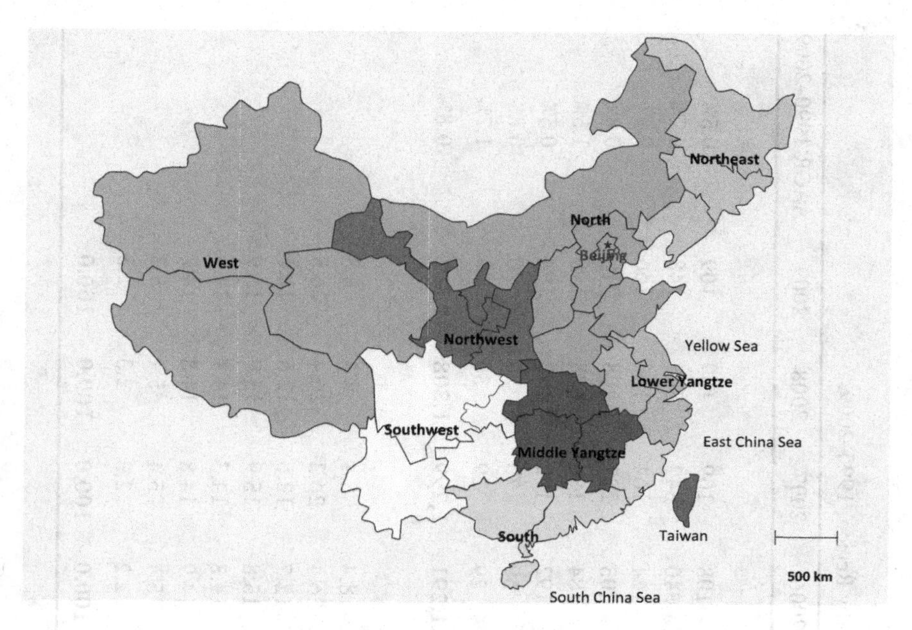

Fig. 9-2. New Division of Regions.

Note: This is an illustrative nonofficial map of China.

9.2. Overview of Regional Economic Development

The total land area of China (mainland), excluding Taiwan, Hong Kong, and Macao, is 9.6 million sq km (3.7 million sq miles). The largest geographic region is the West, followed by the North and the Southwest. The smallest region is the Lower Yangtze region.

The most populous region is the North, with 348 million people, accounting for 26.5% of China's total in 2009, followed by the Lower Yangtze and the Southwest regions. The West (including Tibet) is the least populated region (Table 9-1). In terms of the size of the economy measured by real GDP at the provincial level, the North is the largest region, followed by Lower Yangtze and the South. In comparison, the shares of the West and the Northwest are the lowest (Table 9-2 and Table 9-3). During the past 19 years between 1990 and 2009, the South demonstrated the highest real GDP growth, followed by the Lower Yangtze, the North, and the Middle Yangtze regions.

Table 9-1. Year-end Population by Region, 1990–2009.

	1990	1995	2000	2005	2006	2007	2008	2009	AAGR 1990–2009
Population (million)									
Northeast	100	104	107	108	108	109	109	109	0.5%
North	303	318	331	338	340	342	345	348	0.7%
Middle Yangtze	154	162	166	163	164	164	165	166	0.4%
Lower Yangtze	179	188	198	203	205	207	208	210	0.8%
South	143	154	174	182	184	186	188	190	1.5%
Southwest	178	188	192	192	192	192	193	194	0.5%
Northwest	60	65	67	69	69	70	70	70	0.8%
West	22	24	27	28	29	29	30	30	1.7%
TOTAL	**1,140**	**1,203**	**1,262**	**1,283**	**1,291**	**1,299**	**1,308**	**1,317**	**0.8%**
Share (percent)									
Northeast	8.8	8.6	8.4	8.4	8.4	8.4	8.3	8.3	
North	26.6	26.4	26.3	26.3	26.4	26.3	26.4	26.5	
Middle Yangtze	13.5	13.5	13.2	12.7	12.7	12.6	12.6	12.6	
Lower Yangtze	15.7	15.6	15.7	15.8	15.8	15.9	15.9	15.9	
South	12.6	12.8	13.8	14.2	14.3	14.3	14.4	14.4	
Southwest	15.6	15.7	15.2	15.0	14.9	14.8	14.8	14.7	
Northwest	5.3	5.4	5.3	5.4	5.4	5.4	5.4	5.3	
West	1.9	2.0	2.1	2.2	2.2	2.3	2.3	2.3	
Total	**100.0**	**100.0**	**100.0**	**100.0**	**100.0**	**100.0**	**100.0**	**100.0**	

Table 9-2. Regional GDP in Yuan, 1990–2009.

	1990	1995	2000	2005	2006	2007	2008	2009	AAGR 1990–2009
GDP (constant 2009 bn yuan)									
Northeast	457	724	1,111	1,866	2,123	2,428	2,757	3,108	10.6%
North	1,174	2,202	3,619	6,557	7,502	8,603	9,624	10,739	12.4%
Middle Yangtze	420	751	1,222	2,024	2,284	2,613	2,967	3,368	11.6%
Lower Yangtze	780	1,689	2,852	5,120	5,832	6,696	7,459	8,256	13.2%
South	547	1,290	2,111	3,765	4,315	4,963	5,518	6,113	13.5%
Southwest	483	797	1,139	1,879	2,119	2,423	2,706	3,076	10.2%
Northwest	187	293	454	776	877	1,004	1,147	1,291	10.7%
West	93	156	232	381	425	479	533	580	10.1%
TOTAL	**4,141**	**7,901**	**12,739**	**22,368**	**25,477**	**29,209**	**32,711**	**36,530**	**12.1%**
Share (percent)									
Northeast	11.0	9.2	8.7	8.3	8.3	8.3	8.4	8.5	
North	28.3	27.9	28.4	29.3	29.4	29.5	29.4	29.4	
Middle Yangtze	10.1	9.5	9.6	9.0	9.0	8.9	9.1	9.2	
Lower Yangtze	18.8	21.4	22.4	22.9	22.9	22.9	22.8	22.6	
South	13.2	16.6	16.3	16.8	16.9	17.0	16.9	16.7	
Southwest	11.7	10.1	8.9	8.4	8.3	8.3	8.3	8.4	
Northwest	4.5	3.7	3.6	3.5	3.4	3.4	3.5	3.5	
West	2.3	2.0	1.8	1.7	1.7	1.6	1.6	1.6	
Total	**100.0**	**100.0**	**100.0**	**100.0**	**100.0**	**100.0**	**100.0**	**100.0**	

Table 9-3. Regional GDP in US Dollar, 1990–2009.

	1990	1995	2000	2005	2006	2007	2008	2009	AAGR 1990–2009
GDP (constant 2009 US$ bn)									
Northeast	66.9	106.0	162.7	273.2	310.8	355.5	403.6	455.0	10.6%
North	171.9	322.4	529.9	960.0	1,098.4	1,259.6	1,409.1	1,572.3	12.4%
Middle Yangtze	61.5	109.9	178.9	296.3	334.4	382.6	434.5	493.1	11.6%
Lower Yangtze	114.2	247.3	417.5	749.6	853.9	980.4	1,092.0	1,208.7	13.2%
South	80.1	188.8	309.0	551.2	631.8	726.6	807.9	895.1	13.5%
Southwest	70.7	116.7	166.7	275.1	310.3	354.8	396.2	450.4	10.2%
Northwest	27.4	42.8	66.5	113.6	128.4	147.0	168.0	189.0	10.7%
West	13.7	22.8	33.9	55.8	62.3	70.1	78.1	84.9	10.1%
TOTAL	**606.3**	**1,156.7**	**1,865.2**	**3,274.9**	**3,730.2**	**4,276.6**	**4,789.4**	**5,348.5**	**12.1%**
Share (percent)									
Northeast	11.0	9.2	8.7	8.3	8.3	8.3	8.4	8.5	
North	28.3	27.9	28.4	29.3	29.4	29.5	29.4	29.4	
Middle Yangtze	10.1	9.5	9.6	9.0	9.0	8.9	9.1	9.2	
Lower Yangtze	18.8	21.4	22.4	22.9	22.9	22.9	22.8	22.6	
South	13.2	16.3	16.6	16.8	16.9	17.0	16.9	16.7	
Southwest	11.7	10.1	8.9	8.4	8.3	8.3	8.3	8.4	
Northwest	4.5	3.7	3.6	3.5	3.4	3.4	3.5	3.5	
West	2.3	2.0	1.8	1.7	1.7	1.6	1.6	1.6	
Total	**100.0**	**100.0**	**100.0**	**100.0**	**100.0**	**100.0**	**100.0**	**100.0**	

The richest region in terms of per-capita GDP is the Lower Yangtze region, followed by the South and the North. The Southwest and Northwest are the poorest, with a per-capita GDP well below the national average (Table 9-4). Overall, four regions (the Lower Yangtze, South, North, and Northeast), which are all in Eastern China, are above the national average, and the other four are below it.

The fact that the growth of real GDP in the Southwest and Northwest regions is below the national average suggests that regional income inequality has been growing. In 1990, the per-capita GDP of the Southwest region was 75% of the national average and 59% of the North (the richest region then). In 2009, the Southwest region's per-capita GDP was only 57% of the national average and 40% of Lower Yangtze (the richest region).

China's merchandize exports and imports have been growing rapidly for over two decades. In 2004, the Lower Yangtze region took over the South as China's largest importing region. In 2005, it surpassed the South again to be the largest exporting region (Table 9-5). Together, the Lower Yangtze and the South accounted for 76% of China's total exports and 68% of the total imports in 2009.

If the share of the volume of foreign trade (exports or imports) in total GDP can be loosely regarded as a basic indicator of the "openness" of the economy, South China and the Lower Yangtze region are way ahead of the other regions (see Table 9-6).

China is the largest recipient of foreign investment in the developing world. At the end of 2009, total registered foreign capital in China amounted to US$1.1 trillion, of which nearly 40% was in the Lower Yangtze region, followed by the South at 26% and the North at 17% (Table 9-6). The West and Northwest had only 0.3% and 0.9%, respectively, of the country's total registered foreign capital at the end of 2009. Of the 434,000 foreign-funded enterprises that remained registered at the end of 2009, 31% were located in the Lower Yangtze region, 28% in the South, and 22% in the North.

Table 9-4. Regional Per Capita GDP in US Dollar, 1990–2009.

	1990	1995	2000	2005	2006	2007	2008	2009	AAGR 1990–2009
GDP (constant 2009 US Dollars)[a]									
Northeast	669	1,021	1,527	2,540	2,873	3,276	3,712	4,180	10.1%
North	567	1,014	1,599	2,840	3,228	3,681	4,081	4,515	11.5%
Middle Yangtze	400	677	1,077	1,813	2,042	2,330	2,635	2,978	11.1%
Lower Yangtze	636	1,314	2,111	3,698	4,174	4,745	5,245	5,768	12.3%
South	560	1,228	1,777	3,026	3,430	3,897	4,293	4,715	11.9%
Southwest	397	620	867	1,434	1,615	1,846	2,051	2,320	9.7%
Northwest	454	663	988	1,644	1,849	2,108	2,397	2,688	9.8%
West	622	956	1,254	1,972	2,162	2,391	2,626	2,825	8.3%
Average of All[b]	**532**	**962**	**1,478**	**2,552**	**2,889**	**3,292**	**3,661**	**4,062**	**11.3%**
In Comparison with the National Average (percent)									
Northeast	126	106	103	100	99	100	101	103	
North	107	105	108	111	112	112	111	111	
Middle Yangtze	75	70	73	71	71	71	72	73	
Lower Yangtze	120	137	143	145	145	144	143	142	
South	105	128	120	119	119	118	117	116	
Southwest	75	64	59	56	56	56	56	57	
Northwest	85	69	67	64	64	64	65	66	
West	117	99	85	77	75	73	72	70	
Total	**100**	**100**	**100**	**100**	**100**	**100**	**100**	**100**	

[a]The average exchange rate in 2009 is 6.83 yuan per US dollar.
[b]The average of all regions may be different from the reported national average.

Table 9-5. Merchandise Exports and Imports by Region, 1993–2009.

									AAGR	Trade/GDP
	1993	1995	2000	2005	2006	2007	2008	2009	1993–2009	Ratio in 2009*
Exports (US$ bn)										
Northeast	9.2	11.2	14.5	33.2	38.5	49.7	56.4	42.4	10.0%	9.3%
North	13.4	25.7	39.5	118.4	149.6	190.9	233.4	178.1	17.5%	11.3%
Middle Yangtze	2.9	4.0	4.7	10.7	15.0	20.1	28.0	23.2	13.8%	4.7%
Lower Yangtze	18.6	32.8	73.6	297.8	385.7	490.4	584.5	499.5	22.8%	41.3%
South	43.8	69.3	109.3	280.6	352.1	429.1	475.7	420.2	15.2%	46.9%
Southwest	2.2	3.6	4.1	10.0	13.2	17.9	23.2	20.8	15.0%	4.6%
Northwest	1.0	1.5	2.1	5.8	7.1	8.4	10.2	5.9	12.1%	3.1%
West	0.6	0.6	1.4	5.4	7.7	11.3	19.2	11.4	20.8%	13.4%
Total	**91.7**	**148.8**	**249.2**	**762.0**	**968.9**	**1,217.8**	**1,430.7**	**1,201.6**	**17.4%**	**22.5%**
Imports (US$bn)										
Northeast	7.8	9.4	12.5	31.6	36.7	45.2	59.8	52.7	12.6%	11.6%
North	16.8	27.5	43.9	121.6	149.0	180.5	237.6	218.7	17.4%	13.9%
Mid Yangtze	3.0	3.5	4.2	11.2	12.3	15.7	21.9	19.9	12.5%	4.0%
Lower Yangtze	20.7	26.0	65.5	255.2	306.9	370.7	423.8	366.1	19.7%	30.3%
South	51.3	59.6	92.5	223.2	265.6	316.2	353.3	315.1	12.0%	35.2%

(*Continued*)

Table 9-5. (*Continued*)

									AAGR	Trade/GDP
	1993	1995	2000	2005	2006	2007	2008	2009	1993–2009	Ratio in 2009*
Southwest	2.2	3.4	3.3	8.9	11.4	14.9	19.9	18.6	14.3%	4.1%
Northwest	1.3	1.4	1.5	4.6	5.9	7.7	9.4	9.2	12.9%	4.9%
West	0.8	1.2	1.6	3.5	3.6	5.1	6.9	5.8	13.0%	6.8%
Total	**104.0**	**132.1**	**225.1**	**660.0**	**791.5**	**956.0**	1,132.6	**1,005.9**	**15.2%**	**18.8%**
Total Trade (US$ bn)										
Northeast	17.1	20.6	27.0	64.9	75.2	94.9	116.2	95.1	11.3%	20.9%
North	30.2	53.2	83.4	240.0	298.6	371.4	471.0	396.8	17.5%	25.2%
Middle Yangtze	5.9	7.6	8.9	21.9	27.3	35.8	50.0	43.1	13.2%	8.7%
Lower Yangtze	39.3	58.8	139.1	553.1	692.6	861.1	1,008.3	865.6	21.3%	71.6%
South	95.1	128.8	201.8	503.9	617.7	745.2	829.0	735.3	13.6%	82.1%
Southwest	4.4	7.0	7.4	18.9	24.6	32.8	43.1	39.4	14.7%	8.8%
Northwest	2.3	3.0	3.6	10.3	13.0	16.1	19.6	15.1	12.6%	8.0%
West	1.4	1.8	3.0	8.9	11.4	16.4	26.1	17.1	17.1%	20.2%
Total	**195.7**	**280.8**	**474.3**	**1,421.9**	**1,760.4**	**2,173.7**	**2,563.3**	**2,207.5**	**16.4%**	**41.3%**

*Refers to the ratio of exports or imports to regional GDP.

Table 9-6. Registered Foreign Capital and Foreign-Funded Enterprises by Region at the Year-end, 2008–2009.

	Foreign Capital (US$bn)		Foreign-Funded Enterprises	
Region	2008	2009	2008	2009
Northeast	78.4	85.2	32,380	30,053
North	170.9	188.6	95,269	93,605
Middle Yangtze	43.5	48.1	19,285	19,279
Lower Yangtze	407.2	436.2	135,516	136,350
South	256.9	278.8	123,141	122,720
Southwest	36.6	41.8	20,016	21,814
Northwest	7.7	9.6	7,091	7,811
West	3.3	3.4	2,003	2,377
TOTAL	**1,004.5**	**1,091.8**	**434,701**	**434,009**
Share (percent)				
Northeast	7.8	7.8	7.4	6.9
North	17.0	17.3	21.9	21.6
Middle Yangtze	4.3	4.4	4.4	4.4
Lower Yangtze	40.5	40.0	31.2	31.4
South	25.6	25.5	28.3	28.3
Southwest	3.6	3.8	4.6	5.0
Northwest	0.8	0.9	1.6	1.8
West	0.3	0.3	0.5	0.5
Total	**100.0**	**100.0**	**100.0**	**100.0**

9.3. Regional Distribution of Primary Energy Production

Determined largely by the pattern of resource distribution, the output of each of the primary energy sources is distributed in its own way. Oil and gas production is less evenly distributed than coal and power. The Southwest is unique in hydroelectric development, while the supply of nuclear power is concentrated in only three provinces so far — Zhejiang, Guangdong, and Jiangsu.

Table 9-7. Regional Distribution of Crude Oil Production, 1990–2009.

	1990	1995	2000	2005	2006	2007	2008	2009	AAGR 1990–2009
Output (kb/d)									
Northeast	1,458	1,499	1,407	1,266	1,249	1,200	1,184	1,128	(1.3%)
North	1,055	949	902	1,111	1,160	1,172	1,182	1,240	0.9%
Mid Yangtze	17	17	15	16	16	17	17	16	(0.1%)
Lower Yangtze	18	20	41	38	42	43	40	39	4.1%
South	12	131	279	297	270	255	278	273	17.8%
Southwest	3	5	3	3	4	4	5	4	1.5%
Northwest	48	95	188	371	414	470	508	550	13.6%
West	156	284	409	526	540	565	587	540	6.8%
Total	**2,766**	**3,001**	**3,244**	**3,627**	**3,695**	**3,726**	**3,800**	**3,790**	**1.7%**
Share (percent)									
Northeast	52.7	50.0	43.4	34.9	33.8	32.2	31.2	29.8	
North	38.1	31.6	27.8	30.6	31.4	31.5	31.1	32.7	
Middle Yangtze	0.6	0.6	0.5	0.4	0.4	0.5	0.4	0.4	
Lower Yangtze	0.7	0.7	1.3	1.0	1.1	1.2	1.0	1.0	
South	0.4	4.4	8.6	8.2	7.3	6.8	7.3	7.2	
Southwest	0.1	0.2	0.1	0.1	0.1	0.1	0.1	0.1	
Northwest	1.7	3.2	5.8	10.2	11.2	12.6	13.4	14.5	
West	5.6	9.5	12.6	14.5	14.6	15.2	15.4	14.2	
Total	**100.0**	**100.0**	**100.0**	**100.0**	**100.0**	**100.0**	**100.0**	**100.0**	

9.3.1. *Oil*

The Northeast lost its status as the largest crude oil–producing region in 2009 (Table 9-7). The region had a negative growth in total oil production from 1990 to 2009, and its share in the national total had a sharp decline, from 53% in 1990 to 30% in 2009. The largest oil-producing region is now the North, whose share in the national total also declined during the 1990–2009 period from 38% to 33%. The third largest oil-producing region is the Northwest, where oil production is growing from the Ordos Basin. This is followed by the West, including the Tarim, Junggar, Yumen, Tu-Ha, and Qaidam basins. However, production from the West declined for the first time in 2009. The fastest growing area is the South since 1990, thanks to the surge in offshore oil production, followed by the Northwest, where the promising Ordos Basin is located, and the West. Among the other regions of the country, production was virtually flat in the Southwest and the Middle and Lower Yangtze regions since 2000. Altogether, the eastern part of China, including the Northeast, North, the Middle and Lower Yangtze regions, and the South, is still the dominant producer of crude oil in China. But the western part, consisting of just the West, Northwest, and Southwest, increased its share in total production from 7% in 1990 to 29% in 2009.

9.3.2. *Natural gas*

Until 2005, the Southwest region stood out as China's largest natural gas producer because of the large Sichuan gas field (Table 9-8). In 2006, the West overtook the Southwest as the largest natural gas–producing region in China. From 1990 to 2009, the share of the Southwest region in China's total natural gas production declined notably from 44% in 1990 to 23% in 2009. Of course, both the Northeast and North had sharper declines in shares of the national total, from 29% and 23% in 1990, respectively, to merely 6% and 8% in 2009, similar to the South where the gas production comes entirely from offshore fields. During the same period, the share of the West in the national total rose from 4% in 1990 to 34% in 2009, while the share of the Northwest was up from under 1% to 22%.

9.3.3. *Coal*

While 19 provinces produce at least some oil, as many as 25 provinces in China produce at least some coal. However, the North dominates

Table 9-8. Regional Distribution of Natural Gas Production, 1990–2009.

	1990	1995	2000	2005	2006	2007	2008	2009	AAGR 1990–2009
Output (mmscf/d)									
Northeast	424	473	385	402	377	382	430	481	0.7%
North	343	346	404	468	487	426	439	617	3.1%
Middle Yangtze	7	7	9	11	11	11	53	16	4.2%
Lower Yangtze	4	2	28	65	60	55	47	45	14.0%
South*	0	10	335	504	493	527	601	583	33.7%
Southwest	643	759	883	1,444	1,612	1,863	1,954	1,880	5.8%
Northwest	5	19	208	788	793	1,071	1,392	1,836	37.1%
West	54	120	380	1,248	1,831	2,363	2,700	2,791	23.1%
Total	**1,480**	**1,736**	**2,631**	**4,929**	**5,665**	**6,699**	**7,616**	**8,250**	**9.5%**
Share (percent)									
Northeast	28.7	27.2	14.6	8.2	6.7	5.7	5.6	5.8	
North	23.2	19.9	15.4	9.5	8.6	6.4	5.8	7.5	
Middle Yangtze	0.5	0.4	0.3	0.2	0.2	0.2	0.7	0.2	
Lower Yangtze	0.2	0.1	1.1	1.3	1.1	0.8	0.6	0.5	
South	0.0	0.6	12.7	10.2	8.7	7.9	7.9	7.1	
Southwest	43.5	43.7	33.6	29.3	28.5	27.8	25.6	22.8	
Northwest	0.3	1.1	7.9	16.0	14.0	16.0	18.3	22.3	
West	3.6	6.9	14.4	25.3	32.3	35.3	35.5	33.8	
Total	**100.0**	**100.0**	**100.0**	**100.0**	**100.0**	**100.0**	**100.0**	**100.0**	

*AAGR refers to the period 1995–2009.

the output structure with a 56.3% share of the national total in 2009 (Table 9-9). The fastest growing region in coal production since 1990 is the Northwest, followed by the North and the Lower Yangtze region.

Table 9-9. Regional Distribution of Coal Production, 1990–2009.

	1990	1995	2000	2005	2006	2007	2008	2009	AAGR 1990–2009
Output (mmtpa)									
Northeast	160	161	111	186	207	198	202	197	1.1%
North	557	700	488	1,233	1,306	1,415	1,562	1,660	5.9%
Middle Yangtze	63	100	37	93	98	103	104	107	2.8%
Lower Yangtze	57	72	73	113	113	118	143	152	5.3%
South	28	36	13	29	26	28	27	30	0.4%
Southwest	127	179	79	290	317	326	343	326	5.1%
Northwest	63	82	52	214	256	281	326	390	10.1%
West	24	30	28	45	50	59	81	89	7.1%
Total	**1,079**	**1,360**	**881**	**2,203**	**2,373**	**2,528**	**2,788**	**2,951**	**5.4%**
Share (percent)									
Northeast	14.8	11.8	12.6	8.4	8.7	7.8	7.2	6.7	
North	51.6	51.5	55.4	56.0	55.0	56.0	56.0	56.3	
Middle Yangtze	5.8	7.4	4.2	4.2	4.1	4.1	3.7	3.6	
Lower Yangtze	5.3	5.3	8.3	5.1	4.8	4.7	5.1	5.2	
South	2.6	2.6	1.5	1.3	1.1	1.1	1.0	1.0	
Southwest	11.8	13.2	9.0	13.2	13.4	12.9	12.3	11.0	
Northwest	5.8	6.0	5.9	9.7	10.8	11.1	11.7	13.2	
West	2.2	2.2	3.2	2.0	2.1	2.3	2.9	3.0	
Total	**100.0**	**100.0**	**100.0**	**100.0**	**100.0**	**100.0**	**100.0**	**100.0**	

9.3.4. *Electric power*

Electricity can be primary energy in the form of hydroelectricity and nuclear power, or secondary energy generated by using coal, oil, and other primary energy sources. The most evenly distributed form of power — including both primary and secondary power — is electricity since it is needed in every province. Regional distribution is also in proportion to the level of economic development.

China's electric power generation has been growing rapidly over the past decades. In 2009, the North was the largest electric power–producing region in China, followed by the Lower Yangtze region, the South, and the Southwest (Table 9-10). For the Southwest, the high

Table 9-10. Regional Distribution of Electric Power Generation, 1990–2009.

	1990	1995	2000	2005	2006	2007	2008	2009	AAGR 1990–2009
Output (TWh)									
Northeast	91	121	139	193	210	230	236	243	5.3%
North	184	295	396	762	889	1,058	1,088	1,143	10.1%
Middle Yangtze	66	96	112	231	250	295	314	338	8.9%
Lower Yangtze	109	182	244	496	576	620	675	727	10.5%
South	62	133	202	359	399	457	483	500	11.6%
Southwest	57	104	137	269	326	371	391	460	11.6%
Northwest	38	58	66	137	150	178	198	209	9.4%
West	14	19	32	54	65	74	82	95	10.4%
Total	**621**	**1,008**	**1,329**	**2,500**	**2,866**	**3,282**	**3,467**	**3,715**	**9.9%**
Share (percent)									
Northeast	14.6	12.0	10.4	7.7	7.3	7.0	6.8	6.5	
North	29.6	29.3	29.8	30.5	31.0	32.2	31.4	30.8	
Middle Yangtze	10.7	9.5	8.4	9.2	8.7	9.0	9.1	9.1	
Lower Yangtze	17.6	18.0	18.4	19.8	20.1	18.9	19.5	19.6	
South	10.0	13.2	15.2	14.3	13.9	13.9	13.9	13.5	
Southwest	9.2	10.3	10.3	10.8	11.4	11.3	11.3	12.4	
Northwest	6.1	5.8	5.0	5.5	5.2	5.4	5.7	5.6	
West	2.3	1.8	2.4	2.2	2.3	2.2	2.4	2.5	
Total	**100.0**	**100.0**	**100.0**	**100.0**	**100.0**	**100.0**	**100.0**	**100.0**	

volume and growth of electric power generation are primarily due to the development of hydroelectric power in the region. The Northwest and West have the lowest electricity generation rates in China at present.

In terms of growth rates of electricity generation, the South and Southwest had the highest growth per annum on average during the period 1990–2009, followed by the West and the North.

Distribution of hydroelectricity is different from the distribution of overall electric power. The Southwest dominates the production of hydroelectricity and is also the fastest growing region since 1990. In 2009, the hydroresource-rich Southwest was the largest hydroelectricity producing region in China, accounting for 36.6% of the total, up from 20.9% in 1990 (Table 9-11). While being relatively poor in other energy resources, the Middle Yangtze and the South were the second and third largest hydroelectricity-producing regions. The large share of the South is mainly attributable to the Guangxi Autonomous Region.

9.3.5. *Primary energy production of main sources*

If the production of the above-mentioned primary energy resources (excluding nuclear power) is combined, the North turns out to be the largest producer with 50% of the national total, mainly because of its huge output of coal (Table 9-12). Until 2004, the Northeast was the second largest producer of main primary energy resources, partly because of its large oil production. However, it was surpassed by the Southwest in 2005, which has high natural gas output and more importantly, growing hydroelectricity generation, plus large coal production, and then by the Northwest in 2007, which has seen impressive growth for oil, gas, and coal production. In 2009, the Northwest is the second largest primary energy–producing region, followed by the Southwest and Northeast. The Northwest is also the fastest growing region, followed by the West and Southwest. Altogether, the combined share of the western part of China (consisting of the West, Northwest, and Southwest) in the national total primary energy production of oil, coal, gas, and hydroelectricity, increased from 18.3% in 1990 to 30.1% in 2009.

Table 9-11. Regional Distribution of Hydroelectricity Production, 1990–2009.

	1990	1995	2000	2005	2006	2007	2008	2009	AAGR 1990–2009
Output (TWh)									
Northeast	8.7	13.2	7.6	15.0	11.6	11.6	10.6	10.2	0.8%
North	3.3	4.1	4.8	11.1	14.4	15.9	13.0	13.7	7.8%
Middle Yangtze	37.6	47.2	52.6	112.3	114.2	133.5	166.7	170.0	8.3%
Lower Yangtze	7.0	9.0	7.0	15.0	15.9	14.1	16.1	17.1	4.8%
South	23.2	43.6	48.2	70.5	87.0	88.9	119.4	107.7	8.4%
Southwest	26.4	53.7	73.3	128.3	142.3	166.9	199.9	225.5	11.9%
Northwest	13.0	13.1	14.6	23.3	22.7	26.2	29.2	34.2	5.2%
West	7.5	6.8	14.4	21.5	27.7	28.1	30.4	37.1	8.8%
Total	**126.7**	**190.6**	**222.4**	**397.0**	**435.8**	**485.3**	**585.2**	**615.6**	**8.7%**
Share (percent)									
Northeast	6.9	6.9	3.4	3.8	2.7	2.4	1.8	1.7	
North	2.6	2.1	2.1	2.8	3.3	3.3	2.2	2.2	
Middle Yangtze	29.7	24.8	23.7	28.3	26.2	27.5	28.5	27.6	
Lower Yangtze	5.5	4.7	3.1	3.8	3.6	2.9	2.7	2.8	
South	18.3	22.9	21.7	17.8	20.0	18.3	20.4	17.5	
Southwest	20.9	28.2	33.0	32.3	32.6	34.4	34.2	36.6	
Northwest	10.3	6.9	6.5	5.9	5.2	5.4	5.0	5.6	
West	5.9	3.6	6.5	5.4	6.4	5.8	5.2	6.0	
Total	**100.0**	**100.0**	**100.0**	**100.0**	**100.0**	**100.0**	**100.0**	**100.0**	

9.4. Outlook for Regional Growth of Oil

In this section, we present our forecasts of future growth for oil. We first examine the current situation and future prospects of refining capacity and crude runs by region. Then regional balances of petroleum products are reviewed. Finally, we present the national product balance to 2030, which is derived from all the provinces and regions. The production of refined products for a particular region is heavily affected by the refining capacity available, throughput used, and

Table 9-12. Regional Distribution of Primary Energy Production of Selected Sources,* 1990–2009.

	1990	1995	2000	2005	2006	2007	2008	2009	AAGR 1990–2009
Output (mmboe/d)									
Northeast	3.2	3.2	2.6	3.2	3.4	3.3	3.3	3.2	0.1%
North	6.7	8.0	5.9	13.6	14.3	15.4	16.9	18.0	5.3%
Middle Yangtze	0.7	1.1	0.5	1.1	1.2	1.3	1.3	1.4	3.5%
Lower Yangtze	0.6	0.8	0.8	1.2	1.2	1.3	1.5	1.6	5.3%
South	0.3	0.6	0.6	0.8	0.8	0.8	0.9	0.9	5.2%
Southwest	1.4	2.0	1.1	3.4	3.7	3.9	4.2	4.0	5.5%
Northwest	0.7	0.9	0.8	2.7	3.2	3.5	4.1	4.9	10.7%
West	0.4	0.6	0.8	1.3	1.4	1.7	2.0	2.0	8.7%
Total	**14.1**	**17.3**	**12.9**	**27.3**	**29.3**	**31.1**	**34.1**	**35.9**	**5.1%**
Share (percent)									
Northeast	22.4	18.7	20.1	11.8	11.7	10.5	9.7	8.9	
North	47.6	46.5	45.3	49.7	49.0	49.6	49.5	50.0	
Middle Yangtze	5.1	6.4	3.7	4.2	4.1	4.1	4.0	3.8	
Lower Yangtze	4.3	4.4	6.1	4.4	4.1	4.0	4.4	4.4	
South	2.4	3.3	4.3	2.9	2.6	2.5	2.5	2.4	
Southwest	10.3	11.8	8.4	12.5	12.7	12.6	12.2	11.2	
Northwest	5.0	5.5	6.0	9.9	10.8	11.3	12.0	13.5	
West	3.0	3.6	6.1	4.6	4.9	5.3	5.8	5.6	
Total	**100.0**	**100.0**	**100.0**	**100.0**	**100.0**	**100.0**	**100.0**	**100.0**	

*Include oil, coal, gas, and hydroelectricity.

utilization rate in that region. We first discuss the current regional distribution of refining capacity by region.

9.4.1. *Refining capacity and crude runs*

China's refineries are not evenly distributed and owned. For historical reasons, China's refining industry tends to concentrate in regions with significant crude oil production. During the past two decades, however, China has also built large-scale grassroots refineries or expanded existing refineries in the country's coastal demand centers.

The North has the largest refining capacity by the end of 2010, followed by the Northeast, the Lower Yangtze region, and the South. As the company that dominated the downstream operations, Sinopec alone has nearly 5.1 mmb/d of crude distillation unit (CDU) capacity at the end of 2010, followed by CNPC/PetroChina's 3.4 mmb/d. The combined capacity of others, including those of the other state oil companies such as CNOOC, is 2.8 mmb/d, reflecting the changing pictures of the refining sector.

The regional distribution of crude throughput is similar to the distribution of refining capacity. The average utilization rate for all regions was 75% in 2010. The South, Lower Yangtze, and Northeast regions had relatively high utilization rates of more than 80% while the North had the lowest rate of 62%. The Southwest's refining utilization rate was high, but there are no major refineries in the region.

During the period 2000–2010, China added a total of 5.7 mmb/d to its refining capacity. The North added the most, followed by the South, then the Lower Yangtze region, the Northeast, and the Northwest.

In 2010, the North surpassed the Northeast to have the largest CDU capacity, and it will remain in the No. 1 spot towards 2030. By 2015, the South may take over Northeast to become the No. 2. The shares in the national total for the North and Northeast will both decline towards 2030 while the share for the South will increase.

By 2015, the North, the Northeast, the South and the Lower Yangtze are all expected to have CDU capacities of over 2 mmb/d. The total refining capacity in end 2015 is expected to be 13.8 mmb/d, up by 2.6 mmb/d from end 2010. For all regions and the country as a whole, the refinery utilization rates are expected to be higher at 78.4% in 2015.

By 2020, the North will have a total capacity of more than 4 mmb/d, followed closely by the South. The total refining capacity in end 2020 is expected to be 16 mmb/d, up by 2.2 mmb/d from end 2015. The throughput will reach about 13 mmb/d, with an average national utilization rate of 82%.

By 2030, the total capacity of the North region will increase to about 5 mmb/d while that of the South will increase to 4.6 mmb/d. The total refining capacity in end 2030 is expected to be 19 mmb/d, up by 2.2 mmb/d from end 2015. The throughput will reach about 15 mmb/d, with an average national utilization rate of 81%.

A total of 4.7 mmb/d and 2.9 mmb/d of new or expanded capacity is expected to be added in 2010–2020 and 2020–2030, respectively, under the base-case scenario. The South is expected to lead the way, followed by the Lower Yangtze, the North, and Southwest regions. For crude throughput change, every region is forecast to increase its crude runs by 2030. The South is leading the increase in crude runs between 2010 and 2030, followed by the Lower Yangtze, the North, and the Southwest regions.

9.4.2. *Outlook for regional petroleum product balances*

Regional refined product output is generally proportional to refining capacity in most regions. Compared with production, the consumption of refined products is more evenly distributed in proportion to the population among the eight regions defined in this book, although the consumption rates are still higher in the crude production and refining centers in general.

Owing to the rapid economic growth, the North, the Lower Yangtze, and the South regions are the leading consumers of refined products, which in total account for 69% of the country's total consumption. Looking forward to 2030, the trend will remain about the same, with the three regions accounting for 64% of the 16.1 mmb/d total product consumption in 2030.

However, the situation is not the same if the consumption is broken down into individual products:

> For LPG, the South is the largest consumer at present, followed by the Lower Yangtze, and the North. This pattern — the order of the top three regions — is likely to continue to 2030.
>
> For gasoline, kero/jet, and diesel, the North is the leader of gasoline and diesel use, while the Lower Yangtze region is the largest kero/jet-consuming region at present. These patterns will probably continue to 2030.
>
> As for fuel oil consumption, the South is ahead of the others, followed closely by the Lower Yangtze region. It is expected that the Lower Yangtze region will overtake the South in fuel oil consumption by 2015 and remain the same towards 2030. For "other products," where petrochemical feedstock is included, the North topped the demand in 2010, followed by the Lower Yangtze and the South regions. It is expected that their relative position will stay the same toward 2030.

9.5. Outlook for Natural Gas Production

This section provides an overview of natural gas demand, supply, and balances for the eight regions used in this book for China. Having reviewed each province, autonomous region, and municipality earlier in this book, it is very important to compare these regions to get an integrated outlook under different scenarios and see the overall picture of the natural gas sector development in China.

9.5.1. *Outlook for natural gas production by region*

Under the base-case scenario for 2010–2030, the largest increase in natural gas production in terms of volume is forecast to be the West, home to the vast Tarim Basin. Production from the West is expected to more than double from 2.8 bscf/d in 2009 to 6.2 bscf/d by 2020 and 10.0 bscf/d by 2030. As a result, the share of the West in the nation's total natural gas output is forecast to increase from 34% in 2009 to 37% in 2020 and 43% in 2030 (Table 9.13). In 2010, natural gas production for the West is estimated to have reached 2.9 bscf/d, accounting for 31% of the national total.

The second largest growing area for natural gas production is the Northwest, where the Ordos Basin is located. The output from the Northwest is projected to be nearly doubled from 1.8 mmscf/d in 2009 to 3.8 bscf/d in 2020 and 4.8 bscf/d by 2030. Their share of the nation's total natural gas output is forecast to increase from 22% in 2009 to 23% in 2020 but slightly down to 21% in 2030. In 2010, the natural gas output from the Northwest is estimated to have reached 2.1 bscf/d, 23% of the national total.

The third largest increase in natural gas production in terms of volume will be in the Southwest, increasing from 1.9 bscf/d in 2009 to 3.7 bscf/d in 2020 and 4.5 bscf/d by 2030. Its share in total

Table 9-13. Regional Natural Gas Production Forecast, Base-Case Scenario 2005–2030.

	2005	2009	2010	2015	2020	2025	2030	AAGR 09–30
Output (mmscf/d)								
Northeast	402	481	496	596	607	597	574	0.8%
North	468	617	597	675	748	752	851	1.5%
Mid Yangtze	11	16	16	17	19	20	22	1.6%
Lower Yangtze	65	45	37	39	78	137	186	7.0%
South	504	583	770	1,088	1,486	1,907	2,171	6.5%
Southwest	1,444	1,880	2,282	3,216	3,730	4,184	4,511	4.3%
Northwest	788	1,836	2,143	3,184	3,766	4,444	4,831	4.7%
West	1,248	2,791	2,892	4,247	6,209	8,035	9,978	6.3%
TOTAL	**4,929**	**8,250**	**9,234**	**13,062**	**16,642**	**20,076**	**23,124**	**5.0%**

Note: Data for 2010 are estimates and for 2015–2030 are forecasts.

national production is expected to increase to 25% by 2015, but will decline to 22% in 2020 and 20% in 2030. In 2010, output from the Southwest was 2.3 bscf/d, nearly 25% of the national total.

Another notable growth area in natural gas production is offshore China, thanks to the ambitious plans put forward by CNOOC. This will add the shares to the South and the Lower Yangtze region, which have jurisdiction over the South China Sea and the East China Sea.

Meanwhile, production growth in the mature oil fields in the Northeast, North, and the Middle Yangtze region is expected to be flat, and their shares in the national total are forecast to decline fast. In 2009, the three regions accounted for 14% of the national total production, and their combined share is projected to decline to 8% by 2020 and 6% in 2030. Their production in 2010 is estimated at 1.1 bscf/d, flat from that of 2009. For the Middle Yangtze, despite the slim prospects for natural gas production, the region has the advantage of being located on the routes of natural gas pipelines from the West or the Southwest to the east coast of the country. Under the high-case scenario, production for the West, the Northwest, the Southwest, and the South (offshore China) is expected to be higher. Production is expected to be lower in the same regions under the low-case scenario.

9.5.2. *Outlook for natural gas consumption by region*

Comparing natural gas output by region, the picture for regional consumption is quite different. First, overall consumption is expected to grow at an average annual rate of 7.7% during the 2009–2030 period, which is much faster than the projected 5% growth rate of natural gas production during the same period.

The projected fastest growing region in terms of growth rate is the Middle Yangtze region (12.1% per annum during 2009–2030) though its current consumption is low, followed by the South (10.6% per annum), the Lower Yangtze region (9.4% per annum), and the North (8.2% per annum). In terms of volume change, the biggest increase is projected to be in the North, which accounts for 27% of the incremental demand of the country between 2009 and 2030. This is followed by the South (22.4% of the incremental demand and the Lower Yangtze (21.8% of the incremental demand).

As a result of these forecast developments, the regional structures of natural gas consumption will change continuously. For instance, at present, the three largest natural gas–consuming region (as of 2009) are the North (2.1 bscf/d), the Southwest (1.6 bscf/d), and the Lower Yangtze region (1.3 bscf/d). By 2030, the three largest natural gas–consuming regions are projected to be the North (10.9 bscf/d), the Lower Yangtze region (8.3 bscf/d), and the South (8.2 bscf/d).

Under the high-case scenario, natural gas consumption in many regions is expected to grow fast, largely because of the assumptions of higher economic growth rates, deep natural gas penetration, higher natural gas production, as well as greater and/or earlier imports of liquefied natural gas (LNG) and pipeline natural gas.

Under the low-case scenario, the consumption in many regions is expected to be lower because of slower economic growth, lower output forecasts, and smaller volumes of LNG and pipeline imports. In this scenario, the South, the Northeast, and the North are particularly affected, because of possible delays in LNG and pipeline gas imports.

9.5.3. *Outlook for natural gas balances by region*

At present, the North and the Lower Yangtze regions are the largest natural gas-deficit areas. The West and Northwest are the largest surplus regions, followed in distance by the Southwest. Under the base-case scenario, regional imbalances will be growing rapidly. By 2030, the North, the Lower Yangtze, the South, as well as the Northeast regions will have huge deficits in natural gas supply. In the meantime, the West, the Northwest, and the Southwest are expected to have surpluses of natural gas that can be transported to the regions that are in deficit. However, their surpluses are insufficient, and the import requirements will thus be growing, as demonstrated by the overall deficit of the country.

Under the high-case scenario, although natural gas production is projected to be larger, consumption will be growing even faster, leading to more imports of LNG and pipeline natural gas. Under the low-case scenario, both production and consumption are projected to be low.

One important note about all forecasts is that there can be different combinations of production and consumption cases, which could result in alternative conclusions. For instance, an extreme combination would be high-case domestic production and low-case consumption. That will lead to much less gas imports for China. For another extreme case of low-case domestic production and high-case consumption, then ultra-high gas imports would emerge.

Theoretically, the chances for such combinations are low because of the way we define our scenarios. The primary reason is that China's consumption (note that we use "demand" and "consumption" interchangeably to refer to the same thing—volume of natural gas use) is partially supply driven. If there is insufficient domestic supply while imports are short, there will be no additional consumption. As such, our low-case consumption is in part because of the low natural gas production and less gas imports, while the high-case consumption is related to high-case production as well as more gas (LNG and pipeline gas) imports. Between them are varying assumptions about LNG and pipeline imports. Still, one can come up with numerous other combinations of production versus consumption for comparison, which we will leave to our readers to practice. It is just that in the unique framework of this book, the extreme cases will not occur. Therefore, our conclusions, based on the alternative scenarios presented in this book, encompass a wide range of likelihood with regard to what may happen to the natural gas sector in China over the next 20 years.

chapter 10

Conclusion

This book presents a critical review and an in-depth analysis of all major issues related to China's oil and gas industries, with a general view of economic and overall energy sector developments, as well as a unique focus on energy security issues and regional demand, supply, balances, and future growth. The issues discussed in this book range from structural changes of the oil and gas industry, downstream oil sector developments, and the rules and regulations for oil business, natural gas use, liquefied natural gas (LNG) and pipeline gas imports to energy security, and China's role in the regional and global oil and gas markets.

In short, this book has touched upon every aspect of the oil and gas sector developments — its past, present, and especially future. From the discussions of the past nine chapters, the some key conclusions can be drawn.

10.1. Economic Growth

China continues to show resilience of economic growth after over a quarter century of rapid expansion since 1978. The average annual growth rate (AAGR) of real GDP growth was 9.3% for the 1980s, 10.4% for the 1990s, and 11.0% for the 2000s. In other words, for the past three decades, China managed to achieve an AAGR of over 10%. Can China sustain this high growth rate? Chances are the country does show signs of continuing its GDP at reasonably high rates over the next decade or two but with a high uncertainty. We therefore project that China's AAGR of real GDP for the next two decades between 2010 and 2030 (including actual growth of 9.2% in 201) and be 7.0% under our base-case scenario but with swings from 4.9% under the low-case scenario and 8.1% under the high-case scenario.

10.2. How Fast will China's Oil Demand Grow?

How fast will China grow by 2030? Our base-case scenario shows that China's petroleum product demand (including direct use of crude oil) will grow at an AAGR of 4.2% between 2011 and 2020 and at an AAGR of only 1.5% between 2020 and 2030. As a result, the total demand is forecast to reach 14.0 mmb/d in 2020 and 16.3 mmb/d in 2030. This is equivalent to an average increment of around 480 kb/d each year from 2011–2020 and 230 kb/d from 2020–2030. We forecast a lower demand growth after 2020 under our base case as the Chinese government is currently pursuing an unannounced policy to cap the Chinese oil demand in 2020 at around 13 mmb/d. Although it is unlikely that China can achieve its aggressive target, we expect that there will be major efforts by the Chinese government to slow down demand growth. The Chinese government is considering many policies and regulatory measures to achieve its target. For example, they are liberalizing gasoline and diesel prices. Even under high inflationary pressures, the National Development and Reform Commission (NDRC) has kept increasing retail gasoline and diesel prices corresponding to international crude prices. One of the main objectives is to slow down petroleum product demand. In addition, they could potentially mandate the use of alternative energies or adoption of efficient equipments in the future.

As mentioned earlier, the biggest challenge China and the rest of the region and world face is the uncertainty associated with China's petroleum product demand. The swing in 2020 between high and low cases is in the range of 3 mmb/d and over 5 mmb/d in 2030. This uncertainty affects the business of the downstream refining sector, product trade, infrastructure investments, and demand for crude in a big way. For instance, depending on the final demand and assuming China's current refinery buildup stays, China can swing between a giant product exporter and a huge product importer by 2030. Despite this, our base-case scenario attempts to capture the most likely path for China down the road. As such, all details provided in this book are important to understand this scenario and related factors.

In relation to the above-mentioned scenario, the issue of strategic petroleum reserves (SPRs) is also worth noting. Starting from scratch, China completed and filled the 103 mmb of SPRs Phase I in 2009. It is in the process of building the second phase of SPRs at the moment. It targets to build another 169 mmb for Phase II by 2012/13. Eventually by 2015/2016, the country aims to establish 500 mmb of SPRs, and the impact on the crude oil market will intensify. Nonetheless, similar to the crude filling for Phase I, we expect that the government will continue to approach the crude fillings for Phase II strategically. It is likely that China will import crudes for the SPR Phase II sites when the crude market is relatively loose with weak prices. Therefore, the impact of Chinese SPRs filling will be more to support a weak crude market rather than further pushing up a bullish market. Of course, "weak" or "strong" is up to the interpretation of the Chinese government and national oil companies (NOCs).

10.3. Oil Imports: Crude versus Products

Under the base-case scenario, China's overall net oil import requirements are likely to reach 10.0 mmb/d by 2020, and 12.3 mmb/d by 2030. The question is always how much is likely to be crude oil and how much is refined products. China is now sending a strong signal that the government intends to build sufficient refineries to address the petroleum products needs of the country. In 2010, the net product imports accounted for only 3.4% of the total consumption, down from 11% in 2004. With the refinery buildup, this share may become lower by 2015 and China could switch to be a net product exporter.

As such, the answer is clear. China will continue to be a huge crude oil importer. The share of the Middle Eastern crudes import is forecast to rise from 51% in 2011 to 60% in 2020 and 61% in 2030 even though the Chinese government is making great efforts to diversify its crudes imports sources.

10.4. Oil Production Potential

Compared to the future demand, there is much less uncertainty with regard to China's oil production. The Chinese state oil companies are trying very hard to find enough new reserves to maintain production level, with additional efforts to ensure an overall moderate increase in production. We believe China's oil production is likely to only moderately increase towards 2020, with further marginal growth to 2030. The small growth will mainly come from the offshore area, the Tarim Basin, and the Ordos Basin, while production declines from aging fields in the Northeast and North will continue.

We project that, under the base-case scenario, China's crude oil production is forecast to go up from 4.1 mmb/d in 2011 to 4.2 mmb/d in 2020 and then marginally to 4.3 mmb/d by 2030. Although there is room for China to increase its production further under the high-case scenario, the chances for China's production to decline by 2030 are still there under the low-case scenario. Even if the production targets are met, China's oil import dependence — defined as the net oil (including both crude and products) imports (for the past) or import requirements (for the future) in the country's total petroleum product consumption — is expected to rise rapidly in the future.

10.5. China's Overseas Oil and Gas Investments and Energy Security

Since the recent past, the Chinese state oil companies have been vigorously investing in overseas oil and gas sectors. Some of their investments have paid off. In 2011, the total equity oil held by all Chinese state companies, led by CNPC/PetroChina, amounted to 1.7 mmb/d. In recent years, the Chinese NOCs have increased their overseas investment for oil and gas assets in both numbers and size.

The Chinese State Banks have also signed a total of US$90 billion loan-for-oil/gas deals with large oil and gas producers.

We believe that the achievements made by China do not help a great deal in its energy security. It does, however, give the Chinese state oil companies a growing presence and position in the global upstream sector. For this, they have to make multibillion-dollar investments. For these state companies, these funds are not entirely theirs; if they do not spend the money, the funds will eventually be returned to the government. As such, the motivation is strong for them to spend. We expect that they will continue to take advantage of the government's easy approval to invest more, as long as their duopoly profits at home can be sustained.

10.6. Oil Price Reforms and Trade Regimes

The most pressing issue for China's oil market developments is the oil price reforms. China should be credited for its determination to link crude oil prices with the international market for over a decade. However, there are setbacks on product price reforms. Despite the changing formulas to link up domestic prices with the international markets, the government increased its product prices at a slower rate than the international crude price rise. Furthermore, price changes by the NDRC are widely speculated by the market participants, which lead to products hoarding and thus shortage of petroleum products before the price hike.

Likewise, China has tightly controlled the imports of main products such as gasoline, diesel, jet fuel, and naphtha despite joining the WTO nearly a decade ago. While China continues to claim that it abides by the WTO rules and follows the concessions it made to its trading partners to join the WTO, the effective control of product imports has been restrictive in many ways.

We assume in our study that toward 2030, China will gradually liberalize its oil prices. We also assume that China will allow more room to import main products. However, China may move faster or on the contrary choose to tighten its grip further on oil prices. The impact on foreign investments will be hugely different depending on which direction the policy goes.

10.7. Major Issues Concerning the Chinese Natural Gas Sector and Markets

- **Untapped Natural Gas Resources and Potential Growth in Proven Reserves and Production:** Unlike oil, China's natural gas sector continues to have a bright future for increasing proven reserves and domestic production. China still has huge untapped natural gas resources and the proven reserves — low at present — have room to grow. The low proven reserves-to-resources ratio suggests that there is considerable potential for China to prove and produce more gas. On the other hand, however, the low ratio also indicates that massive investment is needed to turn untapped resources into recoverable proven reserves and ultimately into reality.
- **Unconventional Gas:** Compared with conventional natural gas, China has bigger potential for the development of unconventional gas. While tight gas has already been produced as part of the current natural gas output pool in China, the country is in the early stage of developing CBM and the exploration of shale gas has barely started. Our view is that after 2030, when China's conventional natural gas development slows down, unconventional gas will take over and become a major source of domestic gas supply in China. Will China be another US in terms of CBM and shale gas production? In 10 to 15 years (or faster under the high-case scenario) that is very likely.
- **Uneven Distribution of Natural Gas Resources and Reserves:** The regional distribution of China's natural gas resources and reserves is uneven. The situation is worse compared to a decade ago as more gas is found in the West, the Northwest, and the Southwest, whereas the key consuming regions are in North, East, and South China. Therefore, significant amount of investment in long-distance pipeline infrastructure is essential to ensure gas delivery to the consuming areas.

- **Growing Natural Gas Markets:** Due to the vigorous growth in long-distance pipeline buildup, China's natural gas markets are growing rapidly; regional gas markets and consumption centers are emerging. Nationwide, the market is still fragmented. However, with more domestic production, pipeline imports, and LNG imports, a more integrated market will emerge in China.
- **Natural Gas Pipelines:** China has built slightly more than two-thirds of all its existing natural gas pipelines in the past 10 years over those built during the previous five decades. More is under construction and planned. The decisive move of the government to do all this has ensured the future growth of the natural gas market.
- **Natural Gas Distribution Network:** China has vigorously built the distribution network in cities and towns that receive natural gas. During the past decade, China's distribution network for natural gas in urban areas increased from under 30,000 km (19,000 miles) at the start of 2000 to over 255,000 km (nearly 160,000 miles) at the start of 2011. However, like the main pipelines, China still needs to build more.
- **More Needs to be Done for the Reform of Naturl Gas Prices:** Despite the progress cited earlier, natural gas prices in China are still distorted overall. It is important for the government to speed up the reform and set natural gas prices competitively based on the market.
- **LNG Imports:** China is now one of the major LNG importers in Asia even though it only started in 2006, two years after India. The potential of LNG imports can be massive if the prices are reasonable. Although the current market situation is closer to the buyers' market situation in the sense there are many supply projects chasing buyers, buyers have not been able to force prices substantially lower because costs of project development are three to four times higher than that before 2005. PetroChina, Sinopec, and CNOOC are also brave enough to sign a few expensive deals during sellers' market in 2008. With the actual LNG cargoes arriving under these new deals, it is a test of the affordability of

the Chinese gas market and how far the strategies of "resource pooling" and "price pooling" can go.

- **Regional Natural Gas Production:** China's overall natural gas production is growing rapidly. Between 2000 and 2009, the AAGR of the natural gas output for the country as a whole reached a spectacular 13.6%. However, the growth is uneven. The average annual growth rate (AAGR) of natural gas output for the West is 23.1% and for the Northwest, it was 37.1%. Of the total 2.41 bscf/d gas production growth between 2000 and 2009, the West accounts for 43%, the Northwest for 29%, the Southwest for 18%, and the aggregate of all the other regions for only 10%.
- **Regional Natural Gas Consumption:** Compared to domestic production, China's natural gas consumption is growing even faster. Between 2000 and 2009, the AAGR of China's natural gas consumption was 15.9%. The growth varies widely from region to region again. The AAGR of natural gas consumption for the Lower Yangtze is 53% and for the Southwest was only 6%.

10.8. Challenges for China's Natural Gas Sector Development

There is no doubt that China's natural gas sector continues to have a promising future over the next 15 years — which is the focus of this book — and beyond. However, there exists impediments that may hinder the development of the industry. We summarize these challenges as follows:

- **More Long-Distance Pipelines are Needed:** Despite the rapid build-up of trunklines in recent years, the total length of China's pipelines is far less than that in US and Europe. China still has a long way to go to build sufficient pipelines to distribute the gas. The fact that the Chinese government regulates transportation tariffs and keeps them relatively low does not help the growth of the pipeline business over the long run. Also it is not sustainable in the long run for the state oil companies to have monopolies over major long-distance pipeline projects in China.

- **More Distribution Networks are Needed:** Similarly, massive investment is needed to meet the investment requirements. Here again, the government should loosen up the price control in order to increase competition for gas supply and investment in distribution networks.
- **Reform of the Natural Gas Price Regime:** Here is another issue. NDRC needs to approve all prices for new projects, imported LNG, and future imported pipeline natural gas. The government has been slow in approving projects and assessing market prices. This has often delayed the negotiations of LNG imports and prolonged talks on cross-border pipeline projects. Since China's natural gas consumption is partially supply driven, lack of supply leads to the use of natural gas that is below the desirable levels.
- **Removal of Restrictions on Foreign Investment:** China has, in theory, opened up various segments for foreign investment. In reality, because most upstream and pipeline business is in the hands of the three state oil companies, foreign investment in these areas is constrained. As for gas distribution networks and marketing, city governments are not uniform in their policies, leading to confusion and difficulties for foreign investment.
- **Overall:** The Chinese government still lacks a cohesive natural gas policy to encourage investment in natural gas supply and market expansion.

Natural gas pricing is one of the most important issues concerning the development of and investment in China's natural gas (including unconventional gas) sector. The most expensive domestic gas supply is the Puguang gas, which is priced at about US$10/mmBtu at city gate in Shanghai. This most expensive domestic source is still lower than all the LNG contracts signed in the past five years. Although the Turkmen gas is priced at US$7.7/mmBtu (at Brent crude price of US$80/b) in the Chinese border, its delivered price to Shanghai reaches US$13.1/mmBtu after adding the VAT and domestic pipeline tariff. As the amount of these expensive foreign gas imported to China increases rapidly, the Chinese state oil companies (especially CNPC/PetroChina) will lobby the government to further hike the domestic gas price. However, gas end-users, especially in the fertilizer and power sectors, could potentially have problems in paying higher gas prices as they may not be able to pass on the costs to consumers.

Last but not least, we end the book by touching upon the issue of energy security in terms of limitations for pursuing it. Energy security is one of the central themes and focuses of the book. Narrowly defined, energy security may refer to the security of an individual energy source, particularly oil in the case of China. Broadly speaking, energy security touches upon all aspects of the energy sector as well as the economy. With its economic, environmental, geopolitical, and military dimensions, energy security and how the Chinese government addresses it will have greater impact on the future of the Chinese political, economic, and energy sector developments. However, there are limitations on how far the Chinese government can go to pursue energy security. First and foremost, there is no absolute security. It is only so much China can gain in ensuring adequate, smooth, and clean energy supplies. Secondly, every security measure comes with a cost. Establishing and expanding the SPR system is costly and massive purchase of crude oil to fill up the strategic storage may be a factor for pushing up international crude oil prices from time to time. Investing overseas by Chinese NOCs is not all economical. In fact, Chinese NOCs are facing increasing difficulties in certain countries and their returns there are diminishing with rising political and environmental risks. Regarding diversification of energy imports, it will increase of cost of imports. Thirdly, energy security may be misinterpreted by both policy makers and Chinese state-owned companies for carrying out policies and making investment that fail to promote energy security in the end. For instance, for both overseas investment and diversification of imports, their benefits to energy security per se are highly questionable and debatable. Finally, enhancing one country's energy security could compromise the security of another country (Brown, Mukherji, and Wu, 2008; Phillips, 2011).

To achieve a win-win situation, the Chinese government needs to be careful in designing its energy security policies — at least a good portion of them — absent of severe adverse impacts on other countries. With these limitations in mind, the entire issue of energy security will be better pursued in the long run in the country, which benefits China, the rest of the Asia-Pacific region, and the world at large.

Bibliography

Bambawale, M. J. and B. K. Sovacool, 2011, "China's Energy Security: The Perspective of Energy Users," *Applied Energy*, Vol. 88, pp. 1949–1956.

BP (British Petroleum), 2011a, *Statistical Review of World Energy June 2011*, London, UK.

BP (British Petroleum), 2011b, *BP Energy Outlook 2030*, London, UK.

Brown, J., V. Mukherji and K. Wu, 2008, "The Energy Race Between China and India: Motivations and Potential Opportunities for Cooperation," in The Emirates Center for Strategic Studies and Research, *China, India, and the United States: Competition for Energy Resources*, Abu Dhabi, United Arab Emirates, pp. 223–251.

Chen, X., 2003, "Internal Factors and Policy Elements for Energy Security," *Energy of China* (in Chinese), Vol. 25, pp. 4–14.

Chen, J., J. Cheng and Q. Wu, 2008, "Strategic Evaluation on Security of China's Petroleum: from 1990 to 2006," *China Population, Resources and Environment*, Vol. 18, No. 1, pp. 62–68.

Chen, W., H. Li and Z. Wu, 2010, "Western China Energy Development and West to East Energy Transfer: Application of the Western China Sustainable Energy Development Model," *Energy Policy*, Vol. 38, pp. 7106–7120.

Chu, T., F. Fesharaki and K. Wu, 2006, "China's Energy in Transition: Regional and Global Implications," *Asian Economic Policy Review*, Vol. 1, Issue 1, pp. 134–152.

Clarke, R., 2010, "Chinese Energy Security: The Myth of the PLAN's Frontline Status," *The Letort Papers*, Strategic Studies Institute, United States Army War College, Carlisle, Pennsylvania, USA.

Climate Policy Initiative, 2011, *Review of Low Carbon Development in China: 2010 Report*, February 25, Tsinghua University, Beijing, China.

CNBS (China National Statistical Bureau), 2011, *Statistical Yearbook of China 2011* (and previous issues), Beijing, China.

Downs, E., 2006, "Energy Security Series: China," *Brookings Foreign Policy Studies*, Brookings Institution, December, Washington, D.C., USA.

EIA (Energy Information Administration), 2011a, *International Energy Outlook 2011*, September, Washington, D.C., USA.

EIA (Energy Information Administration), 2011b, *Country Analysis Briefs: China*, May, Washington, D.C., USA.

EIA (Energy Information Administration), 2012, *Short-Term Energy Outlook*, April, Washington, D.C., USA.

EIA (Energy Information Administration), 2011c, *Annual Energy Outlook: With Projections to 2035*, April, Washington, D.C., USA.

FGE (FACTS Global Energy), 2011, *FGE Energy Database*.

Fridley, D., 2008, "Natural Gas in China," in J. Stern (ed.) "*Natural Gas in Asia: The Challenges of Growth in China, India, Japan, and Korea*," pp. 7–65, Oxford University Press, Oxford, UK.

Gao, S., 2003, "China," in *Securing Energy — China's Policy and Its Wider Strategic Implications*, German Council on Foreign Relations, Berlin, Germany.

Garrison, J. A., 2008, *Energy Security Challenges in China and Northeast Asia: Assessing the Strategic Imperative to Cooperate*, paper prepared for the *2008 Northeast Asia Energy Outlook Seminar*, Korea Economic Institute Policy Forum, May 6, Washington, D.C., USA.

Huang Y. and D. Todd, 2010, "The Energy Implications of Chinese Regional Disparities," *Energy Policy*, Vol. 38, pp. 7531–7538.

Huang, Y., D. Todd and L. Zhang, 2011, "Capitalizing on Energy Supply: Western China's Opportunity for Development," *Resources Policy*, Vol. 36, No. 3, pp. 227–237.

IEA (International Energy Agency), 2010, *World Energy Outlook 2010*, Paris, France.

IEA, 2012, *Oil Market Report*, April (and previous issues), Paris, France.

IMF (International Energy Agency), 2011a, *World Economic Outlook Update: Mild Slowdown of the Global Expansion, and Increasing Risks*, June 17, Washington, D.C., USA.

IMF (International Energy Agency), 2011b, *World Economic Outlook: Tensions from the Two-Speed Recovery Unemployment, Commodities, and Capital Flows*, April, Washington, D.C., USA.

Jiang, K., 2011, *Potential, Low-Carbon Growth Pathways for the Chinese Economy*, January, Working Paper, Center for Strategic and International Studies (CSIS), Washington, D.C., USA.

Kennedy, A., 2010, "Rethinking Energy Security in China," *East Asia Forum: Economics, Politics and Public Policy in East Asia and the Pacific*, June 6, Australian National University, Canberra, Australia.

Ladislaw, S., K. Zyla, J. Pershing, F. Verrastro, J. Goodward, D. Pumphrey and B. Staley, 2009, *A Roadmap for a Secure, Low-Carbon Energy Economy: Balancing Energy Security and Climate Change*, Center for Strategic and International Studies (CSIS), Washington, D.C., USA.

Leung, G. C. K., 2011, China's Energy Security: Perception and Reality, *Energy Policy*, Vol. 39, pp. 1330–1337.

Levine, M., N. Zhou and L. Price, 2009, *The Greening of the Middle Kingdom: The Story of Energy Efficiency in China*, Lawrence Berkeley National Laboratory, Berkeley, California, USA.

Lewis, J., 2011, *Energy and Climate Goals of China's 12th Five-Year Plan*, Pew Center on Global Climate Change, March, Arlington, Virginia, USA.

Lewis, S., 2008, *China and Energy Security in Asia*. Paper prepared for the *2008 Northeast Asia Energy Outlook Seminar*, Korea Economic Institute Policy Forum, May 6, Washington, D.C., USA.

Li, F., S. Dong, X. Li, Q. Liang and W. Yang, 2011, "Energy Consumption-Economic Growth Relationship and Carbon Dioxide Emissions in China," *Energy Policy*, Vol. 39, pp. 568–574.

Liao, X., 2006, Central Asia and China's Energy Security, *China and Eurasia Forum Quarterly*, Vol. 4, No. 4, pp. 61–69.

Ma, H., L. Oxley, J. Gibson and W. Li, 2008, "China's Energy Situation in the New Millennium," *Renewable and Sustainable Energy Reviews*, Vol. 13, pp. 1781–1799.

Ma, H., L. Oxley, J. Gibson and W. Li, 2010, "A Survey of China's Renewable Energy Economy," *Renewable and Sustainable Energy Reviews*, Vol. 14, pp. 438–445.

O'Kray, C. and K. Wu, 2010, "Biofuels in China: Development Dynamics, Policy Imperatives, and Future Growth," *IAEE Energy Forum*, Second Quarter, pp. 21–24, International Association for Energy Economics.

Phillips, A., 2011, "Chindia and the Challenges of Energy Security and Strategic Stability," *East Asia Forum: Economics, Politics and Public Policy in East Asia and the Pacific*, May 9, Australian National University, Canberra, Australia.

Price, L., M. D. Levine, N. Zhou, D. Fridley, N. Aden, H. Lu, M. McNeil, N. Zheng, Y. Qin and P. Yowargana, 2011, "Assessment of China's Energy-Saving and Emission-Reduction Accomplishments and Opportunities during the 11th Five Year Plan," *Energy Policy*, Vol. 39, pp. 2165–2178.

Qin, X., 2004, "China's Energy Security Strategies: Role of Transportation," *Energy of China* (in Chinese), Vol. 26, pp. 4–7.

Seligsohn, D., 2011, *The Transformation of China's Energy System: Challenges and Opportunities*, Presented before the Subcommittee on Energy and Power Committee on Energy and Commerce, U.S. House of Representatives, April 4, Washington, D.C., USA.

Song, H., 2005, "Expert's View of the Mid- and Long-Term Energy Conservation Plan," *International Petroleum Economy* (in Chinese), pp. 17–21.

The Climate Group, 2011, *Delivering Low Carbon Growth: A Guide to China's 12th Five Year Plan*, March, HSBC Bank.

Wu, K., 2007, "China's Energy Interest and Quest for Energy Security," in E. V. W. Davis and R. Azizian (eds.), *Islam, Oil, and Geopolitics: Central Asia after September 11*, pp. 123–144, Rowman & Littlefield, Lanham, Maryland, USA.

Wu, K., 2008, "China's Overseas Oil and Gas Investment: Motivations, Strategies, and Global Impact," *Oil, Gas, and Energy Law Intelligence*, Vol. 6, No. 1, p. 9.

Wu, K., 2011, "Special Report: Capacity, Complexity Expansions Characterize China's Refining Industry — Past, Present, Future," *Oil and Gas Journal*, Vol. 109, Issue 10, pp. 27–32.

Wu, K. and F. Fesharaki, 2005a, "As Oil Demand Surges, China Adds and Expands Refineries," *Oil and Gas Journal*, Vol. 103, Issue 28, pp. 20–24.

Wu, K. and F. Fesharaki, 2005b, "Higher Natural Gas Demand Has China Looking Worldwide," *Oil and Gas Journal*, Vol. 103, Issue 27, pp. 50–57.

Wu, K. and F. Fesharaki (eds.), 2007, *Asia's Energy Future: Regional Dynamics and Global Implications*, East-West Center, Honolulu, Hawaii.

Wu, K., F. Fesharaki, T. Hosoe and D. Isaak, 2008, *Strategic Framework for Energy Security in APEC, November*, National Center for APEC, Seattle, Washington, USA.

Wu, K., F. Fesharaki, S. Westley and W. Prawiraatmadja, 2008, "Oil in Asia and the Pacific: Production, Consumption, Imports, and Policy Options," *Asia-Pacific Issues*, No. 85, East-West Center.

Wu, K. and S. Han, 2005, "Chinese Companies Pursue Overseas Oil and Gas Assets," *Oil and Gas Journal*, Vol. 103, Issue 15, pp. 18–25.

Wu, K. and J. Lim, 2007, "Supplying Asia-Pacific Oil Demand: Role of the Gulf," in The Emirates Center for Strategic Studies and Research, *Gulf Oil and Gas: Enduring Economic Security*, pp. 255–285, 2007, Abu Dhabi, UAE.

Wu, K. and C. O'Kray, 2007, "The Implications and Impacts of China's Oil Demand on the Asia Pacific," in The Institute of Southeast Asia Studies, *Energy Perspectives on Singapore and the Region*, pp. 142–155, Singapore.

Wu, K. and I. Storey, 2008, "Energy Security in China's Capitalist Transition — Import Dependence, Oil Diplomacy, and Security Imperatives," Chapter 10 in Christopher A. McNally (ed.), "*China's Emergent Political Economy — Capitalism in the Dragon's Lair*," pp. 190–208, Routledge, London and New York.

Wu, K. and L. Wang, 2009, "Natural Gas Prices in China: An Update," *Hydrocarbon Asia*, Vol. 19, No. 4, pp. 6–13.

Wu, K. and L. Zhang, 2009, "China's Strategic Reserves Capacity to Double in 2011," *Oil and Gas Journal*, Vol. 107, Issue 35, pp. 64–67.

Xinhua News Agency, 2012, *China Oil, Gas, and Petrochemicals*, April 15, (and previous issues), Beijing, China.

Xu, Q., 2007, *China's Energy Diplomacy and its Implications for Global Energy Security*, FES Briefing Paper 13, August, Friedrich-Ebert-Stiftung, Department for Development Policy, Berlin, Germany.

Xu, Y. and Y. Yang, 2004, "Strategic Framework for China's Energy Security," *Energy of China* (in Chinese), Vol. 26, pp. 4–11.

Xuan, X., 2004, "An Analysis of China's Energy Efficiency," *Energy of China* (in Chinese), Vol. 26, pp. 4–8.

Yuan, J. H., J. G. Kang, C. H. Zhao and Z. G. Hu, 2008, "Energy Consumption and Economic Growth: Evidence from China at Both Aggregated and Disaggregated Levels," *Energy Economics*, Vol. 30, pp. 3077–3094.

Yuan, C., S. Liu, Z. Fang and N. Xie, 2010, "The Relation between Chinese Economic Development and Energy Consumption in the Different Periods," *Energy Policy*, Vol. 38, pp. 5189–5198.

Zhang, Z., 2002, "China's Energy Security," in C. Li (ed.), "*China's National Strategies*" (in Chinese), China Social Sciences Press, Beijing, China.

Zhang, Z. X., 2010, "China in the Transition to a Low-Carbone Economy," *Energy Policy*, Vol. 38, pp. 6638–6653.

Zhang, B. and L. Tian, 2010, "Analysis of China's Energy Intensity and Its Forecast," *International Journal of Nonlinear Science*, Vol. 9, No. 3, pp. 320–324.

Zhang, H., D. Zhou and J. Cao, 2011, "A quantitative assessment of energy strategy evolution in China and US," *Renewable and Sustainable Energy Reviews*, Vol. 15, pp. 886–890.

Zhang, J., C. Zhou and H. Ebbers, 2011, "Completion of Chinese Overseas Acquisitions: Institutional Perspectives and Evidence," *International Business Review*, Vol. 20, pp. 226–238.

Zhang, L. and K. Wu, 2011, "Refining Outlook in the Asia-Pacific Region: Implications for Regional Oil Market and Petroleum Product Trade," *International Petroleum Economics* (in Chinese), Vol. 19, No. 5, pp. 27–32.

Zhao, H., 2010, *China's Energy Security Policy and Its International Implication*, paper presented at *Energy Security and Climate Change Workshop*, Beijing, 20–21 October.

Zhao, Z. Y., J. Zuo, L. L. Fan and G. Zillante, 2011, "Impacts of Renewable Energy Regulations on the Structure of Power Generation in China — A Critical Analysis," *Renewable Energy*, Vol. 36, pp. 24–30.

Zhou, Y., C. Rengifo, P. Chen and J. Hinze, 2011, "Is China Ready for Its Nuclear Expansion?," *Energy Policy*, Vol. 39, pp. 771–781.

Zhou, S. and X. Zhang, 2010, "Nuclear Energy Development in China: A Study of Opportunities and Challenges," *Energy*, Vol. 35, pp. 4282–4288.

Zou, G. and K. W. Chau, 2006, "Short- and Long-Run Effects between Oil Consumption and Economic Growth in China," *Energy Policy*, Vol. 34, pp. 3644–3655.

Index